Rugby Annual for Wales
1999-2000

THIRTY-FIRST EDITION

Editor: ARWYN OWEN
Production Editor: JOHN BILLOT

Pontypridd's own Tom Jones sings *Delilah* **to the Wembley watchers before Wales defeated England so dramatically in 1999.** *Huw Evans Picture Agency, Cardiff*

WELCOME FROM

Welcome to this new edition of the Rugby Annual for Wales.

Buy As You View is delighted to continue the long and highly successful line of Rugby Annuals for Wales. The proud heritage and history of our national game has to be recorded in detail. We know that over many years to come our Rugby Annual will be used extensively as an invaluable work of reference, detailing the matches and the players from the schools' DC Thomas Cup to the Rugby World Cup.

Assuredly, Welsh rugby at all levels will continue to progress in this demanding era of professionalism that has proved so difficult to come to terms with.

Buy As You View welcomes the opportunity to present this Rugby Annual to very many enthusiastic readers and are confident it will continue to be enjoyed and respected.

Minor 'Miracles' from Henry's Men

The WRU poster advertising the Wales v South Africa match at Wembley on November 14, 1998 was branded as blasphemous by the Baptist Union of Wales. It showed new coach Graham Henry surrounded by Welsh players under the heading, 'Guide Me O Thou Great Redeemer.' Graham Henry never claimed divine powers, but did guide Wales to an amazing sequence of victories.

There was a first success in Paris for 24 years, a sensational injury-time win over England, double success in Argentina and then the historic first triumph against South Africa to open the Millennium Stadium.

After watching New Zealand defeat the Springboks 28-0 in Dunedin on July 10, 1999, Henry opined that the gap between players of the northern hemisphere and the south was closing rapidly. But he rates the All Blacks favourites for the 1999 World Cup. "The difference between the hemispheres at the moment is the regular intensity of their rugby," he says. "We do not have that yet, but in terms of pure ability we are pretty close to them. Wales are still a step behind the top southern nations, but it is all guesswork until the moment of reckoning. That will come during the World Cup."

EDITOR'S NOTES
by Arwyn Owen

It was rugby to set the pulses racing during the 1998-99 season. We witnessed a memorable revival by Wales under the inspirational guidance of new coach Graham Henry in what proved the most thrilling Five Nations tourney of all time. Excitement very definitely was back on top of the agenda and those breathtaking knife-edge victories over France and England were crowned by that never-to-be-forgotten first triumph in 93 years against South Africa to mark the opening of the partially-completed Millennium Stadium.

Wales went to Argentina to be tested and tempered in the heat of a hostile atmosphere and the regeneration of the side was confirmed. The cool composure of Neil Jenkins, record-breaking goal-kicker and master tactician, made an indelible mark on the national team's performances while the re-emergence of the pack as a force to compare with any in the world game has raised the hopes of our ever-faithful supporters in the build-up to the Rugby World Cup.

Welsh rugby has been in intensive care for so long that the recovery takes some believing; but no-one can dispute that an image transformation has been achieved. Wales A and Wales Under-21 deserve the highest praise for their endeavours in each completing the Grand Slam. Wales Under-19 reached the final of the World Junior (Youth) Cup and Wales Youth won the Triple Crown in the new Four Nations championship. Swansea retained the British Universities Cup. Success came to our game in rich profusion.

We said goodbye to Wembley Stadium, temporary home to the national team during the construction of the new ground in Cardiff, and we watched Tom Jones sing one of his trademark songs, *Delilah*, there before the England match. Perhaps, more appropriately, he should have given a rendition of Cole Porter's *I Get a Kick Out of You* in acknowledgement of Neil Jenkins's amazing feats with his deadly right boot!

There was encouraging news when Cardiff and Swansea signed up with the WRU to return to the Premier Division after a 'sabbatical' season playing against English clubs. Rebels Swansea, of course, regained the SWALEC Cup, defeating Llanelli in the final, though a Stradey star was voted Welsh Player of the Year. This honour went to Chris Wyatt, whose lineout dominance and support running helped distinguish the rise of the national team. Llanelli took the Premier Division title and the WRU Challenge Trophy, which was an impressive double.

Now we welcome teams from all around the world to the fourth Rugby World Cup, the highlight of a season that overlaps two centuries - and Wales, we hope, will continue to improve having at last escaped the hand of our oppressors!

3

Jubilation at Wembley. Welsh players show their delight (or was it relief at their great escape?) after defeating bemused England, who expected to be celebrating another Grand Slam success - until that injury time Scott Gibbs try out of nowhere and Neil Jenkins's cool conversion kick.

Huw Evans Picture Agency, Cardiff

4

COACH HENRY BRINGS BACK
SOME OF THE OLD GLORY

By JOHN BILLOT

Back in 1940, D C Thomson, publishers of the great boys' adventure papers, introduced a comedy series in *The Hotspur*. It featured Pep-talk Polonius, manager of the Imperial School of Gladiators, and his brief was to transform a squad of no-hopers into combat heroes. "Or I'll have him nailed by the ears to the gates of Rome and fed to the lions," warned Trajan. It was said Pep-talk could persuade a caterpillar into imagining it was a crocodile and a crow into singing like a nightingale. Now we have a modern day Polonius: Graham Henry, New Zealand coach extraordinary, has arrived.

He came, saw and almost had his team conquer South Africa at Wembley in his first game in charge. Wales had experienced humiliating record defeats against England (60-26), France (51-0) and South Africa in Pretoria (96-13). Now we saw Wales leading 14-0 as his reborn gladiators stunned the world champions five months after the Springboks had come within four points of running up 100 points. Forget that. Here we had Gareth Thomas racing for a breathtaking try and Neil Jenkins firing over three penalty shots. What a lead! What a match! But before the season was over there were to be two other big games that were even more sensational - and with Wales as winners.

FIVE NATIONS CHAMPIONSHIP 1998-99						
	P	*W*	*D*	*L*	*F*	*A*	*Pts*
Scotland (4)	4	3	0	1	120	79	6
England (2)	4	3	0	1	103	78	6
Wales (3)	4	2	0	2	109	126	4
Ireland (5)	4	1	0	3	66	90	2
France (1)	4	1	0	3	75	100	2
Numbers in brackets indicate finishing positions in previous season.						

True, the old South Africa bogy struck again and Wales lost 28-20. No disgrace in that: and the opportunities had been there to sneak a first ever victory over the Boks. Henry certainly had made his caterpillars perform like crocodiles. "We are not going to be the whipping boys of international rugby any more," forecast happy captain Rob Howley, though he must have pondered that view when Scotland and Ireland came among us and cast doom and gloom throughout the nation yet again.

First, however, there was a pleasing 43-30 verdict over Argentina at Stradey. Though the Pumas' fierce scrum turned the screw and the tourists piled up 19

SIX OF THE BEST WITH 4-TRY FEATS

Gareth Thomas became the sixth Welsh player to score four tries in a match when he stunned Italy in Treviso in March, 1999. The dashing Cardiff wing took his tally of international tries to 18 in 32 appearances. All six players figured as wing three-quarters. The first four-up man was left wing Willie Llewellyn (Llwynypia) against England at Swansea in 1899 to mark an amazing debut. Wales won 26-3.

Reggie Gibbs (Cardiff) crossed for his four against France at the Arms Park in 1908 for a 36-4 success. He would have collected a record fifth try, but dropped the ball in the in-goal area when his legs were knocked from under him when he tried to get closer to the posts. It was 61 years before the next four-try feat. This time Cardiff's Maurice Richards sped in against England in 1969 at the Arms Park with Wales 30-9 winners. Eighteen years on and Ieuan Evans (Llanelli) sizzled away in the 40-9 victory over Canada at Invercargill during the 1987 World Cup. Nigel Walker (Cardiff) repeated the performance during the Welsh record 102 points against Portugal in Lisbon in 1994 in a World Cup qualifying match.

points during the closing 10 minutes, Colin Charvis's second try, from a blistering Scott Gibbs charge, was the turning point. So everything indicated a most encouraging Five Nations campaign with a near-ideal start against what was considered the weakest of the four opponents. Alas, Scotland and Ireland had surprises waiting. The Scots hit Wales with the fastest try in the history of the Five Nations: just 10 seconds from the kick-off to start the Murrayfield match until New Zealander John Leslie scored. The lead swung five times and Scotland won 33-20. Graham Henry summed up, "We were lucky to get second."

Next it was the Battle of the Baldies at Wembley: shaven-headed Craig Quinnell throwing punches like Mike Tyson, being yellow-carded, and then thundering across for a try; Ireland's Keith Wood, equally thinly-thatched, a hooker masquerading as an outside half to take his scrum half's pass, side-step Scott Gibbs and stomp to the posts for a score that will live long in memories for the men in green. A charged-down Neil Jenkins punt gave Ireland a gift seven points. "We lacked discipline," reflected coach Henry. The Roman army, incidentally, had an infallible remedy for indiscipline: they popped the culprit into a sack with a wild boar. This is hardly practical these days, if only because of the scarcity of wild boars. A purple patch for 20 exciting minutes promised to turn the match around for Wales, but Ireland snatched it 29-23 and the words on Welsh lips were "wooden spoon."

The two most arduous matches were yet to come. Were they giving the lions short rations ready for main-course Henry? Wales had not won in Paris for 24 years. What made anyone think it would be any different this time? Especially after the Irish blunder. Yet a great game was to unfold at the magnificent new £270m Stade de France. It was Wales's first visit there and Howley's team put together a superb display. France, aiming for what would be a unique third successive Grand Slam, were totally devastated. Welsh forward heroes hit them

THAT TRY! The score that stunned England at Wembley in 1999 just when they thought they had another Grand Slam in the bag. Scott Gibbs hurtles across during injury time and ace photographer Gareth Everett was on the spot to capture a breathtaking moment for *Huw Evans Picture Agency, Cardiff.* **What a match! What a memory! What a try!**

from every angle: the 20-minute team outlasted the home side with ungovernable fury.

When Craig Quinnell suddenly appeared far out on the right wing to collect the final link pass and flow over for an unforgettable try, France could not believe it. Where did that 19 stone second row come from? Make him a centurion at once! Of course, if Thomas Castaignede's injury-time penalty kick had found the target, Wales would still be seeking that elusive success instead of relishing 34-33 victory.

There was a romp in Treviso for Neil Jenkins to supply a record 30 points and with Gareth Thomas plundering four tries in a 60-21 triumph. All seven replacements went on to savour the Italian job, but we wondered if there would be much to enjoy with England geared for the Grand Slam at Wembley. And when England snapped up a seven points lead before the match was three minutes old, some of the old nightmares began to take shape. Pre-match entertainment by Tom Jones, singing *Delilah*, one of his greatest hits, and Max Boyce with his rugby ballads, looked like bringing the only melodious moments for Welsh fans.

"Our chances of winning are pretty remote," admitted coach Henry and 78,000 watchers saw England lead until 82 minutes had passed. Then, in the second minute of injury time, Scott Gibbs wafted past five tacklers. That wonder-try was goaled by Jenkins, as we expected, as part of his 22 points and a 32-31 win. "England were the better team, but we hung on in there," said coach Henry. Let's hang on to Graham Henry - the lions won't be getting him for their supper!

FIVE NATIONS RESULTS AND TEAMS 1998-99

SCOTLAND v WALES
(Murrayfield)
February 6, 1999. Scotland won by 33 (2G, 3PG, 2T) to 20 (2G, 2PG).

SCOTLAND: G. H. Metcalfe (Glasgow Caledonians); C. A. Murray (Edinburgh Reivers), G. P. J. Townsend (Brive), J. A. Leslie (Glasgow Caledonians), K. M. Logan (Wasps); D. W. Hodge (Edinburgh Reivers), G. Armstrong (Newcastle, capt); T. J. Smith (Glasgow Caledonians), G. C. Bulloch (Glasgow Caledonians), A. P. Burnell (London Scottish), S. Murray (Bedford), G. W. Weir (Newcastle), P. Walton (Newcastle), E. W. Peters (Bath), M. D. Leslie (Edinburgh Reivers). Reps: A. V. Tait (Edinburgh Reivers) for Hodge, D. I. W. Hilton (Bath) for Burnell, S. B. Grimes (Glasgow Caledonians) for Weir, A. C. Pountney (Northampton) for M. D. Leslie.

WALES: S. P. Howarth (Sale); M. F. D. Robinson (Swansea), A. G. Bateman (Richmond), I. S. Gibbs (Swansea), D. R. James (Pontypridd); N. R. Jenkins (Pontypridd), R. Howley (Cardiff, capt); D. R. Morris (Swansea), J. M. Humphreys (Cardiff), C. T. Anthony (Swansea), I. Gough (Pontypridd), C. P. Wyatt (Llanelli), C. L. Charvis (Swansea), L. S. Quinnell (Llanelli), M. E. Williams (Pontypridd). Reps: B. H. Williams (Richmond) for Humphreys, M. J. Voyle (Llanelli) for Gough.

Referee: Ed Morrison (England).

Scorers: For Scotland, John Leslie, Gregor Townsend, Alan Tait, Scott Murray (tries), Kenny Logan (2PG, 2con), Duncan Hodge (1PG). For Wales, Dafydd James, Scott Gibbs (tries), Neil Jenkins (2PG, 2con).

IRELAND v FRANCE
(Dublin)
February 6 1999: France won by 10 (1G, 1PG) to 9 (3PG).

IRELAND: C. M. P. O'Shea (London Irish); J. P. Bishop (London Irish), K. M. Maggs (Bath), J. C. Bell (Dungannon), G. Dempsey (Terenure Coll); D. G. Humphreys (Dungannon), C. D. McGuinness (St Mary's Coll); P. M. Clohessy (Young Munster), K. G. M. Wood (Harlequins), P. S. Wallace (Saracens), P. S. Johns (Saracens, capt), J. W. Davidson (Castres), E. R. P. Miller (Terenure Coll), V. C. P. Costello (St Mary's Coll), D. O'Cuinneagain (Sale). Reps: R. A. J. Henderson (Wasps) for Bell, J. P. Fitzpatrick (Dungannon) for Clohessy, T. Brennan (St Mary's Coll) for Costello.

FRANCE: E. Ntamack (Toulouse); P. Bernat-Salles (Biarritz), R. Dourthe (Stade Francais), F. Comba (Stade Francais), T. Lombard (Stade Francais); T. Castaignede (Castres), P. Carbonneau (Brive); C. Califano (Toulouse), R. Ibanez (Perpignan, capt), F. Tournaire (Toulouse), O. Brouzet (Begles/Bordeaux), F. Pelous (Toulouse), P. Benetton (Agen), T. Lievremont (Perpignan), O. Magne (Brive). Reps: A. Gomes (Stade Francais) for Lombard, S. Marconnet (Stade Francais) for Califano, T. Cleda (Pau) for Pelous.

Referee: Peter Marshall (Australia).

Scorers: For Ireland, David Humphreys (3PG). For France, Emile Ntamack (1T), Thomas Castaignede (1PG, 1con).

WALES v IRELAND
(Wembley)
February 20, 1999. Ireland won by 29 (2G, 2DG, 3PG) to 23 (2G, 3PG).

WALES: S. P. Howarth (Sale); M. F. D. Robinson (Swansea), M. Taylor (Swansea), I. S. Gibbs (Swansea), D. R. James (Pontypridd); N. R. Jenkins (Pontypridd), R. Howley (Cardiff, capt); D. R. Morris (Swansea), B. H. Williams (Richmond), D. Young (Cardiff), J. C. Quinnell (Richmond), C. P. Wyatt (Llanelli), C. L. Charvis (Swansea), L. S. Quinnell (Llanelli), M. E. Williams (Pontypridd). Reps: M. J. Voyle (Llanelli) for M. E. Williams, G. R. Jenkins (Swansea) for B. H. Williams, C. A. Anthony (Swansea) for Young.

IRELAND: C. M. P. O'Shea (London Irish); J. P. Bishop (London Irish), K. M. Maggs (Bath), J. C. Bell (Dungannon), N. K. P. J. Woods (London Irish); D. G. Humphreys (Dungannon), C. D. McGuinness (St Mary's Coll); P. M. Clohessy (Young Munster), K. G. M. Wood (Harlequins), P. S. Wallace (Saracens), P. S. Johns (Saracens, capt), J. W. Davidson (Castres), D. O'Cuinneagain (Sale), E. R. P. Miller (Terenure Coll), A. J. Ward (Ballynahinch). Reps: M. J. Galwey (Shannon) for Johns, J. Fitzpatrick (Dungannon) for Clohessy, V. Costello (St Mary's Coll) for Miller.

Referee: Scott Young (Australia).

Scorers: For Wales, Craig Quinnell, Shane Howarth (tries), Neil Jenkins (3PG, 2con). For Ireland, Kevin Maggs, Keith Wood (tries), David Humphreys (2DG, 3PG, 2con).

8

ENGLAND v SCOTLAND
(Twickenham)
February 20, 1999. England won by 24 (3G, 1PG) to 21 (3G).

ENGLAND: N. D. Beal (Northampton); D. L. Rees (Sale), J. C. Guscott (Bath), J. P. Wilkinson (Newcastle), D. D. Luger (Harlequins); M. J. Catt (Bath), M. J. S. Dawson (Northampton); J. Leonard (Harlequins), R. Cockerill (Leicester), D. J. Garforth (Leicester), M. O. Johnson (Leicester), T. A. K. Rodber (Northampton), L. B. N. Dallaglio (Wasps, capt), R.A. Hill (Saracens), N. A. Back (Leicester). Reps: K. P. P. Bracken (Saracens) for Dawson, D. J. Grewcock (Saracens) for Johnson.

SCOTLAND: G. H. Metcalfe (Glasgow); C. A. Murray (Edinburgh), A. V. Tait (Edinburgh), J. A. Leslie (Glasgow), K. M. Logan (Wasps); G. P. J. Townsend (Brive), G. Armstrong (Newcastle, capt); T. J. Smith (Glasgow), G. C. Bulloch (Glasgow), A. P. Burnell (London Scottish), S. Murray (Bedford), S. B. Grimes (Glasgow), P. Walton (Newcastle), E. W. Peters (Bath), M. D. Leslie (Edinburgh). Reps: D. I. W. Hilton (Bath) for Burnell, A. C. Pountney (Northampton) for Walton.

Referee: D. T. M. McHugh (Ireland).

Scorers: For England, Nick Beal, Dan Luger, Tim Rodber (tries), Jonny Wilkinson (1PG, 3con). For Scotland, Alan Tait (2), Gregor Townsend (tries), Kenny Logan (3con).

FRANCE v WALES
(Paris)
March 6, 1999. Wales won by 34 (2G, 5PG, 1T) to 33 (2G, 3PG, 2T).

FRANCE: E. Ntamack (Toulouse); P. Bernat-Salles (Biarritz), R. Dourthe (Stade Francais), F. Comba (Stade Francais), T. Lombard (Stade Francais); T. Castaignede (Castres), P. Carbonneau (Brive); C. Califano (Toulouse), R. Ibanez (Perpignan, capt), F. Tournaire (Toulouse), O. Brouzet (Begles/Bordeaux), F. Pelouse (Toulouse), P. Benetton (Agen), T. Lievremont (Perpignan), M. Raynaud (Narbonne). Reps: X. Garbajosa (Toulouse) for Bernat-Salles, D. Aucagne (Pau) for Dourthe, S. Marconnet (Stade Francais) for Tournaire, R. Castel (Beziers) for Benetton.

WALES: S. P. Howarth (Sale); M. F. D. Robinson (Swansea), M. Taylor (Swansea), I. S. Gibbs (Swansea), D. R. James (Pontypridd); N. R. Jenkins (Pontypridd), R. Howley (Cardiff, capt); P. J. D. Rogers (London Irish), G. R. Jenkins (Swansea), B. R. Evans (Swansea), J. C. Quinnell (Richmond), C. P. Wyatt (Llanelli), C. L. Charvis (Swansea), L. S. Quinnell (Llanelli), B. D. Sinkinson (Neath). Reps: G. Thomas (Cardiff) for Robinson, A. L. P. Lewis (Cardiff) for Rogers, D. Llewellyn (Ebbw Vale) for Howley.

Referee: Jim Fleming (Scotland).

Scorers: For France, Emile Ntamack (3), Thomas Castaignede (tries), Castaignede (3PG, 2con). For Wales, Colin Charvis, Dafydd James, Craig Quinnell (tries), Neil Jenkins (5PG, 2con).

IRELAND v ENGLAND
(Dublin)
March 6, 1999. England won by 27 (1G, 1DG, 4PG, 1T) to 15 (5PG).

IRELAND: C. M. P. O'Shea (London Irish); J. P. Bishop (London Irish), K. M. Maggs (Baths), R. A. J. Henderson (Wasps), G. Dempsey (Terenure Coll); D. G. Humphreys (Dungannon), C. D. McGuinness (St Mary's Coll); P. M. Clohessy (Young Munster), K. G. M. Wood (Harlequins), P. S. Wallace (Saracens), P. S. Johns (Saracens, capt), J. W. Davidson (Castres), D. O'Cuinneagain (Sale), V. C. P. Costello (St Mary's Coll), A. J. Ward (Ballynahinch). Reps: J. M. Fitzpatrick (Dungannon) for Clohessy, E. R. P. Miller (Terenure Coll) for Costello.

ENGLAND: M. B. Perry (Bath); D. L. Rees (Sale), J. C. Guscott (Bath), J. P. Wilkinson (Newcastle), D. D. Luger (Harlequins); P. J. Grayson (Northampton), K. P. P. Bracken (Saracens); J. Leonard (Harlequins), R. Cockerill (Leicester), D. J. Garforth (Leicester), M. O. Johnson (Leicester), T. A. K. Rodber (Northampton), R. A. Hill (Saracens), L. B. N. Dallaglio (Wasps, capt), N. A. Back (Leicester). Rep: N. McCarthy (Gloucester) for Cockerill.

Referee: Paddy O'Brien (New Zealand).

Scorers: For Ireland, David Humphreys (5PG). For England, Matt Perry, Tim Rodber (tries), Paul Grayson (1DG), Jonny Wilkinson (4PG, 1con).

ENGLAND v FRANCE
(Twickenham)
March 20, 1999. England won by 21 (7PG) to 10 (1G, 1PG).

ENGLAND: M. B. Perry (Bath); D. L. Rees (Sale), J. P. Wilkinson (Newcastle), J. C. Guscott (Bath), D. D. Luger (Harlequins); M. J. Catt (Bath), K. P. P. Bracken (Saracens); J. Leonard (Harlequins), R. Cockerill (Leicester), D. J. Garforth (Leicester), M. O. Johnson (Leicester), T. A. K. Rodber (Northampton), R.A. Hill (Saracens), L. B. N. Dallaglio (Wasps, capt), N. A. Back (Leicester). Reps: N. D. Beal (Northampton) for Rees, M. J. S. Dawson (Northampton) for Bracken, V. E. Ubogu (Bath) for Garforth, M. E. Corry (Leicester) for Hill.

9

FRANCE: E. Ntamack (Toulouse); X. Garbajosa (Toulouse), P. Giordani (Dax), F. Comba (Stade Francais), C. Dominici (Stade Francais); T. Castaignede (Castres), P. Carbonneau (Brive); S. Marconnet (Stade Francais), R. Ibanez (Perpignan, capt), F. Tournaire (Toulouse), O. Brouzet (Begles/Bordeaux), F. Pelous (Toulouse), T. Lievremont (Perpignan), C. Juillet (Stade Francais), R. Castel (Beziers). Reps: C. Califano (Toulouse) for Marconnet, D. Auradou (Stade Francais) for Pelous, M. Raynaud (Narbonne) for Lievremont.

Referee: Colin Hawke (New Zealand). Rep: Jim Fleming (Scotland).

Scorers: For England, Jonny Wilkinson (7PG). For France, Franck Comba (1T), Thomas Castaignede (1PG, 1con).

SCOTLAND v IRELAND
(Murrayfield)
March 20, 1999. Scotland won by 30 (2G, 2PG, 2T) to 13 (1G, 2PG).

SCOTLAND: G. H. Metcalfe (Glasgow); C. A. Murray (Edinburgh), A. V. Tait (Edinburgh), J. A. Leslie (Sanix), K. M. Logan (Wasps); G. P. J. Townsend (Brive), G. Armstrong (Newcastle, capt); T. J. Smith (Glasgow), G. C. Bulloch (Glasgow), A. P. Burnell (London Scottish), S. Murray (Bedford), S. B. Grimes (Glasgow), P. Walton (Newcastle), E. W. Peters (Bath), M. D. Leslie (Edinburgh). Reps: I. T. Fairley (Edinburgh) for Armstrong, D. I. W. Hilton (Bath) for Smith, S. J. Brotherstone (Edinburgh) for Bulloch, A. C. Pountney (Northampton) for Walton, S. Longstaff (Glasgow) for Murray.

IRELAND: C. M. P. O'Shea (London Irish); J. P. Bishop (London Irish), K. M. Maggs (Bath), J. C. Bell (Dungannon), G. Dempsey (Terenure Coll); D. G. Humphreys (Dungannon), C. D. McGuinness (St Mary's Coll); P. M. Clohessy (Young Munster), K. G. M. Wood (Harlequins), P. S. Wallace (Saracens), P. S. Johns (Saracens, capt), J. W. Davidson (Castres), D. O'Cuinneagain (Sale), E. R. P. Miller (Terenure Coll), A. J. Ward (Ballynahinch). Reps: R. A. J. Henderson (Wasps) for Bell, C. D. Scally (UC Dublin) for McGuinness, T. Brennan (St Mary's Coll) for Ward, V. C. P. Costello (St Mary's Coll) for Miller.

Referee: Derek Bevan (Wales).

Scorers: For Scotland, Cameron Murray (2), Gregor Townsend, Stuart Grimes (tries), Kenny Logan (2PG, 2con). For Ireland, penalty try, David Humphreys (2PG, 1con).

FRANCE v SCOTLAND
(Paris)
April 10, 1999. Scotland won by 36 (4G, 1PG, 1T) to 22 (2G, 1PG, 1T).

FRANCE: E. Ntamack (Toulouse); X Garbajosa (Toulouse), P. Giordani (Dax), F. Comba (Stade Francais), C. Dominici (Stade Francais); T. Castaignede (Castres), P. Carbonneau (Brive); C. Califano (Toulouse), R. Ibanex (Perpignan, capt), F. Tournaire (Toulouse), O. Brouzet (Begles/Bordeaux), T. Cleda (Pau), R. Castel (Beziers), C. Juillet (Stade Francais), C. Labit (Toulouse). Reps: T. Lombard (Stade Francais) for Giordani, D. Aucagne (Pau) for Castaignede, C. Laussucq (Stade Francais) for Carbonneau, S. Marconnet (Stade Francais) for Califano, D. Auradou (Stade Francais) for Cleda, P. Benetton (Agen) for Castel.

SCOTLAND: G. H. Metcalfe (Glasgow); C. A. Murray (Edinburgh), A. V. Tait (Edinburgh), J. A. Leslie (Glasgow), K. M. Logan (Wasps); G. P. J. Townsend (Brive), G. Armstrong (Newcastle, capt); D. I. W. Hilton (Bath), G. C. Bulloch (Glasgow), A. P. Burnell (London Scottish), S. Murray (Bedford), S. B. Grimes (Glasgow), A. C. Pountney (Northampton), S. Reid (Leeds), M. Leslie (Edinburgh). Reps: G. Graham (Newcastle) for Hilton, P. Walton (Newcastle) for Pountney, A. Reed (Wasps) for S. Murray.

Referee: Clayton Thomas (Wales).

Scorers: For France, Emile Ntamack, Christophe Juillet, Christophe Dominici (tries), Franck Comba (1PG), David Aucagne (2con). For Scotland, Martin Leslie (2), Alan Tait (2), Gregor Townsend (tries), Ken Logan (1PG, 4con).

WALES v ENGLAND
(Wembley)
April 11, 1999. Wales won by 32 (2G, 6PG) to 31 (2G, 4PG, 1T).

WALES: S. P. Howarth (Sale); G. Thomas (Cardiff), M. Taylor (Swansea), I. S. Gibbs (Swansea), D. R. James (Pontypridd); N. R. Jenkins (Pontypridd), R. Howley (Cardiff, capt); P. J. D. Rogers (London Irish), G. R. Jenkins (Swansea), B. R. Evans (Swansea), J. C. Quinnell (Richmond), C. P. Wyatt (Llanelli), C. L. Charvis (Swansea), L. S. Quinnell (Llanelli), B. D. Sinkinson (Neath). Reps: N. J. Walne (Richmond) for Thomas, A. L. P. Lewis (Cardiff) for Rogers, D. Young (Cardiff) for Evans.

ENGLAND: M. B. Perry (Bath); D. D. Luger (Harlequins), J. P. Wilkinson (Newcastle), B. J. Mather (Sale), S. M. Hanley (Sale); M. J. Catt (Bath), M. J. S. Dawson (Northampton); J. Leonard (Harlequins), R. Cockerill (Leicester), D. J. Garforth (Leicester), M. O. Johnson (Leicester), T. A. K. Rodber (Northampton), R. A. Hill (Saracens), L. B. N. Dallaglio (Wasps, capt), N. A. Back (Leicester). Rep: V. E. Ubogu (Bath) for Garforth.

Referee: Andre Watson (South Africa).

Scorers: For Wales, Shane Howarth, Scott Gibbs (tries), Neil Jenkins (6PG, 2con). For England, Dan Luger, Steve Hanley, Richard Hill (tries), Jonny Wilkinson (4PG, 2con).

TIME FOR EUROPE TO FIND NEW CHAMPIONS

Can a northern hemisphere country capture the Rugby World Cup for the first time? New Zealand (1987), Australia (1991) and South Africa (1995) have collected the coveted William Webb Ellis Trophy and the odds appear stacked strongly in favour of the prize going south of the equator yet again. England are the most formidable of the European countries now that France have fallen by the wayside with a tame pack; while Scotland, for all that they won the 1999 Five Nations title, do not impress as likely giant-killers of the big boys from the southern hemisphere.

Overall, there has been a decline in standards. New Zealand suffered a string of defeats and there has been much muttering in the Land of the Long White Cloud that the glory days are gone and they never should have allowed Graham Henry to be lured to Wales. South Africa were given a rare old fright by Wales at Wembley in November 1998. The Springboks found themselves looking down the barrel of a 14-0 deficit before they pulled themselves into winning shape.

Then South Africa suffered that astonishing first defeat at the hands of an inspired Welsh team to mark the opening of the new super-stadium in Cardiff on June 26, 1999. Once the wave of Springbok forwards had dashed in vain against the Welsh goal-line, thrown back by fearless tacklers, there was no Plan B to save them.

HOW WALES FARED IN RUGBY WORLD CUP

1987

Ireland	W 13-6	(Wellington)
Tonga	W 29-16	(Palmerston North)
Canada	W 40-9	(Invercargill)
England	W 16-3	(Brisbane)
NZ	L 6-49	(Brisbane)

Play-off for 3rd place:

| Australia | W 22-21 | (Rotorua) |

1991

Western Samoa	L 13-16	(Cardiff)
Argentina	W 16-7	(Cardiff)
Australia	L 3-38	(Cardiff)

1994 (RWC qualifying rounds)

| Portugal | W 102-11 | (Lisbon) |
| Spain | W 54-0 | (Madrid) |

1994 (Seeding rounds)

| Romania | W 16-9 | (Bucharest) |
| Italy | W 29-19 | (Cardiff) |

1995

Japan	W 57-10	(Bloemfontein)
NZ	L 9-34	(Johannesburg)
Ireland	L 23-24	(Johannesburg)

Wales's overall RWC record:

P16 W11 D0 L5 Pts for 448 Pts against 272

Considered favourites by many to retain the Bill Ellis Trophy, South Africa suddenly found themselves with major problems. These were underlined in the first match of the 1999 Tri-Nations series when New Zealand worked them over quite considerably to win 28-0 in Dunedin on July 10. The fact that the Springboks failed to register a point was of considerable significance. Did it mean that the All Blacks were regrouping and it was woe betide all who stood in their way?

Australia, who had piled up 56 tries in 13 test matches during 1998, failed to cross England's line at Twickenham in November of last year, but stole a 12-11 win four minutes from the end with a 40-yard penalty shot by John Eales. Skipper Lawrence Dallaglio commented brusquely, "We can stand toe to toe with these top nations, but unless we start producing actual wins instead of narrow defeats or draws, we cannot start talking seriously about winning World Cup 1999."

Welsh chances do not rate significantly when comparisons are made, though it can be unwise to under-rate a team toned and tempered by such a cool customer as Graham Henry and, of course, with Neil Jenkins ever lurking with a ready boot to blast goals between the posts.

ENGLAND'S FRIGHT AND RECORD

Italy put the frighteners on England at Huddersfield on November 22, 1998 before the home side scraped a 23-15 verdict to finish top of the RWC qualifying zone. Dan Luger and Will Greenwood scored tries; Paul Grayson converted both and kicked three penalty goals. Diego Dominguez provided all the Italian points with a drop shot and four penalty goals. They had a try disallowed when Alessandro Troncon appeared to reach the goal-line. Italy conceded 25 penalties, but still felt they were better than England on the day.

A week earlier, in their opening qualifying fixture, England had raised their record tally for a cap match, defeating Netherlands 110-0 at Huddersfield, where 9,000 saw Jeremy Guscott score four of the record 16 tries. Neil Back also crossed for four tries, the first time an England forward had achieved this feat since George Burton against Wales in 1881. Paul Grayson's 30 points came from 15 conversions.

Derek and Clayton with Elite Refs

Derek Bevan, who has refereed a world record 37 major international matches, and fellow WRU ref Clayton Thomas are in the squad of 16 to officiate during the 1999 Rugby World Cup. It will be Mr Bevan's fourth such event. In the inaugural 1987 RWC he controlled two group games. He was in charge of the 1991 final when Australia defeated England at Twickenham; and refereed the 1995 semi-final between South Africa and France in Durban. Mr Thomas is involved in his second RWC : he did the 1995 group match Italy v Argentina.

IEUAN'S RECORD IS 14 WORLD TRIES

Ieuan Evans, Wales's record holder for number of full caps, tries and times as captain of his country, also is the record try scorer in Wales's Rugby World Cup games (including two qualifying matches and two seeding fixtures). Wonder wing Ieuan piled up 14 RWC tries, including four against Canada in the pool clash of 1987. The only other four-try Welsh scorer is Nigel Walker, who swooped in the qualifying match against Portugal in Lisbon in 1994, when Wales stormed to their record score of 102-11. Neil Jenkins has scored most RWC points with a tally of 117 made up of 21 penalty goals, 24 conversions and two drop-shots. Paul Thorburn, who won the third-place play-off match against Australia in 1987 during the fifth minute of injury time with a superb conversion of Adrian Hadley's corner try, accumulated 37 goal points.

Scotland swamped Portugal 85-11 at Murrayfield, watched by probably the smallest crowd at an international match in Scotland: the recorded gate was just 5,961. The fact that Scotland said they would not award caps for their two qualifying games obviously devalued the matches; and Portugal responded by fielding second string players to save their star performers for the match against Spain. Jamie Mayer scored three of the 13 Scots' tries. The score was four points short of the Scottish record 89 against Ivory Coast three years earlier. The next match brought 85-3 success over Spain. Kenny Logan scored five tries, the most since the Scottish record by George Lindsay against Wales 111 years earlier in 1887.

Ireland won their opening qualifier 70-0 against Georgia with 10 tries and a record total at Lansdowne Road. Then Ireland defeated Romania 53-35 with two tries by Jonathan Bell; two penalty tries helped boost the tally. Ireland were worried that their defence conceded five tries.

● RWC chairman Leo Williams (New Zealand) warned that over-zealous refereeing could impair events in 1999 and stressed that RWC must never become a festival of whistle blowing. At one time he was concerned at scare stories circulating which suggested the Millennium Stadium would not be completed in time. Contingency plans were made should it not be possible to stage the final in Cardiff.

WORLD CUP 1999

POOL A

Saturday, Oct 2	Spain v Uruguay	Galashiels
Sunday, Oct 3	Scotland v South Africa	Murrayfield
Friday, Oct 8	Scotland v Uruguay	Murrayfield
Sunday, Oct 10	South Africa v Spain	Murrayfield
Friday, Oct 15	South Africa v Uruguay	Glasgow
Saturday, Oct 16	Scotland v Spain	Murrayfield

POOL B

Saturday, Oct 2	England v Italy	Twickenham
Sunday, Oct 3	New Zealand v Tonga	Bristol
Saturday, Oct 9	England v New Zealand	Twickenham
Sunday, Oct 10	Italy v Tonga	Leicester
Thursday, Oct 14	New Zealand v Italy	Huddersfield
Friday, Oct 15	England v Tonga	Twickenham

POOL C

Friday, Oct 1	Fiji v Namibia	Beziers
Saturday, Oct 2	France v Canada	Beziers
Friday, Oct 8	France v Namibia	Bordeaux
Saturday, Oct 9	Fiji v Canada	Bordeaux
Thursday, Oct 14	Canada v Namibia	Toulouse
Saturday, Oct 16	France v Fiji	Toulouse

POOL D

Friday, Oct 1	Wales v Argentina	Cardiff
Sunday, Oct 3	W Samoa v Japan	Wrexham
Saturday, Oct 9	Wales v Japan	Cardiff
Sunday, Oct 10	Argentina v W Samoa	Llanelli
Thursday, Oct 14	Wales v W Samoa	Cardiff
Saturday, Oct 16	Argentina v Japan	Cardiff

POOL E

Saturday, Oct 2	Ireland v USA	Dublin
Sunday, Oct 3	Australia v Romania	Belfast
Saturday, Oct 9	USA v Romania	Dublin
Sunday, Oct 10	Ireland v Australia	Dublin
Thursday, Oct 14	Australia v USA	Limerick
Friday, Oct 15	Ireland v Romania	Dublin

QUARTER-FINAL PLAY-OFFS

Weds, Oct 20	Runner-up Pool B v Runner-up Pool C (H)	Twickenham
Weds, Oct 20	Runner-up Pool A v Runner-up Pool D (G)	Murrayfield
Weds, Oct 20	Runner-up Pool E v Third Best (F)	Lens

QUARTER-FINALS

Saturday, Oct 23	Winner D v Winner E (M)	Cardiff
Sunday, Oct 24	Winner A v Winner H (J)	Paris
Sunday, Oct 24	Winner C v Winner F (L)	Dublin
Sunday, Oct 24	Winner B v Winner G (K)	Murrayfield

SEMI-FINALS

Saturday, Oct 30	Winner J v Winner M	Twickenham
Sunday, Oct 31	Winner K v Winner L	Twickenham

THIRD-PLACE PLAY OFF

Thursday, Nov 4	Play-off between losing semi-finalists	Cardiff

FINAL

Saturday, Nov 6		Cardiff

KICKER MASON WINS IT FOR
GALLANT ULSTER UNDERDOGS

Thousands swarmed on to the pitch in Dublin on January 30, 1999 to mob their heroes. Ulster had defeated Colomiers 21-6 to become the first Irish team to win the European Cup and Lansdowne Road enjoyed a record attendance for the tourney of a capacity 49,000. The first Euro Cup had seen 21,800 watch Toulouse edge Cardiff 21-18 after extra time at Cardiff Arms Park National Stadium in 1996. There were 41,664 to witness Brive defeat Leicester 28-9 at the same venue in 1997 and 36,500 watched Bath's 19-18 victory over Brive in Bordeaux in 1998.

Ulster's astonishing march of success brought north and south together in Dublin after the Belfast boys had defeated Toulouse twice and then knocked out the tourney favourites, Stade Francais, in the semi-final 33-27 at Ravenhill. Simon Mason kicked a decisive 23 points with five penalty goals, two dropped goals and a conversion. He finished top scorer in the tournament with 144 points.

CRACKLED WITH TENSION

Mason was the match winner again in the final as he planted over six penalty shots and David Humphreys dropped a goal. There were no tries in the game and Laurent Labit and Mickael Carre fired over penalty goals for the French champions. Ulster midfield man Jonathan Bell said, "We simply never expected to be in the final. Our success has lifted rugby in our province and in the nation." It was by no means a classic contest, with defences dominating, but it often crackled with tension.

"It is quite disrespectful for people to say that if the English had taken part we would never have won it," said Ulster coach Harry Williams. "We would love English clubs to be back in next season, but I don't want to detract from our achievement - we are the first family team to win the European Cup."

ULSTER: S. Mason; S. Coulter, J. Cunningham, J. Bell, A. Park; D. Humphreys (capt), A. Matchett; J. Fitzpatrick, A. Clarke, R. Irwin, M. Blair, G. Longwell, S. McKinty, A. Ward, T. McWhirter. Reps: S. McDowell for Cunningham, G. Leslie for Irwin, D. Topping for McWhirter.

COLOMIERS: J. L. Sadourney (capt); M. Biboulet, S. Roque, J. Sieurac, B. Lhande; L. Labit, F. Galthie; S. Delpuech, M. Dal Maso, S. Graou, G. Moro, J. M. Lorenzi, B de Giusti, P. Tabacco, S. Peysson. Reps: D. Skrela for Lhande, M. Carre for Labit, P. Pueyo for Peysson.

Referee: Clayton Thomas (Wales).

England's clubs declined to take part in this 1998-99 competition. Initially, the French clubs appeared doubtful of whether to participate, but had a change of heart. Inevitably, the English absence devalued the event.

Three Welsh clubs went to the quarter-finals in the two Euro competitions, but that was a match too far for them. In the Cup, Pontypridd were humiliated by their heaviest defeat of all time 71-14 against Stade Francais at Stade Jean Bouin Stadium. An awesome display of power and pace brought 10 home tries

15

TOULOUSE WIN BY RECORD 108-16, BUT PROUD EBBW TAKE REVENGE

Toulouse trounced Ebbw Vale by a Euro record 108-16 with 16 tries on September 19, 1998. Wing Michel Marfaing scored four tries. But a shock awaited the French club in the return pool fixture on November 7. Ebbw were 19-11 winners - their only Euro success - as Jason Strange converted a penalty try and kicked four penalty goals.

Unpleasant scenes followed. Referee Ed Murray, who had sent off Toulouse prop Cyril Vancheri for kicking (banned 28 days) was jostled by French players. A touch judge also appeared to be pushed, as were police officers as they stepped in to protect the match officials. One policeman had his helmet knocked off. In the clubhouse, there were further incidents and the visitors left without attending the after-match function.

Euro Cup director Roger Pickering was reported to be making a formal complaint against Toulouse forward Franck Tournaire for alleged threatening behaviour towards Scottish touch judge Rob Dickson. Toulouse apologised and were ordered to pay £2,600 in costs at their hearing and reprimanded. They were let off lightly compared to the £15,000 fines paid by Pontypridd and Brive the previous season, and £10,000 by Pau and Llanelli after violent matches. The disparity did not go without notice.

with Italian international fly half Diego Dominguez a dynamic influence. He scored 31 points with two tries, nine conversions and a penalty goal. Ponty put 12 international players on the field and scored the most spectacular try with a length-of-field attack that Gareth Wyatt finished off.

Neil Jenkins (who went off at half time with shoulder trouble) converted one try and Gareth Wyatt the other. Geraint Lewis also crossed. "It is shattering because you never want to be involved in a defeat like that," admitted coach Dennis John after this December 12, 1998 day of disaster.

Llanelli failed 34-17 in their quarter-final at Perpignan. The Scarlets had asked permission to include new signings Byron Hayward and Scott Quinnell in their line-up, but this was refused because the registration date had expired.

LLANELLI SCRAPE INTO QUARTERS

Llanelli won three and lost three in their pool, but scraped into the quarters by rallying in Donnybrook after Leinster roared into a 21-0 lead. Refusing to admit defeat, the Scarlets came back from the dead to win 34-27 with tries from each of the three Boobyer brothers, Neil, Ian and Roddy. Earlier, Leinster had inflicted Llanelli's first home defeat in Euro competition 33-27 with a Gordon Darcy try in the second minute of injury time.

Stephen Jones's four penalty goals helped Llanelli defeat Begles/Bordeaux 22-10 before the Scarlets lost 49-3 to Stade Francais at Lille. The return with

16

FINAL EUROPEAN CUP POOL TABLES

POOL A

	W	D	L	F	A	Pts
Stade Francais	5	0	1	219	117	10
Llanelli	3	0	3	113	180	6
Begles/Bordeaux	2	0	4	141	124	4
Leinster	2	0	4	127	179	4

Results: *Llanelli 27, Leinster 33; Llanelli 22, Begles/Bordeaux 10; Stade Francais 49, Llanelli 3; Begles/Bordeaux 48, Llanelli 10; Llanelli 17, Stade Francais 13; Leinster 27, Llanelli 34.*

POOL B

	W	D	L	F	A	Pts
Perpignan	5	0	1	238	108	10
Munster	4	1	1	144	108	9
Neath	1	1	4	118	194	3
Padova	1	0	5	79	169	2

Results: *Neath 33, Perpignan 51; Munster 34, Neath 10; Padova 28, Neath 17; Neath 18, Munster 18; Neath 16, Padova 3; Perpignan 60, Neath 24.*

POOL C

	W	D	L	F	A	Pts
Ulster	4	1	1	197	168	9
Toulouse	4	0	2	234	103	8
Edinburgh R	2	1	3	179	146	5
Ebbw Vale	1	0	5	114	307	2

Results: *Toulouse 108, Ebbw Vale 16; Edinburgh Reivers 41, Ebbw Vale 17; Ebbw Vale 28, Ulster 61; Ebbw Vale 16, Edinburgh Reivers 43; Ulster 43, Ebbw Vale 18; Ebbw Vale 19, Toulouse 11.*

POOL D

	W	D	L	F	A	Pts
Colomiers	4	0	2	176	121	8
Pontypridd	3	0	3	160	141	6
Benetton Treviso	3	0	3	142	150	6
Glasgow Cal.	2	0	4	121	187	4

Results: *Glasgow Caledonians 21, Pontypridd 43; Pontypridd 32, Colomiers 27; Pontypridd 13, Benetton Treviso 22; Colomiers 35, Pontypridd 21; Benetton Treviso 33, Pontypridd 19; Pontypridd 32, Glasgow Caledonians 3.*

Quarter-finals:	*Colomiers 23, Munster 9*	*Perpignan 34, Llanelli 17*
	Stade Francais 71, Pontypridd 14	*Ulster 15, Toulouse 13*
Semi-finals:	*Colomiers 10, Perpignan 6*	*Ulster 33, Stade Francais 27*
Final:	*Ulster 21, Colomiers 6*	*(at Lansdowne Road, Dublin)*

Begles/Bordeaux brought the French team revenge 48-10, but a below strength Llanelli inflicted a first cup defeat of the season on Stade Francais 17-13 at Stradey with full back Jonathan Williams, on loan from Bath, landing four penalty goals on debut. Prop Phil Booth scored the try.

Only 600 saw Pontypridd open with 43-21 victory over Glasgow Caledonians at Partick Thistle soccer ground, and half of those were Ponty fans. Neil Jenkins supplied 23 points. Jenkins was on target in the next match with 22 goal points for a 32-27 verdict against Colomiers - their first success over French opponents in the Euro Cup - in an intensely exciting contest.

Italian champions Treviso dismayed Pontypridd on a wet night at Sardis Road to win 22-13 with South African No 8 Adriaan Richter in irresistible form. Neil Jenkins missed four penalty shots and offered to stand down as captain if it meant someone could inspire the team to better performances. He was persuaded to remain in command.

Jenkins accused his forwards of being "a disgrace" as they lost 35-21 at Colomiers. Team manager Eddie Jones added his criticism, "They couldn't win a raffle!" Ponty hopes of reaching the quarters for the first time suffered a setback with a third consecutive defeat, this time 33-19, at Treviso with fly half Francesco Mazzariol scoring 23 points. However, a 32-3 win over Glasgow sent them to the quarter-finals as Jenkins hit over five penalty goals.

FINAL EUROPEAN SHIELD POOL TABLES

POOL A

	W	D	L	F	A	Pts
Narbonne	6	0	0	228	98	12
Caerphilly	4	0	2	167	154	8
Perigueux	3	0	3	168	119	6
Connacht	3	0	3	129	156	6
Racing CF	3	0	3	127	184	6
Rovigo	1	0	5	108	156	2
Newport	1	0	5	123	183	2

Results: *Caerphilly 31, Perigueux 28; Racing CF 37, Newport 21; Newport 12, Connacht 31; Rovigo 34, Caerphilly 14; Caerphilly 17, Narbonne 31; Perigueux 31, Newport 16; Newport 27, Rovigo 18; Racing CF 20, Caerphilly 31; Narbonne 31, Newport 17; Caerphilly 39, Connacht 8; Newport 30, Caerphilly 35.*

POOL B

	W	D	L	F	A	Pts
Montferrand	5	0	1	303	86	10
Bourgoin	5	0	1	222	86	10
Dax	5	0	1	163	124	10
Castres	3	0	3	229	101	6
Roma	2	0	4	117	213	4
Aberavon	1	0	5	86	287	2
Spain	0	0	6	65	288	0

Results: *Castres 87, Aberavon 10; Aberavon 12, Roma 30; Montferrand 97, Aberavon 13; Aberavon 28, Dax 41; Spain 6, Aberavon 18; Aberavon 5, Bourgoin 26.*

POOL C

	W	D	L	F	A	Pts
Brive	5	0	1	241	102	10
Agen	4	0	2	231	93	8
Pau	4	0	2	211	87	8
Biarritz	4	0	2	187	124	8
Bridgend	2	0	4	158	206	4
Dinamo Bucharest	2	0	4	131	246	4
Portugal	0	0	0	73	374	0

Results: *Bridgend 17, Agen 32; Dinamo Bucharest 45, Bridgend 43; Bridgend 45, Portugal 24; Pau 45, Bridgend 21; Biarritz 45, Bridgend 12; Bridgend 20, Brive 15.*

Quarter-finals
Bourgoin 29, Agen 19
Brive 43, Caerphilly 12
Montferrand 66, Dax 13
Narbonne 30, Pau 13

Semi-finals
Bourgoin 26, Brive 23
Montferrand 27, Narbonne 21

Final
Montferrand 35, Bourgoin 16   (at Lyon)

Neath opened with a 51-33 home defeat by Perpignan and coach Lyn Jones summed up, "Most players in Wales have to be dictated to rather than make decisions themselves. Until our players become decision-makers we will never be able to perform on the European or world stage." Neath's only success came 16-3 against Padova at the Gnoll. Geraint Evans was the try scorer. Matthew McCarthy converted and Luke Richards kicked three penalty goals.

European Shield

Caerphilly carry flag for Wales

Montferrand won the newly-named European Shield 35-16 against Bourgoin in front of 32,000 at Stade Gerland in Lyon on February 27, 1999. Bourgoin were outplayed up front and outscored 3-1 on tries. Gerald Merceron kicked 20 Montferrand points with six penalty goals and conversion of a penalty try. Wing Jimmy Marlu and scrum half Christophe Larrue scored their tries. Jim McLaren was try scorer for the losers with Benjamin Boyet firing over three penalty goals and a conversion.

Caerphilly carried the flag for Wales. They were the first Welsh club to reach the last eight of this second division of Euro competition and prevented the

French making a clean sweep. However, Brive, defeated finalists in the Cup the previous season, overwhelmed Caerphilly 43-12 in their quarter-final meeting with seven tries. The only reply was four penalty goals by Brett Davey.

The Green Army won four of their six pool games and opened impressively with a 31-28 verdict against Perigueux, though Caerphilly skipper Nathan Jones was sent off, together with visitors' hooker Lancelot Eymard, and suspended for 21 days. Another Caerphilly early bath participant was wing Sean Marshall at Rovigo, where the Italians were 34-14 winners. Outside half Paul Williams crossed for the Welsh club's try.

A second reverse followed. Narbonne were on top 34-17 at Caerphilly with home tackling unexpectedly fragile. But the next three games brought victories. Chris John dropped a goal and Davey kicked 23 points with seven penalty goals and a conversion of Christian Ferris's try to dispose of Racing Club 31-20 in Paris. Davey struck again in the 39-8 win over Connacht with a try in his 24 points. And yet again it was full back Davey to dominate the scene in a 35-30 success at Newport: he landed 22 points, including conversions of tries by Sean Marshall and Chris John.

Aberavon were hammered 87-10 in their opening match at Castres; but worse followed with a record 97-13 defeat at Montferrand, conceding 15 tries. The Wizards' only success came 18-6 against Spain in El Ferol. Newport also managed just one victory - 27-18 against Rovigo.

Bridgend surprised everyone with a 20-15 verdict over Brive. Chris Stephens, Adrian Durston and Owain Thomas scored tries. Gareth Bowen converted one and kicked a penalty goal. Their trip to play Dinamo Bucharest proved a journey of woe. Passport trouble meant they had to leave No 8 Owain Lloyd at Heathrow and then Andrew Williams was left behind in Bucharest because he mislaid his passport! He had to wait until the following day to get a replacement from the British Embassy.

There was a massed brawl on the ramshackle ground in temperatures of near 90 degrees and, without hot water or toilets at the ground, Bridgend had to rush back to their hotel to shower. The luckless home players had to go without an after-match meal because of lack of funds, though Bridgend were provided with food. And Bridgend lost 45-43 as the home side kicked a penalty goal in the ninth minute of injury time. Not a happy experience.

WELSH CLUBS' EURO CUP DATES

Nov 19/21: Swansea v Padova, Wasps v Llanelli, Munster v Pontypridd, Cardiff v Harlequins, Northampton v Neath. **Nov 26/28:** Toulouse v Swansea, Llanelli v Bourgoin, Pontypridd v Colomiers, Montferrand v Cardiff, Neath v Edinburgh. **Dec 10/12:** Swansea v Bath, Ulster v Llanelli, Saracens v Pontypridd, Cardiff v Treviso, Neath v Grenoble. **Dec 17/19:** Bath v Swansea, Llanelli v Ulster, Pontypridd v Saracens, Treviso v Cardiff, Grenoble v Neath. **Jan 7/9:** Swansea v Toulouse, Bourgoin v Llanelli, Colomiers v Pontypridd, Cardiff v Montferrand, Edinburgh v Neath. **Jan 14/16:** Padova v Swansea, Llanelli v Wasps, Pontypridd v Munster, Harlequins v Cardiff, Neath v Northampton. **April 15:** Quarter-finals. **May 6:** Semi-finals. **May 27:** Final.

Crowds flock to watch Cardiff and Swansea play the English

Rebels with a cause. That was the catchword for Cardiff and Swansea while playing friendly games during the whole of the 1998-99 season against England's premier clubs. This Welsh defection was identified by some as revolutionary. Others claimed their action gave impetus to the need to introduce a British League. The absence of two of the great clubs of Welsh rugby certainly damaged the credibility of the WRU premier division, which became a straight fight for the title between Llanelli, the ultimate champs, and Pontypridd, who emerged runners-up.

Cardiff were unbeaten at home by any opponents, but suffered nine away defeats against English clubs (eight of them consecutively) and lost at Swansea 31-15. Some fixtures brought large attendances to the Arms Park and St Helen's. There were 10,000 to watch Cardiff win their first home game 40-19 against England cup-holders Saracens, compared with an aggregate attendance of 8,200 in the WRU premier division's four matches. "If all we were doing was sustaining mediocrity, I don't think people would support us," stated Cardiff chief executive Gareth Davies.

Swansea v Newcastle was the battle of the champions: Swansea as Welsh title winners of the previous season, Newcastle as England's equivalent. The Whites were 26-14 winners watched by 7,350. It was try for try, but Arwel Thomas kicked 18 penalty points and popped over a drop-shot.

But when Swansea suffered their first defeat 28-13 at Richmond's new 'home' at Madejski Stadium, Reading, skipper Scott Gibbs growled, "We are professionals, but we played like a bunch of amateurs. I am furious!" Only Saracens 32-25 and London Scottish 27-12 won at St Helen's; and there were seven away defeats - Richmond, Sale, Bath, Saracens, Newcastle, Gloucester and 40-19 at Cardiff.

Cardiff were the first team to win at Welford Road when nearly 10,000 attended on a Friday night to see the Welsh visitors take a 35-20 decision against Allied Dunbar leaders Leicester. Cardiff's 24-3 home victory over Bath in front of 12,250 saw Victor Ubogu ordered off for dissent after 39 minutes. Bath coach Andy Robinson was so incensed he had to be persuaded to send his team out for the second half when he wanted to end events there and then. It was pointed out he would disappoint the large crowd.

English clubs fielded numerous second choice players on frequent occasions, which devalued some games. Cardiff's away defeats were by Sale (twice), Newcastle, Richmond, Wasps, Northampton, Saracens, Bath and London Irish, who won 50-40.

WRU BRING IN NZ STAR COACH HENRY

The WRU spent three months on a global search for a national coach to replace Kevin Bowring and appointed New Zealander Graham Henry, aged 52, at the end of July 1998 on a five-year contract worth around £250,000 per year. England had tried to sign him a year earlier. Henry, a former Auckland schoolteacher, enjoyed an impressive coaching pedigree. He inspired Auckland to 86 victories in 108 matches between 1992-98, 22 victories in the Ranfurly Shield, three national provincial championships and directed Auckland Blues to the Super-12 title in 1996 and 1997.

Steve Black joined the team in October 1998 from Newcastle as conditioning expert. Former Wales captain David Pickering was appointed Wales team manager, also in October 1998.

<u>WRU National League</u>

LLANELLI TOP AGAIN AFTER SIX YEARS
By JOHN BILLOT

A unique triple crown beckoned for Llanelli: League championship, Challenge Cup and SWALEC Cup. It was not to be as the SWALEC Cup proved a tie too far. So the Scarlets had to settle for the other notable landmarks of a generally troubled season for Welsh rugby. Llanelli made sure of the title in the fourth of their six play-off matches with a 37-11 home victory over born-again Neath to bring the prize back to Stradey after a six-year interlude. They burned off the challenge from Pontypridd, who disappointingly recorded just one success during their six play-offs in the absence of skipper Neil Jenkins, recovering from a shoulder operation.

It was always going to be a duel between Llanelli and Ponty as the only pair possessing the wherewithal to become champions. The absence of Cardiff and Swansea, who rejected the WRU demand to sign loyalty contracts and took themselves off to play a series of friendly matches throughout the season against the top English clubs, inevitably devalued the premier division.

BONUS POINTS SYSTEM SCRAPPED

Play-offs were introduced to spice events and provide additional fixtures, but made only one difference to the finishing order of the leading four teams with Neath vaulting over Ebbw Vale to take third place. Ironically, if the bonus system had not applied, Ebbw would have been third. At the end of the season, the premier division clubs requested the WRU to abolish the unpopular bonus points and this was accepted.

The method was instigated for season 1995-96 to encourage exciting, open play. Eddie Jones, chairman of the premier clubs, explained, "People have

BRETT KEEPS CAERPHILLY ON COURSE

Full back Brett Davey accumulated 384 points (including 10 tries) in all Caerphilly matches during 1998-99, playing in 28 of the 34 fixtures. He helped his team defeat Newport five times, including the Euro Shield tie, and register four victories over Aberavon. For the second successive season Davey topped the premier division scoring chart. His closest rival was Llanelli's Byron Hayward with 196 points.

Caerphilly, formed on August 26, 1887, have forced their way into the elite bracket of Welsh rugby with a team of part-time professionals. They were Div 4 runners-up in 1994, runners-up in Div 3 in 1995, Div 2 runners-up in 1996, Div 1 champs in 1998 and now best of the rest behind the top four 1999 premier division sides.

forgotten the most important thing in the game - winning. The bonus system has become too much of a mathematical complication and a distraction. We want bonus points removed entirely from league games. We want win, lose or draw."

The four leading teams in the premier division met each other on a home and away basis in the play-off stage while the four teams in the lower half of the division competed against each other similarly to decide relegation. Pontypridd captain Neil Jenkins commented. "Having six play-off matches in late April and beginning of May is too much for the players. We do not have the strength in depth of some clubs and have to recruit in the summer if we are to compete with the best."

Neath, who were reported to be broke in the late summer of 1998, made a miraculous return to viability after 13 players had departed for pastures new. They certainly made events hum on the field and defeated both leaders, Llanelli and Pontypridd, at the Gnoll twice. The WRU permitted dual registration so that players could appear for two clubs on permit and this often eased problems in key positions when injuries struck.

RECORD 28 TRIES BY NEIL EDWARDS

Dunvant were Div 1 champs with a league record tally of 151 tries to pass the 137 by Caerphilly the previous season. Revitalised Pontypool made great efforts to challenge the leaders in Div 1 and the presence of player/coach David Bishop was of vital importance. Veteran of a thousand charges and, like Napoleon's Marshal Ney, the 'Bravest of the Brave', Bishop announced yet again that his playing days were over. But we all know that when the battle rages at its hottest and Pooler are in need of a champion, he will be the first to answer the call.

Abercynon had their special hero in skipper and No 8 Neil Edwards. He scored a league record 28 tries for a season in leading his club to the Div 2 title. Among other notable records we witnessed seven tries by Pontypridd wing Rhys Shorney against Aberavon and a 116-7 Div 2 victory by Ystradgynlais over Kenfig Hill as the highest score in the leading divisions.

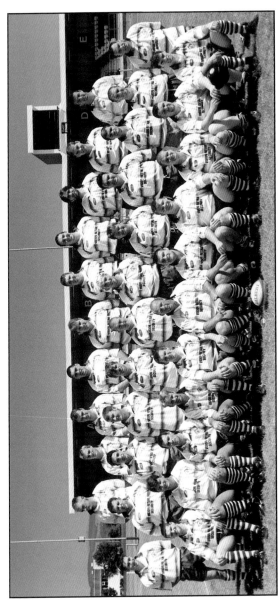

Caerphilly RFC. Back row (left to right): Brett Davey, Adam Palfrey, Martin Liddiart, Danzi Niblo, Ian Gardner, Jarrod Lougher, Antony Evans, Adrian Wainwright, David Duly, Roger Bidgood. Middle row: Jonathan Hooper, Robert Benson, Nigel Berbillion, Chris John, Chris Bridges, Darryl Williams, Ben Watkins, Tim Carless, Phil Ager, Darren Starr, Paul Williams, Owen Robbins. Front row: Steffan Jenkins, Nathan Jones (capt), Wayne Bray, Paul Phillips, Chris Murphy, Robert Bilton, Chris Ferris, Stuart Price, Sean Marshall, Richard Jasper, Richard Wintle.

Huw Evans Picture Agency, Cardiff

23

WEEK 1: Llanelli and Ebbw Vale, who climaxed the previous season with the SWALEC Cup final at Bristol, clashed again, this time to open the new season and with Llanelli once more victors. It was 35-18 after Ebbw had dominated the first half with two tries by wing Alun Harries. Stephen Jones supplied 15 goal points for the Scarlets. Neil Jenkins was on target with 13 goal points in Pontypridd's 23-3 success at Caerphilly. Caerphilly, record league try scorers the previous season with 137, failed to score one this time. Newport, reprieved from relegation by the decision of Cardiff and Swansea to opt out of the WRU National League, failed at home as Neath crushed them 36-8. Bridgend saw off Aberavon 45-10. The Wizards had won just one of their last 23 meetings with Bridgend.

WEEK 2: Pontypridd were the only unbeaten team after defeating Llanelli 22-15 as Ponty confirmed their role as championship favourites. But team boss Eddie Jones stressed, "We are disappointed with the way we are playing. We are making too many errors." Wing Rhys Shorney collected a debut try and Martyn Williams also crossed with Neil Jenkins hitting four penalty goals. Stephen Jones provided the Scarlets points with five penalty goals. Llanelli's Tony Copsey was sin-binned and then sent off four minutes into injury time. Newport registered their first league victory for 16 months. It came 47-5 at Aberavon with seven tries. Full back Gareth King (2), Nicky Lloyd (2), Gary Hicks, Martin Llewellyn and Rod Snow were the men who did the damage. Byron Hayward doomed Bridgend as the Ebbw Vale outside half dropped a goal from near the touchline after three minutes of injury time. Hayward provided 18 points (five penalty goals and a drop-shot) in a 23-20 verdict. David Llewellyn was Ebbw's try-getter. Gareth Cull kicked five Bridgend penalty goals and skipper Chris Stephens crossed for the try. Caerphilly registered a 21-18 success at Neath.

WEEK 3 (midweek): Full back Brett Davey, Caerphilly's Red Eminence, and the league's record scorer, produced another match-winning display in a 28-20 success at Newport. He kicked 13 points and set up two of the three tries by Chris Murphy, Richard Wintle and Paul Williams. For the 13th consecutive occasion Bridgend failed against Pontypridd. Inevitable defeat came 52-24 as Ponty collected six tries, including one by Greg Prosser as the giant lock sold an extravagant dummy. Neil Jenkins landed 22 points for Ponty to go top of the table, but they lost full back Kevin Morgan with a badly fractured left thumb. No 8 Scott Eggar scored both Neath tries at Stradey before Llanelli finished 30-20 winners with tries by Stephen Jones (2), Wayne Proctor (2) and Garan Evans. Full back Nick Stork pounced for Aberavon's try, but it could not save them from 29-5 home defeat by Ebbw Vale. Alun Harries collected two Ebbw tries.

WEEK 4: Former UWIC wing Rhys Shorney swept in for a premier/Div 1 record seven tries as Pontypridd hammered Aberavon 64-28. The previous best in the top divisions had been six by Llanelli's Ieuan Evans at Maesteg in October 1992; although Marc Evans obtained seven tries for Kidwelly in a Div 5 match at Hendy in the 1995/96 season. Shorney's second hat-trick took just eight minutes. The other three home tries came from Jason Lewis, Andrew Lamerton

The non-stick interior of every Tefal pan is guaranteed against blistering
or peeling during normal use.

and Neil Jenkins. Skipper Jenkins converted seven tries. No 8 Richard Morris gave the Wizards the lead with a try before Shorney shimmered into devastating action. Byron Hayward totted up 27 points with three tries and six conversions in Ebbw Vale's 57-17 victory over Newport.

Neil Boobyer's two tries spearheaded Llanelli to 51-20 success at Caerphilly after Brett Davey had fired his side into an 8-0 lead with a try and penalty shot. There were only some 2,000 at the Gnoll to see Neath overpower Bridgend 38-9. Home wing Delme Williams eluded four tackles to score a memorable try and Luke Richards kicked 18 points.

WEEK 5: Inspired by a brilliant display from skipper Kingsley Jones, Ebbw Vale became the first league team to defeat Pontypridd. Ebbw edged it at 24-23, but success was marred by Mark Jones felling Ponty's Ian Gough three minutes from the end. Jones marched and Gough needed an operation to repair a damaged right eye socket. It was a spine-tingling contest with the home side deserved winners. Byron Hayward supplied 14 points with four penalty goals and a conversion of one of the tries by Chay Billen and former Ponty wing David Manley. Ponty's tries came from Rhys Shorney and Gareth Wyatt. Neil Jenkins converted both tries and added three penalty shots. Newport, without a win at Stradey in 21 seasons and trailing 54-0, hit back with four tries, but were overwhelmed 68-26. Wayne Proctor scored two of the 10 home tries. Stephen Jones crossed for one try and converted nine for 23 points. Newport had prop Rod Snow ordered off six minutes from the end for a second late tackle. Aberavon led 20-10 at half time through two tries by fly half Richard Lewis, converted by Nick Stork; but visitors Neath powered away to win 37-27. Luke Richards contributed 22 Neath points. Star goal-kicker Gareth Cull missed four out of five penalty attempts and Bridgend were held to a 24-all verdict by visitors Caerphilly. Brett Davey landed 14 Caerphilly points, but missed a penalty shot five minutes from the end that would have snatched victory.

WEEK 6: All matches played later because of waterlogged pitches. Brett Davey supplied 19 goal points and Chris Brown and Richard Wintle each crossed twice for Caerphilly to slam Aberavon 49-19. A penalty try for a collapsed scrum four minutes into injury time gave Ebbw Vale 22-20 victory at Neath. Although the home side outscored Ebbw 3-1 on tries (two by hooker Mefin Davies, one by wing Delme Williams), Jason Strange angled in five penalty goals and converted the penalty try. Neil Boobyer's three sparkling tries proved the highlight as Llanelli turned on second half power to add 32 points in a 47-11 verdict over Bridgend. Pontypridd, much weakened because of injuries, held off Newport's stirring late rally at Rodney Parade to squeeze a 16-13 victory. Kevin Morgan and Ngalu T'au were Ponty try-getters and Gareth Wyatt fired over two penalty shots.

WEEK 7: Neath were no match for Pontypridd at muddy Sardis Road, where the visitors had not won for six years. It was 44-7 and Neath had two players sin-binned in the second half. Referee Nigel Whitehouse first binned Dale Jones for persistent infringement and two minutes later despatched full back Geraint Evans to cool his heels. Bridgend wing Owain Thomas ripped away for three tries to inspire a 30-24 victory over Newport, who now can claim just two successes against Bridgend in 12 meetings. Centre Matthew Watkins scored a sensational Newport try with a 90-yard interception. The lead changed five times at Ebbw Vale before Caerphilly lost 24-19. They were kept in contention by Brett Davey, who provided 14 points. Jason Strange, taking over kicking duties with Byron Hayward having joined Llanelli, landed three home conversions and a penalty shot. Cerith Rees scored a try and converted a penalty try, but could not save Aberavon from 48-12 home defeat by Llanelli.

WEEK 8: Pontypridd went top because Llanelli lost at Ebbw Vale. Ponty pulverised Caerphilly 55-15 with wing Gareth Wyatt whipping over for three of the eight tries. Neil Jenkins kicked 15 points. Ebbw Vale avenged their only defeat to date against the Scarlets, winning 24-20. Fly half Jason Strange collected 19 points, including a try. David Llewellyn was the other try-getter. Stephen Jones kicked five penalty goals for Llanelli and replacement centre Salesi Finau crossed for their try. Full back Nick Stork's try proved the turning point as Aberavon registered their first success. After 10 encounters with Bridgend without a win, the Wizards made it at 16-6. They had waited seven seasons for victory. Newport, with just one win at Neath during the previous 15 years, failed again, this time 30-13.

WEEK 9: Pontypridd had Dale McIntosh ordered off right at the end for a dangerous challenge on Rupert Moon and Llanelli's 24-16 success saw them displace Ponty at the top. Some Ponty players were visibly annoyed at losing their second game and skipper Neil Jenkins was

HOW THEY FINISHED

PREMIER DIVISION

	W	D	L	T	B	Pts
Llanelli	15	1	4	104	18	64
Pontypridd	12	0	8	80	10	46
Neath	12	0	8	68	8	44
Ebbw Vale	12	1	7	58	7	44
Caerphilly	10	2	8	63	5	37
Bridgend	9	2	9	61	5	34
Newport	5	0	15	63	8	23
Aberavon	2	0	18	51	4	10

DIVISION ONE

	W	D	L	T	B	Pts
Dunvant	24	1	5	151	24	97
Bonymaen	22	2	6	120	23	91
Pontypool	23	0	7	101	11	80
Treorchy	16	2	12	113	14	64
Cross Keys	18	1	11	88	7	62
Merthyr	16	2	12	87	9	59
Llandovery	15	2	13	104	9	56
Tredegar	16	1	13	84	6	55
Rumney	12	1	17	92	14	51
Newbridge	14	0	16	72	6	48
Abertillery	12	2	16	69	10	48
UWIC	12	1	17	74	5	42
Blackwood	10	1	19	87	9	40
Tondu	10	1	19	68	7	38
SW Police	9	1	20	71	1	29
Maesteg	2	0	28	45	2	8

DIVISION TWO

	W	D	L	T	B	Pts
Abercynon	20	0	6	114	20	80
Llanharan	19	0	7	119	22	79
Ystradgynlais	18	2	6	121	21	77
Whitland	21	0	5	98	12	75
Tenby Utd	17	0	9	105	15	66
Rhymney	16	0	10	89	11	59
Mountain Ash	15	0	11	55	5	50
Llantrisant	12	1	13	68	11	48
Narberth	13	0	13	65	5	44
Oakdale	8	0	18	63	10	34
St Peter's	8	0	18	73	9	33
Wrexham	9	1	15	52	3	31
Kenfig Hill	3	0	23	48	2	11
*Pyle	0	0	25	28	1	-5

(*Pyle had 6 pts deducted) Wrexham v Pyle not played)

physically restrained by teammates as he protested vigorously to referee Derek Bevan. "I am very disappointed with the amount of penalties given against us and disappointed with the way the game was handled," stressed Ponty coach Dennis John. Byron Hayward, signed from Ebbw Vale, marked his debut for Llanelli with eight penalty goals; Jenkins fired over three penalty shots and converted Kevin Morgan's try in front of 4,000 night watchers. Former Neath half backs Chris Bridges and Chris John helped defeat their old club 33-22 at Caerphilly, where Roger Bidgood and Chris Ferris scored home tries (plus a penalty try) and Brett Davey kicked 18 points. Ebbw Vale's second defeat came unexpectedly at Bridgend 23-14. Sam Greenaway and Chris Winn scored tries in Bridgend's third win. Newport registered their second success, accounting for Aberavon 36-16.

WEEK 10: All played later after heavy rainfall. Llanelli suffered their fourth defeat in their last five visits to the Gnoll, going down 24-21. Matthew Pearce, on loan from London Welsh, kicked 14 points and Mike Turner scored both home tries. Jonathan Hawker collected two of the eight Ebbw Vale tries in defeating Aberavon 52-17. Pontypridd's record win over Bridgend came 73-14 with full back Kevin Morgan collecting three of the 11 tries. Neil Jenkins scored 23 points. Two fine tries by back row forward Chris Brown set Caerphilly up for their second success against Newport, this time by a 40-25 margin.

WEEK 11: Newport's revenge for a 57-17 hammering was a totally unexpected jolt for third-placed Ebbw Vale. Shaun Connor coolly calculated his line of flight and sent a winning drop-shot sailing between the Ebbw posts from some 25 yards six minutes into injury time. So it was 30-29 and only Newport's third win. Their two previous successes had been against bottom team Aberavon. Connor finished with 15 points from kicks. Jason Strange fired over 19 Ebbw points. Bridgend's fifth successive defeat by Neath came 20-17 at the Brewery Field through a decisive Darren Case penalty goal. It was 17-all, but Bridgend could not escape the Gnoll team's grip. Only one win has come Bridgend's way during 16 meetings with the Blacks. No 8 Shawn van Rensberg, centre David Tueti and wing Case were the try-getters. Gareth Wyatt, deputising for Neil Jenkins, collected 14 points as Pontypridd won 49-21 in the Aberavon mud. It brought Ponty's ninth consecutive victory over the Wizards. Leaders Llanelli rattled up 10 tries to rout Caerphilly 62-7 with Chris Wyatt snapping up a hat-trick.

WEEK 12: Aberavon have not won at the Gnoll for 15 seasons. Though the Wizards led 10-0 on this latest visit, two tries by New Zealander Brett Sinkinson launched Neath's revival and Delme Williams added three tries for a 63-24 decision. Played later, Llanelli were 30-11 winners at Newport with 15 points from Byron Hayward. Neil Boobyer's punch sent Newport skipper Sven Cronk to hospital for six stitches beneath an eye. A second try by Chris Higgs two minutes from the end rescued Bridgend in a 31-all draw at Caerphilly. Brett Davey kicked 16 home points; Gareth Cull landed 16 for Bridgend. Ceri Sweeney, deputising for Neil Jenkins, kicked 11 vital points for Pontypridd to defeat Ebbw Vale 21-9.

WEEK 13: Three tries in six minutes right at the end by defiant 14-man Neath had Ebbw Vale gasping. But Ebbw held out for a 25-24 decision. Neath

Anthony Sullivan, the Great Britain RL wing, shows his paces for Cardiff. The Arms Park club signed him on a three-month loan contract from St Helens RL club, but had to release him in January. Cardiff would have kept him had he been available.

Huw Evans Picture Agency, Cardiff

had lock Mike Turner ordered off after only 17 minutes, but they refused to submit even though trailing 25-3. Shane Williams inspired the fightback with two tries and Richard Johnson added another in injury time. Bridgend battled with great determination before going down 32-17 to Llanelli at the Brewery Field. Neil Jenkins provided 21 points and full back Kevin Morgan swooped for two tries as Pontypridd hit Newport 31-16. Two tries by wing Richard Wintle helped Caerphilly win 27-24 at Aberavon, where the Wizards rallied purposefully after trailing by 15 points.

WEEK 14: One of the most thrilling contests of the season saw Neath's record score in matches against Pontypridd. The home side were surprise winners 53-31 with two penalty tries awarded by Robert Davies. Ponty also were stunned by the irrepressible drive of the superb Gnoll forwards with outstanding scrum half Mark Davies snapping inspiringly at their heels. Shane Williams, Geraint Evans, John Colderly and Leighton Gerrard crossed and Matthew Pearce converted four of the tries and fired over four penalty goals and a drop-shot for 23 points. At one stage it was 31-all. What a match! Three tries by Wayne Proctor, and 13 in all, produced a blistering record win for Llanelli in matches against Aberavon. It ended 83-10. Jason Strange kicked 14 points as Ebbw Vale won 24-13 at Caerphilly. A dismal performance by Bridgend cost them a 33-0 defeat at Newport.

PLAY-OFFS: Llanelli clinched the title by defeating Neath 37-11 in their fourth play-off match at Stradey. Byron Hayward kicked 17 points and Rupert Moon, Craig Warlow, Hywel Jenkins and Chris Wyatt scored the victors' tries. Neath had four players sin-binned. This success meant Llanelli maintained an unbeaten home record in the league and they did not lose a home fixture after the Euro Cup reverse 33-27 on September 19, 1998.

The Scarlets' first play-off game produced their only defeat in this new stage of the tournament: Neath stole a shock 32-17 decision at the Gnoll, which was only Llanelli's second defeat in all matches since they lost their Euro Cup quarter-final 34-17 away to Perpignan on December 12. Incidentally, Llanelli's defeat at the Gnoll was their third successive failure there. This time Matthew Pearce kicked 17 points.

Next up, Llanelli won 42-3 at Ebbw Vale with Byron Hayward totting up 22 points against his old clubmates. The former Welsh amateur light-middleweight boxing champion scored a try, converted four, kicked two penalty goals and popped over a superb 45-yard drop-shot. Salesi Finau crossed for two of the five tries as Ebbw Vale wilted. The best try, a bobby-dazzler, was obtained by American flanker David Hodge on the end of a string of five passes, and launched by prop John Davies.

Pontypridd could not deflect Llanelli from their title aim at Sardis Road and the visitors triumphed 42-12. Chris Wyatt was a two-try star and Hayward supplied 17 goal points. Weakened Ponty had to use scrum half Paul John as outside half deputy for Neil Jenkins and John put over four penalty goals as their only points.

Following their title-winning performance against Neath, Llanelli were jolted by Ebbw Vale's spirited resistance at Stradey. Indeed, it was only a penalty goal by Hayward five minutes from the end that saw the Scarlets scrape a

LEADING LEAGUE SCORERS 1998-99

MOST POINTS

Jason Williams (Newbridge) Div 1..........304
Matthew Silva (Pontypool) Div 1............285
Paul Jones (Mtn Ash) Div 2.....................274
Ioan Bebb (Cross Keys) Div 1.................259

Brett Davey (Caerphilly) Prem Div 257
David Love (Ystradgynlais) Div 2....................252
Wayne Jervis (Llanharan) Div 2........................247
Phil Withers (Abertillery) Div 1.......................223

MOST TRIES

Neil Edwards (Abercynon) Div 2 28
*Tevita Manaseitava (Dunvant) Div 1.......24
+ Mark Jones (Llandovery) Div 1 23

* Includes 3 for Pyle
+ Includes 1 each for Builth Wells and Llanelli
(Statistics apply to top three divisions only)

Stuart Harris (Ystradgynlais) Div 2 22
Chris Batsford (Bonymaen) Div 1 18
Adrian Killa (Dunvant) Div 1 18

desperate 23-all draw. In their final encounter, Llanelli disposed of Pontypridd for a fourth time in five meetings during the season (including the SWALEC Cup) in a most entertaining tussle at Stradey. It was 41-22 with seven home tries a week before Llanelli faced Swansea in the cup final. There were some 3,000 spectators to see captain Robin McBryde presented with the crystal glass League Trophy at the end of the match.

Pontypridd won only one of their six play-off matches, but they had established a seven point lead over third-placed Ebbw Vale and this proved enough to give them runner-up spot. Ponty's only play-off success came 34-29 over Ebbw Vale at Sardis Road. It was a thrilling contest with Ebbw leading 29-27 until the closing minutes, when wing Geraint Lewis crossed for his second try and Gareth Wyatt converted to the great relief of the Ponty faithful.

Ponty's first play-off saw Dafydd James race 70 yards for the most spectacular try at Ebbw Vale, but it could not save his side from 36-23 defeat. Another blow followed at the Gnoll with Neath 33-21 winners. Wing Shane Williams scored three tries and Matthew Pearce found the Ponty posts with 18 points. The return clash with Neath brought the visitors their first success at Sardis Road for seven years. Hooker Mefin Davies (2) and scrum half Mark Davies were Neath try men and Pearce kicked a penalty goal and drop-shot. Neath edged Ebbw Vale at the Gnoll 43-39 in a thrill-packed contest with wings Shane Williams and Delme Williams each scoring two home tries; but Neath lost the return 38-16 with Jason Strange kicking 18 Ebbw points.

Gareth Cull's 26 points from nine kicks - and never a miss - brought Bridgend a 31-25 decision against Caerphilly. Bridgend had prop Jason White ordered off after 24 minutes for punching, but the 14 men held out. Sam Greenaway's three tries spearheaded Bridgend to their first away league success of the season 68-26 at Aberavon with Cull contributing 23 points. Next, Gareth Jones's two tries encouraged Bridgend to 28-18 victory at Newport.   Cull's penalty goal two minutes from the end gave Bridgend a 32-30 verdict in a tense tussle at Caerphilly, where Brett Davey supplied 20 points. In the return with Newport, Gareth Jones again went in for two tries in a 55-29 win. With time fast running out, Aberavon led 33-32 at Bridgend, but in the second minute of injury time, Steve Ford pounced for his second try and Bridgend were 37-33 winners. Cerith Rees collected 18 Aberavon pints.

Caerphilly completed their five victories over Newport with first a 33-16 success at Rodney Parade (Davey 20 points) and then a 36-22 decision on waterlogged Virginia Park. Roger Bidgood obtained a try hat-trick as Caerphilly crushed Aberavon 65-13 (Davey 35 points) and Bidgood followed with another three tries in the 29-26 verdict at Aberavon, Bidgood's final try clinching a late victory.

Aberavon were in front 12-10 at the interval at Rodney Parade before Newport rallied to win 57-19 with Shaun Connor scoring two of the eight tries. Matt Cardy also crossed twice. Scott Mitchell's 22 points included a try. He snapped up two tries in 23 points at Aberavon, but could not prevent the Wizards winning 40-38 for their second victory of the season. Cerith Rees scored a try in his 20 home points.

DIVISION ONE

WEEK 1: Rumney, with ex-Pontypridd and Wales jumper Mark Rowley, a prominent new recruit, defeated UWIC 22-15. Dunvant's 50-6 victory over Maesteg featured 15 points by Mark Thomas. Two Austin Howells late penalty goals sealed Tredegar's fate 19-14 at Tondu. Pontypool were away to a rare winning start, accounting for Merthyr 20-13. Jason Williams fired over 16 points as Newbridge won 31-12 at SW Police. For the third successive season, Cross Keys disposed of Blackwood in the opening match: this time 28-18 at Blackwood. Played later, Treorchy stopped Abertillery 21-13. Bonymaen were 24-20 winners at Llandovery.

WEEK 2: A hat-trick of penalty goals and a drop-shot by outside half Jeremy Lloyd earned Merthyr an unconvincing 22-18 success over Tredegar. Wing Andrew Loring raced in for a spectacular 40-yard try for the winners. Maesteg led 12-11 at half time before visitors Treorchy powered to 49-12 victory. Carl Hammans and wing Gareth Martin each obtained two tries for the Zebras as 38 points came in the closing 25 minutes. David Evans contributed 14 goal points. Cross Keys produced a stunning second half display to defeat Llandovery 29-17. Coach David Rees enthused, "It was the best 40 minutes of rugby at Pandy Park for many years." Pontypool crashed 17-0 at Bonymaen, where a delightful last-minute try by former Rhigos fly half Stuart Davies was the highlight. SW Police lost to visitors Rumney 27-10. Former Wales wing Steve Ford snapped up two tries for Rumney. Outside half Jason Williams sparkled with 21 points, including a try, as Newbridge stopped Abertillery 31-23. Tondu, promoted from Div 2, fell 36-20 to visitors Dunvant. Blackwood were 30-11 victors at UWIC.

WEEK 3: A David Evans penalty goal two minutes from the end earned Treorchy a tense 11-8 decision against Tondu. Wings Jonathan Young and David Batsford swooped for the tries that produced Bonymaen's 17-14 success at Tredegar. Cross Keys lost their first game, going down 21-15 at Pontypool as Phil Ford's first try for Pooler clinched it. There was a first defeat also for Newbridge, beaten 30-16 at Rumney. Former Welsh international players Steve

A Tongan side-step! Llanelli centre Salesi Finau lets fly with a piston hand-off that Ebbw Vale flanker Gareth Green probably felt for a week afterwards. Ouch!

Huw Evans Picture Agency, Cardiff

Ford, Mark Rowley and Glen George were among the try scorers. A first win for Abertillery came 39-3 against Maesteg with two tries by centre Stuart Pennell. Leaders Dunvant were 18-9 winners against Merthyr. Injury-hit UWIC suffered 43-10 at Llandovery. Blackwood dominated SW Police 29-12.

WEEK 4: Newbridge raised their highest league tally in beating Maesteg 57-14. Jason Williams became the sixth player to pass 1000 league points as he totted up 22, including two tries. Leaders Rumney defeated Blackwood 27-7, spearheaded by Lee Abdul's two tries. Gafyn Cooper, deputy kicker for rested Ioan Bebb, put over three decisive conversion shots as Cross Keys fought off the challenge of Tredegar 21-18. Wings Andrew Loring and Neil Morgan, full back Grant Davies and scrum half Richard Williams crossed for Merthyr tries in a 26-11 verdict over Treorchy. Two tries by Matthew Rowlands failed to save UWIC from home defeat 26-10 by Pontypool. SW Police obtained their first point of the season in a 25-all draw with visitors Llandovery. Bonymaen were 29-19 winners against Dunvant. Abertillery won 22-17 at Tondu.

WEEK 5(midweek): Colin Lewis and Huw James each scored two tries as Llandovery schemed the first defeat of visitors Rumney 32-20. Tredegar's first success came 38-35 against UWIC with Dai Davies and Paul Hudson both crossing for two tries to establish a 38-7 lead before the students made their amazing rally, spearheaded by two Paul Jones tries. Maesteg failed 15-13 against visitors Tondu. Pontypool were 22-10 winners against SW Police, fired by David Bishop's two dummying tries from close range. Bonymaen's first defeat came 30-5 at Treorchy. Played later, Jeremy Lloyd's penalty shot with the last kick of the match earned Merthyr an 11-all draw at Abertillery. Matthew Veater's two tries encouraged Blackwood to 30-12 victory over Newbridge. Dunvant had lock Mark Glover ordered off, but still powered to 46-29 victory over Cross Keys at Broadacre. Keys trailed 29-3 at half time, but stormed back with Steve Gardner getting two tries. Emyr Harris and Tevita Manasateiva each crossed for two home tries.

WEEK 6: Dunvant became leaders with a 51-16 victory at UWIC. Although Dunvant had skipper Richard Llewellyn ordered off for punching just before half time, Adrian Killa snapped up three of their seven tries and Mark Thomas supplied 16 goal points. Rumney nosed ahead 16-0 at Riverside Park, but Pontypool crowned their impressive rescue act with a David Bishop drop-shot in the last minute for a 25-22 verdict. SW Police registered their first win 30-20 at Tredegar with Mark Cox on target with 15 points. Six penalty goals by Ioan Bebb saw Cross Keys defy Treorchy 18-17 after the Zebras had scored three tries. Jason Williams's 19 points launched Newbridge to 34-16 success against Tondu. Stuart Davies popped over two drop shots and a couple of penalty goals for Bonymaen to topple Abertillery 12-3. Llandovery won 17-8 at Blackwood. Maesteg lost 21-9 at Merthyr.

WEEK 7: Llandovery had prop Arwel Evans ordered for an early bath, but still snatched a 23-20 verdict to inflict Newbridge's first home defeat. Daniel Stead's injury-time try stole it for the Drovers. Cross Keys led 21-12 at Abertillery before Phil Withers ensured home success 27-21 with 19 points, including a try and two drop-shots. Blackwood's rip-roaring second half rally gave Pontypool an anxious time, but Pooler held on for a 33-32 decision. Daniel

Fofana's two spectacular tries could not prevent Merthyr's 31-19 triumph at Tondu. Former Wales Youth scrum half Paul Young was driven across by his forwards for a try five minutes from the end and Matthew Chapman converted for Tredegar's 26-20 victory over Rhymney. Chapman's 21 points included a try. Bottom team Maesteg crashed 39-12 to visitors Bonymaen. Chris Batsford and Dean Evans each scored two Bonymaen tries. Leaders Dunvant defeated SW Police 41-17. Key Police players were absent, on duty at Welsh farmers' protest demonstrations.

WEEK 8: Bonymaen replaced Dunvant as leaders with a hurricane blast to destroy Tondu 50-15. Scrum half Graeme Alexander snapped up two of the eight tries and Stuart Davies contributed 15 points, including a try. Although wing Lee Abdul was clawed down inches short after a 90-yard interception run, Rumney kept up the pressure to topple Dunvant 16-11 - and Abdul scored a late try. Newbridge inflicted Merthyr's first home reverse 31-17 with 16 goal points from Jason Williams. Ioan Bebb supplied 16 points as Cross Keys thundered to 51-0 victory over Maesteg. After five successive league wins, Pontypool were nudged out 26-22 at Llandovery. Tongan recruit Feao Vunipola scored a debut try for Pooler. SW Police surprised Treorchy 17-15 with tries by Sean Legge, Richard Gregory and Steve Rees. Abertillery lost 30-22 at UWIC. Unyielding defence earned Tredegar a 25-all draw at Blackwood.

WEEK 9: Bonymaen lost for the second time, but retained top spot. They failed by a whisker at Merthyr 23-22 as Jeremy Lloyd's penalty shot went over right at the end. Two tries by Anthony Rees inspired Dunvant to 31-22 success over persistent Blackwood. Pontypool's first victory at Newbridge for almost four years came 25-6 with 10 goal points from Matthew Silva. Stuart Hancox kicked 14 points to render vital aid for Llandovery in a 39-30 decision against Tredegar. Former Wales and Neath lock Glyn Llewellyn could not save Maesteg from home defeat 54-13 by UWIC. The return of playmaker David Evans revitalised Treorchy for a 25-0 win over Rumney, though the Zebras had Gavin Owen sent off. No 8 Eddie Lewis collected his first Cross Keys try in a 23-13 success at Tondu. Abertillery were 33-8 winners against SW Police with 15 Phil Withers goal points.

WEEK 10: Dunvant took over at the top because they won 32-15 at Llandovery in the only match played. Mark Thomas's 17 points included a try. Played later, Pontypool defeated Tredegar 30-11 with Matthew Silva kicking 15 points. After 10 successive league defeats, SW Police were 37-29 winners over Maesteg with 24 points from Matthew Brown, on permit from Pencoed. Ioan Bebb kicked 18 points for Cross Keys to defeat Merthyr 33-24. Rumney stopped Abertillery 25-11. UWIC beat Tondu 29-17. Treorchy triumphed 30-17 at Blackwood. Bonymaen equalled their league best with a 60-27 verdict against Newbridge at Parc Mawr. Wings Chris Batsford and Paul John each scored two tries and Stuart Davies kicked 15 points.

WEEK 11: Bonymaen lost their first home game 30-6 with Gafyn Cooper collecting 15 Cross Keys points. The lead changed hands six times before Tredegar snatched their first away success 18-16 at Newbridge. Matthew Chapman decided the issue with a penalty shot in the last few minutes. Tredegar had scrum half Paul Young dismissed for reckless use of the boot. Merthyr's 20-

15 verdict over UWIC featured tries by No 8 Mark David and fly half Adam Rosser, who also dropped a goal. Played later, Tondu were 27-10 winners over SW Police with impressive Daniel Fofana's try setting them on the way. David Evans kicked 10 vital points so Treorchy edged Llandovery 25-24. Referee Peter Rees showed the red card to Pontypool's David Bishop - and he wasn't even playing. Bishop, Pooler's player/coach was protesting that sin-binned scrum half Manu Vunipola had been off for 12 minutes instead of 10. The ref ordered Bishop off the bench and into the crowd. Pooler lost 27-23 at Dunvant with Simon Daniel contributing 17 points. Scrum half Lloyd Paget scored a late try for Maesteg to shock Rumney 32-31. Abertillery were 23-5 winners against Blackwood.

WEEK 12: Maesteg secured their long-awaited first success 21-19 at Blackwood. Full back Ed Griffiths scored both Old Parish tries. Richard Davies converted one and put over three penalty goals. Matthew Silva was the star for Pontypool in a 30-21 decision against Treorchy. The full back scored a try, converted three, kicked two penalty goals and added a drop shot for 20 points. No 8 Geraint Gladwyn snapped up both Abertillery tries in a 32-22 verdict at Llandovery. For the first time SW Police registered a league win against Merthyr. It was 27-20 as Ian Hemburrow stormed across for his 63rd try - a league record for a forward. Tondu lost 33-18 at Rumney and the visitors had Nathan Strong dismissed after 20 minutes. Leaders Dunvant won 32-22 at Tredegar with Adrian Killa a two-try getter. Bonymaen were held to 14-all at UWIC, where David Hawkins scored two Bonymaen tries. Cross Keys suffered their first home defeat, going down 20-9 to Newbridge, with four players sin-binned.

WEEK 13: Bonymaen struck peak form to wreck Rumney 60-0. Paul John snapped up four of the nine tries in his first appearance of the season. Veteran scrum half David Bishop scored the first try to set Pontypool on the way to 38-8 success at Maesteg. Newbridge had captain Matthew Taylor ordered off in the first half and lost their fourth consecutive home match, going down 35-27 to UWIC. Wing Chris Howells went in for two tries as Cross Keys defeated SW Police 30-12. Skipper Nick Davies led the way with two tries as Merthyr blasted Blackwood 22-5. Llandovery, trailing 7-6 at the interval, unleashed a searing scoring burst to savage Tondu 41-18. Abertillery took a 21-11 decision against Tredegar.

WEEK 14: Jonathan Bryant's eight goal points were decisive as Merthyr snatched a 23-22 decision at Rumney. Wing Neil Morgan scored two Merthyr tries. After six successive defeats, Tondu registered a 12-5 victory at Blackwood with Daniel Fofana collecting two tries. Gerald Williams obtained a hat-trick of tries as Bonymaen won 36-14 at SW Police. Abertillery, winners in three meetings with Pontypool the previous season, failed 35-17. Matthew Silva totted up 20 home points, including a try. For the fifth time, Maesteg were overwhelmed by a half-century of points: it was 57-15 at Llandovery. Stuart Hancox converted seven of the eight tries and added a penalty goal. Leaders Dunvant were 41-26 winners against Newbridge. Deiniol Evans was a two-try getter for Dunvant. Matthew Chapman kicked 14 points to give Tredegar the verdict 19-7 over Treorchy. Ioan Bebb, in his 100th appearance for Cross Keys, supplied 15 points in a 20-13 success at UWIC.

Brett Davey, Caerphilly's deadly match-winner with his goal-kicking. The accomplished full back holds WRU National League records for most points in a season and most points in a match. He also enjoys the distinction of being Wales's Most Overlooked Player of the Year. Joined Pontypridd for 1999-2000 season.

Huw Evans Picture Agency, Cardiff

WEEK 15: Tondu assistant coach and former Wales wing Glen Webbe forecast his team would shock Pontypool. They did, becoming the first team to win on Pooler territory. It was 30-22 with Austin Howells (2) and Glyn Welsh scoring tries and Gethin Watts providing 15 goal points. Second-placed Bonymaen scraped an 8-7 decision at Blackwood through a penalty goal in the closing moments by Stuart Davies after Chris Lay had converted Wayne Simms's home try. Richard Langmead's 18 goal points proved decisive as Treorchy fought off Newbridge's late rally to snatch it 33-30. Leaders Dunvant chopped up a half-strength Abertillery 64-3 with nine tries. Colin Ellis collected two of the seven Cross Keys tries as they won 45-15 at Rumney. Llandovery's resolute recovery rescued them 18-14 against Merthyr with Mark Jones and Paul Jones snatching vital tries. UWIC were 8-5 winners at SW Police. Played later, Maesteg lost 52-11 to Tredegar (played at Ebbw Vale) with scrum half Paul Young scoring three tries. Martin Jones kicked 17 points.

WEEK 16: It was marching orders for Pontypool hooker Feao Vunipola, a Tongan international, at Merthyr and Pooler went down 27-17 for Merthyr to avenge earlier defeat. Blackwood also took revenge. They won 22-19 at Cross Keys with full back Dean Brown scoring a vital try. Abertillery's first home defeat came 38-10 as Treorchy stormed to their second away victory of the season. Richard Langmead totted up 18 points, including two tries. Jason Williams scored all the Newbridge points in a 13-7 verdict over SW Police. Simon Greedy collected two tries for Rumney to win 37-7 at UWIC. Matthew Chapman's penalty goal could not deflect defeat and Tredegar went down at home 6-3 as Gethin Watts and Karl Hocking found the target with penalty shots for Tondu. Leaders Dunvant destroyed Maesteg 66-0 at the Old Parish ground while Bonymaen accounted for Llandovery 29-5.

WEEK 17: Cross Keys won 17-13 in driving rain at Llandovery with Andrew Price securing the decisive try. Hooker Simon Delaney scored his first try to help Dunvant fight off Tondu 19-10. Played later, Newbridge lost 9-3 at Abertillery. Matthew Silva provided all the points for Pontypool to pip Bonymaen 22-21. He converted his try and kicked five penalty goals. Wayne Simms scored two tries as Blackwood stopped UWIC 29-7. Treorchy trounced Maesteg 55-0 with eight tries. Rhymney's 25-20 home defeat by SW Police meant the Riverside Park team managed just one victory from their final eight games. The relegated Police scored a spectacular length-of-the-field try by skipper Mark Cox. Merthyr won 31-10 at Tredegar.

WEEK 18: Merthyr hung on tenaciously for revenge 24-19 against leaders Dunvant at The Wern with two tries each by Stefan Jenkins and Neil Morgan. Newbridge found themselves 8-0 in front before Rumney, inspired by coach Mike Watkins's illuminating half-time pep-talk, stole it 14-11 through a try by Max Ryce. Jason Williams's two home penalty goals saw the Newbridge kicker become the first league player to reach 200 points for the season. Treorchy were 37-10 winners at Tondu with wing Gareth Martin crossing twice. Bonymaen registered the double 20-0 over Tredegar. Abertillery won 23-10 at Maesteg. Played later, Cross Keys shocked Pontypool 10-6 as Ioan Bebb converted prop Darren Crimmins's try and added a penalty goal. Phil Sparrow's late penalty goal meant SW Police beat Blackwood 22-19. UWIC surprised Llandovery 43-32 with 23 points by John Welch.

WEEK 19: Top team Dunvant deflected the challenge of second-placed Bonymaen 17-12 with tries by Adrian Killa and Phil Middleton. Simon Daniel converted both and landed a penalty goal. Full back Chris Lewis and Mark John crossed for Bonymaen; Stuart Davies converted one. Scrum half Shane Pinch's two tries behind a driving Tredegar pack produced 25-12 success against Cross Keys. Mark Jones racked up a hat-trick of tries as Llandovery ripped into SW Police 39-8. Maesteg missed five penalty shots and lost 12-10 to visitors Newbridge. Prop Shaun Mason and wing Mark Addis crossed for the winners. Outside half Simon Davies darted down the blind-side for the decisive try in Rhymney's 17-10 victory at Blackwood. Pontypool pounded UWIC 44-22. Treorchy registered revenge over Merthyr 32-20. Tondu lost 32-14 at Abertillery.

WEEK 20: Two tries by Richard Field and one by hooker Feao Vunipola saw Pontypool win 20-7 at SW Police. Merthyr took command in the second half to defeat Abertillery 31-22 with two tries by Neil Morgan. Newbridge impressed with a revenge 27-5 decision against Blackwood. There was a try hat-trick from wing Mark Addis. Outside half Stuart Davies scored 13 points, including a try, as Bonymaen topped Treorchy 18-10. The Zebras suffered a catalogue of injuries, including former Wales star David Evans stretchered off with a damaged rib. Tondu stopped Maesteg 20-3 with tries by Daniel Fofana, Nathan Strong and Karl Hocking. Played later, Dunvant won 28-24 at Cross Keys as Simon Daniel made a decisive contribution with 18 points. No 8 Chris Hughes scored two tries as Llandovery won 26-19 at Rumney. Tredegar were 29-12 winners at UWIC.

WEEK 21: Merthyr's two penalty tries, converted by Tommy Price, brought a lucky 14-12 win at Maesteg. A hotly-disputed penalty award during injury time saw Matthew Silva on target with the winning kick for Pontypool 18-15 against Rumney. Silva landed all the Pooler points with five penalty shots and a drop-goal. Rumney's Keith Lee crossed and they were awarded a penalty try. Two tries by Paul Morris saved Treorchy as they trailed 25-13. The Zebras forced a 25-all draw with visitors Cross Keys. Tondu clamped an unbreakable grip through their forwards to beat Newbridge 22-3. Richard Morgan and Karl Hocking each crossed for two tries. Phil Middleton's three tries saw leaders Dunvant triumph 39-13 against UWIC. A penalty try in the closing minutes enabled Bonymaen to draw 19-all at Abertillery. Opposing outside halves Phil Withers (Abertillery) and Stuart Davies each kicked 14 points. Blackwood's power pack paved the way for 27-13 victory at Llandovery. Tredegar avenged earlier defeat 27-13 at SW Police.

WEEK 22: Mark Thomas scored 16 points as Dunvant won 47-6 at SW Police. A long, late penalty goal by Glyn Welsh earned Tondu an 18-all draw at Merthyr. Played later, Newbridge lost 22-18 at Llandovery where wing Tracey Lewis and Huw Thomas crossed and there also was a penalty try for the Drovers. A late second try by Matthew Silva, which he converted after kicking a penalty goal for all Pontypool's points, brought a tense 15-13 verdict at Blackwood. Wing Paul John's three tries pointed the way for Bonymaen to take Maesteg 49-12. Full back Gareth Davies crossed for two tries for the Old Parish. Cross Keys beat Abertillery 34-18. Shane Pinch, Andrew Smereon and Andy Jewitt each snapped up two tries in Tredegar's 40-27 success at Rumney. UWIC played their sixth game in a fortnight and it produced 21-15 victory over Treorchy. The Zebras had skipper Paul Morris sent off when they were leading 12-6 and the students sealed success with two tries in the last five minutes, both by Julian Moroney.

WEEK 23: Ioan Bebb scored all the Cross Keys points in a 22-19 win at Maesteg to pass 1000 league points. Matthew McCarthy obtained two of Pontypool's nine tries in a 62-17 demolition of Llandovery. Adrian Killa collected a try hat-trick in Dunvant's 73-0 success against Rumney. But it was tight at Abertillery before the home side edged UWIC 12-11 with Phil Withers converting one of the tries by prop Peter Harriman and No 8 Geraint Gladwyn. Revenge for Treorchy came 67-19 against SW Police with 17 goal points from David Evans. Bonymaen were 28-6 winners at Tondu. Blackwood lost 17-8 at Tredegar. Merthyr avenged earlier defeat 24-6 at Newbridge.

WEEK 24: No 8 Stuart Jarman's hat-trick of tries set Tredegar up for 34-15 success against Llandovery with Martin Jones supplying 14 goal points. Leaders Dunvant were 65-17 winners at Blackwood with 14 points from Mark Thomas. Gavin Owen's two tries from close range augured well for Treorchy at Rumney, but the home side hit back to make it 22-all with tries by Steve Ford and Ben Atkins. Tondu snatched a surprise 19-13 verdict at Cross Keys. Two tries by wing Phil Sparrow proved the flight-path to 23-21 victory for SW Police over Abertillery. Pontypool's forward power wore down Newbridge 17-7. Chris Batsford was a two-try getter as Bonymaen blasted Merthyr 47-3. Played later because their players were on strike, Maesteg lost to UWIC 22-10.

WEEK 25: A last-minute try by hooker Lee Gardner brought Cross Keys 21-18 success at Merthyr. Leaders Dunvant drew 17-all at Llandovery. The Drovers could have stolen it with a late penalty, but Aled Williams's shot whispered just wide. Jason Williams kicked 13 points and Gareth Bisp and Alan Lucas crossed to enable Newbridge to dispose of Bonymaen 23-8. Centre Lee Abdul's try and a Jonathan Mason drop-shot earned Rumney 8-0 victory at Abertillery. Played later, Treorchy battered Blackwood 53-15. UWIC were 18-5 winners at Tondu. Maesteg went down again at home as SW Police won 31-21. An injury-time try by centre Dai Davies, converted by Matthew Chapman, saw Tredegar stop Pontypool 18-13.

WEEK 26: Tondu led 18-0 at SW Police, but an amazing recovery brought a 20-18 home victory as Phil Sparrow crossed with the final move of the game. John Apsee, customarily a centre, figured at No 8 and scored another Police try. Treorchy were 32-31 winners at Llandovery thanks to 17 points by Richard Langmead. John Welch kicked 13 points for UWIC to surprise Merthyr 23-10. The match was played at Cardiff RFC ground. Martin Ackerman scored two tries as Blackwood stopped Abertillery 30-22. Played later, Bonymaen (two tries by wing Paul John) avenged earlier defeat with 35-12 success at Cross Keys. Newbridge wing Mark Addis and Tredegar scrum half Shane Pinch each snapped up a try hat-trick, but visitors Newbridge lost 34-27 as the goal kicking of Martin Jones proved decisive. Maesteg lost 62-29 at Rumney. Pontypool avenged earlier defeat with a 24-11 decision over champions Dunvant. Will James, Matthew Silva and Danny Barrier scored Pooler tries.

WEEK 27: Matthew Silva's drop-shot in the eighth minute of injury time

40

The Man from Nowhere! Scott Gibbs materialises through a shocked England defence en route to score THAT Wembley try.

Huw Evans Picture Agency, Cardiff

stole Pontypool an anxious 20-17 decision at Treorchy. A dazzling move brought Rob Sidoli the outstanding try of the match in Merthyr's 41-20 win over SW Police. Mark Purdue's Dunvant took another step towards the division title with a 26-13 victory against Tredegar. Mark Bowcott's two tries could not save Rumney from 34-12 defeat at Tondu. Darren Wright lanced through for the winning try as Abertillery disposed of Llandovery 24-19. Matthew Veater crossed twice in Blackwood's 27-10 success at Maesteg. Cross Keys failed 24-10 at Newbridge. Bonymaen dispatched UWIC 23-3.

WEEK 28: Leaders Dunvant were 46-27 winners over Treorchy and in the process set a Div 1 record try aggregate of 138 to pass Caerphilly's 137. Dunvant battled back from 20-7 down with two tries by Fijian centre Tevita Manaseitava. John Colderley, borrowed from Neath, was among the Treorchy try-getters. Pontypool scourged Maesteg 67-3 as Mark Cawley (3) and David Bishop (2) led the way with tries. Matthew Silva supplied 17 points. Gareth Jones's two tries spearheaded Bonymaen to 19-10 success at Rumney. No 8 Jamie Sims surged over during injury time to bring Blackwood a 33-29 verdict over Merthyr after the lead swung five times. Tredegar avenged earlier defeat against Abertillery 25-24 with Martin Jones kicking 20 points, including three drop-shots. Javed Nolan scored the home try. Wing Ian Perryment's two tries enabled Newbridge to win 28-20 at UWIC. Llandovery won 29-20 at Tondu with two Tracey Lewis tries. Ioan Bebb's 15 points in Cross Keys 50-31 success at SW Police saw him top his club record of 323 set the previous season. Craig Clements collected three Keys tries.

WEEK 29: Bonymaen's all action back row of Chris Powell (4), David Hills (2) and Andy McPherson shared all seven tries between them in the 41-0 success over weakened SW Police. Jeremy Lloyd converted Richard Sheppeard's injury time try to bring Merthyr their first double over Rumney. It was 29-28 with Jonathan Mason supplying 18 Rumney points. Leaders Dunvant suffered their first reverse for three months as they flopped 23-13 at Newbridge. Paul Jones and Matthew Taylor scored home tries and Jason Williams kicked 13 points. Tongan hooker Feao Vunipola snapped up two tries in the first two minutes as Pontypool scraped in 19-17 at Abertillery. Tondu's determined fightback from 22-3 down could not save them as visitors Blackwood took a 34-20 verdict with 14 goal points from Dean Brown. Tredegar stole a 25-20 victory at shocked Treorchy. UWIC also sprang a surprise 27-0 at Cross Keys. Llandovery were 52-5 winners at Maesteg.

WEEK 30: Bonymaen, after winning the Tovali Cup in midweek against Dunvant, rattled up nine tries while defeating Blackwood 59-22. Wings Paul John and Chris Batsford, skipper Mark John and full back Dean Evans were each two-try getters for Bonymaen. Tondu led 24-22 before visitors Pontypool snapped up a late try by replacement prop Graham Woodward and a Matthew Silva penalty goal for 30-24 victory. Steve Gardiner led the way with two tries as Cross Keys stopped Rumney 54-26. Dunvant were 30-23 winners at Abertillery with 15 points from Simon Daniel, including a try; UWIC recorded their third win in a week with a 28-24 decision against SW Police. Dan Batty's two drop shots proved decisive for the students. Neil Bundock scored two Police tries. Llandovery registered a 37-28 success at Merthyr. Tredegar won 40-21 at Maesteg. Played later, Newbridge defeated visitors Treorchy 21-10.

WEEK 1: Llantrisant, Div 3 champions the previous season with just three defeats, lost their opening match in this new division, going down 25-21 to visitors Tenby. Neil Truman was a two-try scorer for the winners. Rhymney also promoted, suffered the same fate, failing at home 20-18 against Whitland. However, Oakdale marked their promotion with a 14-7 verdict at Abercynon. Llanharan snatched an 18-13 decision at Mountain Ash through tries by Denver Thompson and David Griffiths. Wrexham, fast-tracked through from Div 5 East, won 18-10 at Pyle as Graham Spence kicked eight decisive points and scored a try. Ystradgynlais were 18-0 winners at St Peter's with Bleddyn Howells swooping for two tries. Shane Williams's three tries set Narberth en route to 57-14 victory over Kenfig Hill.

WEEK 2: Llanharan's Chris Rees snapped up two tries in defeating St Peter's 21-9. Narberth surprised Wrexham, winning there 20-12 with two tries by Chris McDonald. Wayne Booth's goal-kicking helped Rhymney triumph 15-5 at Pyle. Rob Parfitt's two tries could not save Oakdale from home defeat 23-17 by Tenby. Mountain Ash won 20-3 at Kenfig Hill. Llantrisant were 17-0 winners at Ystradgynlais. Whitland failed at home, going down 13-3 to Abercynon.

WEEK 3: Paul Jones supplied 14 goal points for Mountain Ash to defeat Wrexham 39-10. Wayne Booth's two penalty goals were vital in Rhymney's 16-12 verdict at Narberth. St Peter's ran in eight tries to win 53-24 against Kenfig Hill. Whitland walloped Pyle 51-10. Leaders Abercynon were 24-16 winners at Tenby. Llantrisant accounted for Llanharan 15-6. Ystradgynlais defeated Oakdale 20-10.

WEEK 4: Abercynon, the only unbeaten side in the division, defeated Pyle 20-10 with two tries by skipper Neil Edwards. Paul Jones monopolised the scoring as Mountain Ash won 22-13 against Rhymney. He produced a try, converted, kicked three penalty goals and added a drop-shot for 19 points. Whitland were 9-6 winners at Narberth with Stephen Pearce on target with a dropped goal and two penalty shots. Tenby went down at home 15-7 as David Love fired over four Ystradgynlais penalty goals and a drop-kick. Eubie Snyman's two tries helped Wrexham account for St Peter's 39-12. Denver Thomson's two tries paved the way for Llanharan's 32-6 success at Oakdale. Kenfig Hill lost 18-0 at Llantrisant.

WEEK 5: Former Wales and Swansea flanker Alan Reynolds scored a try for Whitland in their 15-3 success over Mountain Ash. Leaders Llantrisant were 41-13 winners at Wrexham with 13 goal points by Kevin Jenkins. Oakdale recorded their first victory 27-5 at Kenfig Hill. Robert Barnett was a two-try getter. Neil Edwards inspired Abercynon with two tries in a 35-25 decision at Ystradgynlais. There were nine tries for Rhymney in a 47-18 win over St Peter's. Only one was converted. Tenby shook Llanharan to their first home defeat 17-12. Narberth won 24-16 at Pyle.

WEEK 6: With Abercynon suffering their first defeat, going down 35-27 to visitors Narberth (Lee Rogers 15 Narberth points), Llantrisant climbed to top spot with a 21-10 verdict over Rhymney. Kevin Jenkins scored 13 points. Neil Forrester contributed 16 points for Pyle at Mountain Ash, but his side lost 33-26. Stuart Harris's two tries helped Ystradgynlais edge Llanharan 37-36. David Love put over 14 points for the winners. Justin Price landed 18 points for Tenby to blast Kenfig Hill 53-12. Whitland, in second place, triumphed 38-30 at St Peter's. Oakdale lost 13-6 to visitors Wrexham.

WEEK 7: Whitland were 23-7 winners against leaders Llantrisant to take over top spot. Steve Pearce kicked 13 points. Andrew Thomas skewered over for three tries as Tenby triumphed 48-13 at Wrexham. Tries by Steve Dodd and Denver Thomson paved the way for Llanharan to inflict Abercynon's second defeat 18-8. Bottom team Kenfig Hill suffered a home drubbing 67-13 as Ystradgynlais poured through for 11 tries. Narberth fought off a vigorous Mountain Ash challenge 25-16. St Peter's recorded their second success 32-6 at Pyle. Played later, Rhymney defeated Oakdale 24-22. Two Royston O'Reilly tries helped swing it.

WEEK 8: All fixtures played later because of waterlogged grounds. Llanharan's record league victory 83-0 over Kenfig Hill featured four tries each by wings Dewi Decaux and Scott Bowen. Wayne Jervis converted nine. Llantrisant swamped Pyle 71-0 with 11 tries. Three tries from close-up scrums by No 8 Neil Edwards spearheaded Abercynon to 21-6 success over Mountain Ash. Abercynon were aided by former Wales lineout jumper Mark Rowley, on permit from Rumney. Wayne Booth's goal-kicking helped Rhymney to a surprise 32-14 win at Tenby. St Peter's defeated Narberth 23-5 with Chris Norman collecting two tries. Wrexham lost at Ystradgynlais 43-0. Oakdale went down 36-15 at Whitland. Nolan Goodman scored a try-hat-trick for Whitland.

WEEK 9: Pyle bowed to their heaviest league reverse 63-7 at Oakdale. Jeff Relf scored 14 points, including two tries. Tenby replaced Whitland as leaders with a 15-13 verdict, helped by a penalty try against the Whitland visitors. Wayne Jervis kicked his fourth penalty goal right at the end to give Llanharan 12-9 victory at Wrexham in a game of no tries. Paul Jones supplied 19 points as Mountain Ash defeated St Peter's 34-16. Ystradgynlais were 28-14 winners at Rhymney. Played later, Narberth defeated Llantrisant 29-7. Scrum half Chris McDonald scored two tries. Abercynon won at Kenfig Hill 76-10 with a salvo of 12 tries. Skipper Neil Edwards scored four of them.

WEEK 10: A thumping victory by Tenby Utd 34-0 at Pyle took them to the top of the table with Justin Price scoring two tries in his 14 points. Ystradgynlais were 11-7 winners at Whitland as David Love dropped a goal and put over a penalty shot. Paul Jones slotted in two drop-goals in his 14 points for Mountain Ash to defeat Llantrisant 24-14. Chris Monk's three tries spearheaded Wrexham to 40-18 success at Kenfig Hill. Robbie Savage was on target with 13 goal points to edge Abercynon through 23-18 against St Peter's. Llanharan triumphed 27-8 over Rhymney. Oakdale lost 22-16 at Narberth.

WEEK 11: Ystradgynlais displaced leaders Tenby by blasting Pyle 59-5. Stuart Harris's four tries catapulted the winners to the top and David Love joined in with 19 points, including a try. Wayne Booth took centre stage with two tries in his 26 points for Rhymney to subdue Kenfig Hill 41-10. Justing Price's 14

New Zealander Brett Sinkinson charges at Italian defenders in Treviso in 1999. He qualified for Wales through a Welsh grandfather and proved a tireless and tenacious worker for his adopted country and for revitalised Neath as a flank forward.

Huw Evans Picture Agency, Cardiff

goal points saw Tondu defeat Narberth 24-12. Graham Spence fired over 13 points as Wrexham shaded Abercynon 28-25. Huw Locke's two drop shots helped Llantrisant fight off St Peter's 26-16. Paul Jones kicked a decisive nine points for Mountain Ash to triumph 24-16 at Oakdale. Whitland were 28-18 winners at Llanharan.

WEEK 12: Ystradgynlais were shaded 16-15 at Narberth, but still stayed top. Chris McDonald and Daniel Griffiths scored home tries and Lee Rogers hit over two penalty shots. Tenby also lost, but remained in second spot. They went down 20-7 at Mountain Ash, where Paul Jones supplied 15 points, including a try. Neil Lewis was on the mark with three tries for Abercynon to lambast Llantrisant 44-10. Llanharan's 56-3 victory at Pyle featured a hat-trick of tries by Dewi Decaux. Kenfig Hill crashed 55-0 at Whitland, where Frank Setaro slipped away for three tries. Chester Robinson's two tries helped St Peter's fight off Oakdale 26-23. Rhymney were on top 25-16 at Wrexham.

WEEK 13: With Ystradgynlais losing at Mountain Ash, Tenby Utd took over the lead by winning 34-14 at St Peter's. Chris Morgan scored three Tenby tries. Paul Jones obtained all the points for the Old Firm in the 19-18 victory over Ystradgynlais. His collection included two drop shots and a try. Llanharan closed up on the leaders with a 29-3 verdict at Narberth. Neil Edwards was a two-try scorer as Abercynon accounted for home side Rhymney 29-19. Robbie Savage added 14 goal points. Three penalty goals by Kevin Jenkins eased Llantrisant home 14-8 against Oakdale. Kenfig Hill held off Pyle 15-8. Played later, Whitland defeated Wrexham 43-18 with two Simon Thomas tries.

WEEK 14: Pace-setting Tenby displayed their awesome all-round power to rout Llantrisant 67-0, but it was knife-edge stuff at Llanharan before the home side edged it 17-14 against Mountain Ash. Ystradgynlais's finishing proved deadly as they devastated St Peter's 52-14. Played later, Rhymny just failed at Whitland despite a furious fightback. Whitland held on for a 28-24 decision. Abercynon were 45-6 winners at Oakdale. Narberth's power paid off for a 33-15 decision at Kenfig Hill.

WEEK 15: Tenby were grateful to Justin Price for nine vital goal points in their 29-23 win over Oakdale. Second-placed Ystradgynlais could only draw 3-3 at Llantrisant. David Love kicked the visitors' penalty goal; Huw Locke put over a drop-shot for Llantrisant. Bottom team Pyle were hit by Rhymney's Operation Try-Storm: there were 11 tries in a 64-0 demolition and Matthew Pizey scored three of them. Paul Jones supplied 17 goal points as Mountain Ash mangled Kenfig Hill 42-3. Steve Pearce's 15 points included a try in Whitland's 25-12 verdict at Abercynon. Played later, Colin Phillips collected two tries as Narberth defeated Wrexham 28-17. Wayne Jervis's 13 points were decisive in Llanharan's 28-20 decision at St Peter's.

WEEK 16: An Alan Reynolds hat-trick of tries spearheaded Whitland to 63-12 success with 11 tries at Pyle. Replacement hooker Steve Langdon went over for a last-minute try which Wayne Jervis converted for Llanharan to steal 18-17 victory against Llantrisant. Mountain Ash had wing Lee Meredith sent off and lost 13-3 at Wrexham. A high scoring contest saw Kenfig Hill register only their second win as they defeated visitors St Peter's 38-33. Narberth were 12-3 winners at Rhymney. Played later, Ystradgynlais won 35-8 at Oakdale.

46

Abercynon's 58-5 victory over Tenby brought them the division title on May 11 with Neil Edwards scoring four of the nine tries to finish top try-scorer in the top divisions with 28.

WEEK 17: Tenby's gathering bid for the tile was enhanced by 16-11 victory at Ystradgynlais. There was a try each, but Justin Price kicked 11 decisive points. Llanharan closed on the leaders with a 37-0 decision against Oakdale. Wayne Jervis contributed 13 points. Abercynon were 41-0 winners at Pyle with Neil Edwards and Darryl Hughes each snapping up three tries. Llantrisant's Kevin Jenkins fired over 10 winning points at Kenfig Hill for a tense 25-21 verdict. Mike Buckingham was the only try getter as Whitland despatched Narberth 10-0. Wrexham gained 17-13 success at St Peter's. Rhymney edged out Mountain Ash 15-14.

WEEK 18: It was three tries each when the two top teams clashed at second-placed Tenby, but Justin Price fired over two conversions to shade leaders Llanharan 19-18, though the visitors stayed in top spot. Narberth, in irrepressible form, cut up Pyle 56-0 with three of their 10 tries by Anthony Rees. David Love's nine goal points, including a drop shot, saw Ystradgynlais steal it 14-13 at Abercynon. Mark Bryant's two tries helped Llantrisant batter Wrexham 38-0. Whitland were 20-6 winners at Mountain Ash. Kenfig Hill lost 27-0 at Oakdale. Rhymney defeated St Peter's 32-12.

WEEK 19: Llanharan accounted for Ystradgynlais 32-10 with two tries by full back Anthony Donovan. Wing Mark Evans also crossed for two tries for Whitland to take a 32-13 verdict against St Peter's. Oakdale failed 23-17 at Wrexham. Glenn Blackmore was the key man with his goal shots. Scrum half John Fowler's two tries saw Mountain Ash triumph 31-16 at Pyle. Rhymney shaded it 13-10 against Llantrisant through Wayne Booth's decisive goal kicking. Abercynon won 24-17 at Narberth. Played later, Tenby took a 36-19 verdict at Kenfig Hill with four tries by flanker Andrew Thomas.

WEEK 20: Ystradgynlais shattered the league record, punishing Kenfig Hill 116-7 with a league record-equalling 18 tries. Full back Nigel Williams plundered four tries and Stuart Harris three with skipper David Love firing in 13 conversions. Leaders Dunvant were shocked to their third defeat, this time 44-0 at Abercynon. Tenby were 51-12 winners over Wrexham with two tries by Chris Morgan and 14 points by Justin Price. Rhymney failed 23-20 at Oakdale as Jonathan Williams kicked 13 decisive points. St Peter's sparkled to beat Pyle 59-22. Ben Thomas was a three-try scorer for the Rocks. Whitland won 16-3 at Llantrisant. Mountain Ash defeated Narberth 27-17.

WEEK 21: Scrum half Greg Jones led the way with a try hat-trick as leaders Llanharan were 63-8 winners at Kenfig Hill. Wayne Jervis was responsible for 18 points. Justin Pinch, on his 100th appearance for Rhymney, snapped up the vital try to edge Tenby 20-19. Colin Phillips scored his 50th league try to cement Narberth's 12-3 success against St Peter's. Neil Edwards's two tries inspired Abercynon's 30-12 decision at Mountain Ash. Llantrisant triumphed 38-22 at Pyle with Rhodri Evans and Huw David each collecting two tries. David Love's 13 points rescued Ystradgynlais in a 13-all draw at Wrexham. Whitland won 25-13 at Oakdale.

WEEK 22: Steve Pearce kicked Whitland to 15-6 victory over Tenby with four penalty goals, but then suffered an ear injury in a ruck and went to hospital to have it stitched back. Lee Cobner added the other home penalty goal. Leaders Llanharan swamped Wrexham 58-21. Wayne Jervis collected 23 points, including three tries. Denver Thomson also was a try hat-trick man. Wing Gareth Davies snaffled four tries as Abercynon crushed Kenfig Hill 77-7. Robbie Savage supplied 17 points. Rhymney had Wayne Booth ordered off after just 10 minutes and Ystradgynlais won 27-14. Jason Alford provided 18 points for Llantrisant to defeat Narberth 28-13. Mountain Ash profited from their visit to St Peter's 25-20. Oakdale were 52-12 winners at Pyle.

WEEK 23: Wing Steve Hartland swooped for five of the 14 tries in Tenby's 86-5 rout of Pyle. Three tries by No 8 Lloyd Griffiths helped Ystradgynlais topple Whitland 25-12. Llantrisant scrum half Ian Worgan pounced for two tries, but it could not prevent 22-20 defeat by visitors Mountain Ash, for whom Paul Jones kicked 17 points. Leaders Llanharan lost 20-12 at Rhymney, but stayed on top. Full back Darren Worgan was a two-try getter for the winners. Brendan A'Hearn crossed twice as Oakdale hit Narberth 41-17. Abercynon were 19-16 winners at St Peter's. Kenfig Hill failed 29-24 at Wrexham.

WEEK 24: Leaders Llanharan owed it to scrum half Graham Pritchard for the decisive try to edge a 20-15 decision at Whitland. Three penalty tries helped Ystradgynlais win 45-10 at Pyle. Paul Jones was on target with 11 points for Mountain Ash, but they lost 23-16 to visitors Oakdale. Abercynon were awarded two penalty tries as they disposed of Wrexham 29-7. Rhymney were 31-24 winners at Kenfig Hill. St Peter's held off a keen Llantrisant challenge 28-23. Narberth could not prevent 15-11 defeat by visitors Tenby.

WEEK 25: A hat-trick of tries by speedy Scott Bowen spelt trouble for bottom team Pyle and Llanharan went on to a blistering 85-9 victory with 15 tries. Anthony Donovan also crossed for three tries for the leaders. Second-placed Ystradgynlais applied relentless pressure in disposing of Narberth 55-11 with 20 points from Dave Love, including two tries. John Styles collected two tries for Whitland as they won 43-32 in a thriller at Kenfig Hill. Rhymney saw off Wrexham 43-13 with two tries by Matthew Pizey. Another two-try man was Tenby's Jon Dodd, but it could not save his team from 30-26 defeat by visitors Mountain Ash. Paul Jones assembled 20 points for the Old Firm, including two drop shots. Abercynon were 25-6 winners at Llantrisant. St Peter's won 18-13 at Oakdale.

WEEK 26: Leaders Llanharan were 50-7 winners over Narberth with two tries by wing Dewi Decaux. Scott Eggar's try hat-trick saw Whitland triumph 46-8 at Wrexham. Jonathan Williams obtained 17 points for Oakdale in a 27-8 verdict against Llantrisant. Lloyd Griffiths's two tries helped Ystradgynlais dispose of Mountain Ash 48-25. Abercynon suffered a surprise home defeat 17-13 by Rhymney. St Peter's won 29-25 at Tenby. There were 15 points for Mark Jones in Kenfig Hill's 20-10 success at Pyle.

NATIONAL LEAGUE RECORDS

	CHAMPIONS			BIGGEST VICTORIES
	Prem Div	**Div 1**	**Div 2**	Ystradgynlais 116-7 v Kenfig Hill
1991	Neath	Newport	Dunvant	Div 2 1998-99
1992	–	Swansea	SW Police	Felinfoel 106-14 at Cardiff Quins
1993	–	Llanelli	Dunvant	Div 5 1996-97
1994	–	Swansea	Treorchy	**HIGHEST TEAM AGGREGATE IN SEASON**
1995	–	Cardiff	Aberavon	1090 Caerphilly (Div 1) 1997-98
1996	–	Neath	Dunvant	**MOST TEAM TRIES IN SEASON**
1997	–	Pontypridd	Aberavon	151 Dunvant (Div 1)... 1998-99
1998	Swansea	Caerphilly	Tredegar	
1999	Llanelli	Dunvant	Abercynon	*All records apply to top divisions*

Neil Jenkins joins Cardiff as Wales's highest paid player

After winning 67 Wales caps while playing for Pontypridd, Neil Jenkins signed up with Cardiff in July 1999 in a four-year contract that made him the highest paid rugby player in Wales. It was estimated to be worth around £125,000 per annum. Pontypridd received some £200,000 transfer fee.

Jenkins, who scored a record 2,943 points in 213 Ponty appearances, said, "I owe Ponty everything, but I have found it hard to get motivated with them for the last couple of years. Carrying on would not be fair to the people at the club or to the best supporters in the land." The 28-year-old outside half, who had been with Pontypridd for 14 years, since he was aged 15, added, "I want to win trophies and feel I have a chance to do that with Cardiff. I have had probably my best year for Wales, but it just didn't happen for Ponty."

There was a technical hiccup over the transfer, which resulted in Ponty Director of Rugby Eddie Jones resigning "on principle".

Cardiff's Lee Jarvis rejoined his former Sardis Road club to replace Jenkins. Jarvis scored a record aggregate 1,143 points in 87 matches for Cardiff.

Swansea, 1999 SWALEC Cup winners. Standing (left to right): Ben Evans, Lee Jones, J. Griffiths, Andrew Moore, T. Maullin, P. Moriarty, C. van Rensburg, M. Taylor, D. Morris, R. Rees, C. Wells, M. Robinson, Lee Davies. In front: Rhodri Jones, D. Weatherley, Arwel Thomas, G. Jenkins, J. Plumtree (director of rugby), Scott Gibbs (capt), Baden Evans (chairman), Andy Booth, Dean Thomas, C. Charvis, C. Anthony, K. Hopkins (coach).

Huw Evans Picture Agency, Cardiff

Tricky Thomas 'dropped in' and the rebel yell was SWANSEA!

By JOHN BILLOT

Two twinkling drop-goals by Arwel Thomas garnished Swansea's third cup victory and dashed Llanelli ambitions of a record 11th success in their 14th final. Arwel finished with 15 points and the Lloyd Lewis Memorial Award as man-of-the-match. Behind the erosive power of a superb pack, the outside half delighted with his master-class display; and that deadly dummy which shredded the defence and let in Tyron Maullin for a try was the turning point. From then on Llanelli, trailing 24-10 just before the interval, were adrift on the river of no return.

There was a full house of 14,500 at Ninian Park, home of Cardiff City AFC (the new national stadium was still in process of completion) on May 15, 1999. With a bit of a civil war going on in Welsh rugby, this final was billed as between the Rebels and the Loyalists. Swansea, like Cardiff, had taken no part in the WRU premier division, playing instead against English major clubs in a series of friendly fixtures.

Many considered a forecast of likely winners too close to call, though Llanelli, with their unmatchable cup pedigree, and total suppression of Cardiff's pack in the semi-final, looked to have a slight edge. In the aftermath of Cardiff's inconsolable discomfort, it had been suggested they had played too many soft games against below strength English opponents.

But Swansea captain Scott Gibbs refuted this theory. After the ravaging of Llanelli, suffering the biggest cup final defeat in the tourney's 28 years, Gibbs insisted, "Our games have been far more meaningful than any games in the

---

TEAMS IN THE 1999 CUP FINAL

SWANSEA	LLANELLI
David Weatherley	Byron Hayward
Richard Rees	Wayne Procter
Mark Taylor	Salesi Finau
Scott Gibbs (capt)	Nigel Davies
Matthew Robinson	Garan Evans
Arwel Thomas	Stephen Jones
Rhodri Jones	Rupert Moon
Darren Morris	Martyn Madden
Garin Jenkins	Robin McBryde (capt)
Ben Evans	John Davies
Tyrone Maullin	Chris Wyatt
Andy Moore	Mike Voyle
Paul Moriarty	Hywel Jenkins
Lee Jones	Scott Quinnell
Colin Charvis	Ian Boobyer
Reps: Clive van Rensburg, Chris Anthony, James Griffiths, Dean Thomas, Lee Davies, Andy Booth, Chris Wells.	*Reps:* Marcus Thomas, Vernon Cooper, Phil Booth, Tony Copsey, Aled Thomas, Chris Warlow, Iwan Jones

Referee: Robert Davies (Dunvant)

domestic league in Wales. From what I have seen, Llanelli have been playing against boys all season. They were outweighted, outmuscled and outplayed today. We would rather play our Anglo-Welsh friendly games again than go back into the Welsh premier division. That doesn't excite me."

Colin Charvis was one of many Swansea heroes. He was not included in the original line-up, having been out for five weeks since fracturing a cheekbone against England. But Swansea took the risk, called him in late and his response was to snap up the first two tries, running close support for dynamic Mark Taylor, who tortured the defence on feet of fire.

Byron Hayward put the Scarlets ahead with a penalty goal, but missed four other shots, and Arwel's first drop-goal and conversion of both Charvis's tries nosed the Rebs 17-3 in front. Wayne Proctor's smooth overlap try to the corner, superbly converted by Hayward, trimmed the lead. Then Arwel's mesmerising dummy for Maullin's try, which Arwel goaled, signalled the end.

WRU CHALLENGE CUP WINNERS

1972 Neath bt. Llanelli 15-9
1973 Llanelli bt. Cardiff 30-7
1974 Llanelli bt. Aberavon 12-10
1975 Llanelli bt. Aberavon 15-6
1976 Llanelli bt. Swansea 16-4
1977 Newport bt. Cardiff 16-15

1987† Cardiff bt. Swansea 16-15
1988 Llanelli bt. Neath 28-13
1989 Neath bt. Llanelli 14-13
1990 Neath bt. Bridgend 16-10
1991 Llanelli bt. Pontypool 24-9
1992 Llanelli bt. Swansea 16-7

SCHWEPPES CUP

1978 Swansea bt. Newport 13-9
1979 Bridgend bt. Pontypridd 18-12
1980 Bridgend bt. Swansea 15-9
1981 Cardiff bt. Bridgend 14-6
1982* Cardiff 12, Bridgend 12
1983 Pontypool bt. Swansea 18-6
1984 Cardiff bt. Neath 24-19
1985 Llanelli bt. Cardiff 15-14
1986 Cardiff bt. Newport 28-21

SWALEC CUP

1993 Llanelli bt. Neath 21-18
1994 Cardiff bt. Llanelli 15-8
1995 Swansea bt. Pontypridd 17-12
1996 Pontypridd bt. Neath 29-22
1997 Cardiff bt. Swansea 33-26
1998 Llanelli bt. Ebbw Vale 19-12
1999 Swansea bt. Llanelli 37-10

Winners on more tries rule, † Extra time

Scarlets' skipper Robin McBryde graced the sin-bin for a sample of stamping and Marcus Thomas went on as specialist hooker deputy (Ian Boobyer took the 10-minute punishment so that only 14 men remained). Arwel flighted over his second drop from around 40 yards and followed with a penalty goal when Salesi Finau provided one of his familiar imitative acts of the executioner and the head in the basket. Dean Thomas, who had stood down when Charvis was cleared for action, went on as replacements and pounced for an injury time try which Lee Davies converted to complete Llanelli's heaviest defeat in 141 cup ties.

Nigel Davies, aged 34, announced his retirement after playing in a record nine cup finals for the Scarlets, but will keep his registration in case of future need during his duties as backs coach at Stradey.

The use of all 14 replacements was a first for a WRU cup final and must make governing bodies wonder if the process is being abused. To call players on to the pitch for the last few minutes in a cup final or international match is not what the replacement system is all about.

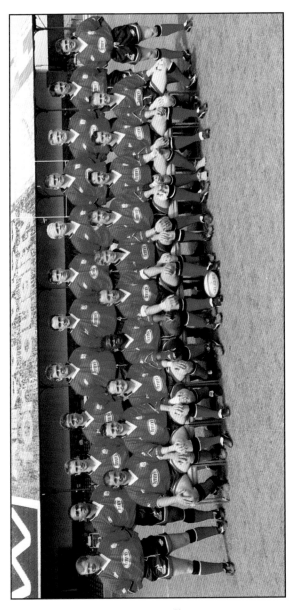

Llanelli, defeated SWALEC Cup finalists 1999. Standing (left to right): Marcus Thomas, Salesi Finau, W. Proctor, Iwan Jones, T. Copsey, C. Wyatt, M. Voyle, S. Quinnell, V. Cooper, P. Booth, Nigel Davies, Aled Thomas. Seated: J.D. Davies, Stephen Jones, I. Boobyer, M. Madden, Robin McBryde (capt), G. Evans, H. Jenkins, R. Moon, B. Hayward, C. Warlow.

Huw Evans Picture Agency, Cardiff

It was designed initially to replace injured players; then extended to tactical substitutions. Now it is being used for team bonding. Before long we could see whole squads being put on to enjoy fleeting minutes! Is it a match we are watching or a party?

SEMI-FINALS: It all started so encouragingly for Cardiff: 10 points ahead after 15 minutes against Llanelli at the Brewery Field. But that was the end for the Rebels. Their forwards were in thrall to the more dynamic Scarlets' pack for the remainder of the game and Llanelli coach Gareth Jenkins expressed the view that a season of playing friendly fixtures against major English clubs, who mostly fielded their reserves, had deprived Cardiff of their cutting edge of competition. The Stradey side recorded their biggest cup success in 10 meetings with Cardiff, at 39-10, with Byron Hayward providing 24 goal points. There was a penalty try at a scrum; Mike Voyle snapped up a gift try when passing broke down, and Scott Quinnell, in his most impressive form since returning to Stradey, also crossed. Cardiff's try came from wing Craig Morgan. Lee Jarvis converted and put over a penalty shot. Referee Clayton Thomas aired his yellow card, sending Llanelli's Hywel Jenkins and Cardiff's Rob Howley and Derwyn Jones for 10 minutes each in the sin-bin. Cardiff still lead 6-4 in cup victories over the Scarlets, but this was clearly Cardiff's most dismal display. It was the Martini-Henry against the assegai.

Cross Keys, in their first semi-final, were another team in bondage as Swansea overwhelmed them 60-3 at Sardis Road. Player/coach David Rees, at outside half, dropped a sparkling goal for Keys; but Swansea romped away with eight tries, three of them by wing Matthew Robinson. Richard Rees (2), Mark Taylor, Tyrone Maullin and Dean Thomas also crossed. Arwel Thomas kicked 16 points and Lee Davies converted the last two tries.

SEVENTH ROUND: Referee David Davies sent Ponty captain Neil Jenkins packing to the sin-bin for 10 minutes for dissent in a ferociously contested Sunday tussle which Llanelli edged 22-17 at Sardis Road watched by 7,000. Right at the end, Llanelli scrum half Rupert Moon also was sentenced to sin-bin occupation for killing the ball in front of the posts with Ponty desperately seeking the score that would save them. The Scarlets were allowed to bring on Aled Thomas for the specialist scrum half role while forward Hywel Jenkins went off to leave 14 men. Llanelli held out and now lead Pontypridd 8-2 in cup meetings. Jenkins came back for the final 10 minutes, but could not inspire a rescue operation. His side led 12-3 and again at 17-16 when wing Gareth Wyatt went around Salesi Finau to cross in the corner. However, that and four Jenkins penalty goals were just not enough. Prop John Davies surged away for the Llanelli try and Byron Hayward converted and kicked five penalty goals. "Our defence won the match," praised Llanelli coach Gareth Jenkins. "It was a question of not getting involved in the referee's decisions. We did that better than Ponty, which was a big factor in our success. Referees will always make unpopular decisions. You've got to cope with that." Pontypridd coach Dennis John stated, "We had the game won, but allowed ourselves to get frustrated by some 50-50 decisions which was our own fault.".

Player/coach David Bishop, aged 38, chugged on to the field earlier in the second half than he might have wanted, but Pontypool were trailing 19-6 in front of 8,000 excited fans and if one man could lift Pooler it was the charismatic

Centre Mark Taylor was a searing seeker of gaps for Swansea and Wales during 1998-99. He produced his most dynamic form with remarkable consistency, helping to spear Swansea to the cup and Wales to notable successes. Here he is in Cup final action.

Huw Evans Picture Agency, Cardiff

GARETH ON TARGET FOR WASPS' FIRST

After five finals without success, Wasps at last won the coveted cup, defeating Newcastle 29-19 at Twickenham on May 15, 1999. Outside half Alex King and wing Josh Lewsey were Wasps try-getters. Canada star Gareth Rees, playing at full back, converted both tries and put over four penalty goals. There was also a King dropped goal. Newcastle's brilliant young outside half Jonny Wilkinson, who had kicked 11 goals for England in two Twickenham matches during the season (and never a miss), fired in four penalty shots and converted the try by Va'aiga Tuigamala.

Bish. But the task was beyond even this rugby superman. The home side managed daring late tries by Matthew Silva and full back Joel Griffin which Silva, who kicked four penalty goals, converted. Two streakers made an appearance in the closing stages, symbolic of the way Pontypool had been stripped of their cup hopes by a 52-26 margin. Giant South African forward Tyrone Maullin powered over for two tries as Swansea put out the previous season's defeated finalists Ebbw Vale 42-14. Arwel Thomas, a dominating figure, provided 17 goal points. A dazzling dummy by Arwel set up wing Matthew Robinson for one of his two tries and Richard Rees also crossed. Leighton Olsen and Richie Collins were Ebbw's try-getters and Jason Strange added the conversions. This avenged Swansea's cup reverse in the same stage at Ebbw Vale the previous season and was the Whites sixth cup win in seven meetings with Ebbw. Cross Keys reached the semi-finals for the first time with 17-12 success at Tredegar. A controversial penalty try saw Tredegar take a 12-10 lead after Keys went 10-0 up. Scrum half Tom Walsh retrieved the situation with a smart try, which Ioan Bebb converted. Wing Julian Vernalls crossed for the other Keys try. Bebb converted and popped in a penalty shot. In addition to the home penalty try, Anthony Forrest crossed and Martin Jones converted one.

SIXTH ROUND: Pontypool's first win over Neath for six years produced a riveting contest. "We knew we could do it," enthused Pooler player/coach David Bishop, who went on as scrum half for the final 20 minutes. "It was like old times here." With the crowd baying their warcry, "Pooler, Pooler!" the home side edged out the premier division team 15-14 with tries by lock Alex Brown and wing Martin Cawley. Matthew Silva converted one and kicked a penalty goal. Matthew Pearce had a chance to steal it for Neath three minutes into injury time but missed the penalty shot. Wayne Proctor snapped up four of the 15 tries as Llanelli saw off Div 4 Llanhilleth 91-0 with the referee terminating events a few minutes early to save further suffering. Skipper Robin McBryde, in his first full game for eight weeks, crossed for three tries. Events went to extra time at Blackwood before Martin Jones fired over his fourth penalty goal and Tredegar

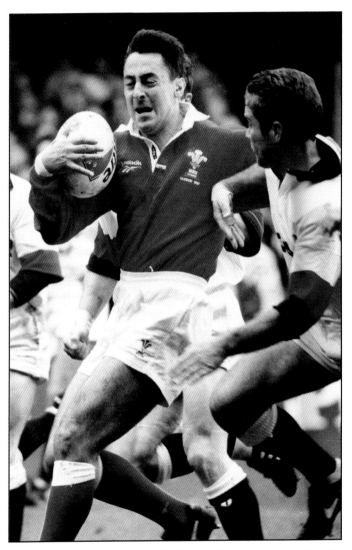

Nigel Davies in action against England. He played in a record nine cup finals for Llanelli, but was on the losing side in 1999. The 34-year old veteran and a legend at Stradey retired to concentrate on coaching.

Huw Evans Picture Agency, Cardiff

were through 12-9. Chris Lay kicked three home penalty goals.

Cardiff struggled desperately for 20-12 success at Aberavon. The Wizards had not defeated Cardiff since 1987, but trailed only 13-12 going into the closing seconds. Then Gareth Thomas broke away and raced 50 yards. Paul Burke converted. Simon Hill, on the other wing, crossed for two tries. Aberavon had given their most resolute display of the season and Cerith Rees kicked four penalty goals. Bridgend, forging in front 10-0, were magnificently defiant before losing at home 43-16 to Swansea, for whom Arwel Thomas contributed 16 points. Loose forward Geraint Lewis swooped for three tries to help Pontypridd (who rested Neil Jenkins) put out Bonymaen 47-12. Gerald Williams and Lee Carlsen crossed for Bonymaen. Cross Keys had few problems winning 39-11 against Tondu with two tries by flanker Steve Gardner. Ebbw Vale, on the wrong end of a 12-0 scoreline in the Virginia Park mud, struck back through pack power to squeeze a 20-15 verdict over Caerphilly. A try by full back Jonathan Williams doomed the home heroes.

FIFTH ROUND: Llanelli surpassed their previous cup tally of 80-0 with a 100-0 verdict against Ynysybwl. Compassionate referee Colin Saunders called a halt seven minutes early. Hooker Marcus Thomas, signed from Pontypridd, scored a try hat-trick on debut as the Scarlets raised 16 tries. Stephen Jones converted 10 of them. Newport had never conceded so many points in a cup tie (previously 56-0 at Pontypridd) and never scored so many points and lost. Swansea defeated them 60-38 after a stirring Newport rally had seen them recover from 38-3 down to make a rare old fight of it. Kyle Nicholls snapped up a hat-trick of tries for the visitors and Gareth King and Matthew Watkins also crossed. Swansea finished strongly with Richard Rees, a former Newport wing, collecting three tries. Brett Davey supplied 23 points as Caerphilly toppled neighbours Bedwas 53-10. Bedwas had 11 former Caerphilly players in their line-up.

Pontypool had prop Graham Woodward, on loan from Newport to make his debut for Pooler, dismissed for butting Alan Reynolds, and scraped a nail-biting 15-13 decision at Whitland with tries by wing Matt Cawley and flanker Danny Hurford. Home kicker Stephen Pearce missed two close range penalty shots during the closing stages. Cardiff were unimpressive as they eased to 33-3 victory over Abertillery. Bridgend also appeared lacklustre in winning 29-0 at Nantymoel. Bradley Watts crossed for Ystrad Rhondda's try, but visitors Aberavon tipped them out 37-7. Pontypridd rested skipper Neil Jenkins, but won comfortably 41-0 at Cwmllynfell. Jason Strange contributed 21 points as Ebbw Vale knocked out Pontypool Utd 61-3. Tongan centre David Tuieti was the star for Neath with two tries as they won 47-3 at Penygraig. Wing Chris Batsford swooped for four tries and Gareth Jones converted 11 for Bonymaen to blast UWIC 82-19. Gareth Jones also pounced for two tries in his 32 points. Cross Keys stopped Trimsaran 38-7 with two tries by Chad Bushell. Replacement Emyr Richards scored Trimsaran's try. Rumney disappointed in losing 35-14 at Tredegar. Shane Pinch was a two-try home scorer and Mark Jones converted five tries.

FOURTH ROUND: Gareth Wyatt contributed 21 points, including one of the 11 tries, as Pontypridd put out Aberavon Quins 71-15. Newport had lock Gareth Taylor ordered off and had to play almost half the match with 14 men. However, they managed a 25-19 decision at Llanharan through a late Matt

Rhodri Jones helped Swansea to success against Llanelli in the 1999 SWALEC Cup final at Cardiff City's Ninian Park. The scrum half's consistency also earned him selection for the Welsh team's tour to Argentina.

Huw Evans Picture Agency, Cardiff

Cardey try. Denver Thomson scored the home try. Wayne Jervis converted and landed four penalty goals. Cardiff won 40-22 at Llandovery as Paul Burke collected 20 points, including two tries. Div 3 East Risca led Swansea 8-0 before the visitors found their rhythm and a 57-8 success. Prop Andrew Davies scored the home try. Scott Gibbs crossed for three of the nine Swansea tries. Cross Keys surprised Div 1 leaders Dunvant 25-14. Cerith Rees produced 19 points to help Aberavon dispose of Carmarthen Quins 49-22.

Ystrad Rhondda coach Nigel Bezani played his first game of the season and was sent for an early bath; but his team secured a 19-13 verdict over SW Police with a decisive try by Paul Morris. Ebbw Vale assembled an impressive tally 73-15 against Treherbert with three tries by wing David Manley. Bonymaen shocked Newbridge out 51-12 with 26 points from fly half Stuart Davies. Llanelli piled up the points 80-0 at Pontyclun with three tries each by Wayne Proctor and Daniel Rogers. Two second half tries by acting-captain Phil Ager helped Caerphilly reach an anxious 29-19 verdict at Narberth. A 40-yard solo try at the end by centre Lloyd Davies against his former teammates saw Bridgend scrape into the next round 29-24 against Treorchy. Neath were 46-15 winners at Wrexham after the home side grabbed the lead in just 35 seconds with a try by Kevin O'Toole. Shawn van Rensburg was a two-try getter for Neath. Matthew Silva supplied 24 points for Pontypool to overwhelm Rhigos 64-6. Maesteg ended Abercwmboi's unbeaten record in this December tie 29-5.

EARLIER ROUNDS: Cardiff and Swansea were instructed to enter the tournament in the second round because they had opted out of the WRU National League. Inevitably, their opponents would be outclassed. Swansea recorded their record cup score 100-7 at Div 5 West Amman Utd. Referee Derek Bevan blew up five minutes early 'to save further punishment'. There were 16 Swansea tries, three of them by wing Simon Davies. Lee Jones included two tries in his 22 points. Steve Liles put the village team ahead with a try inside the first minute and Nick Griffiths converted in front of a crowd of around 1,500. Cardiff were 93-0 winners away to Div 7 side Cilfynydd. Rugby league star Anthony Sullivan, on three-month loan from St Helens, snapped up two debut tries on the wing. Liam Botham and Matthew Wintle each scored three of the 15 tries and Lee Jarvis topped 1000 career points for Cardiff with a try and two conversions. Gilfach Goch won 59-15 at Penarth.

Cardiff's 84-10 demolition of Seven Sisters in the third round saw Leigh Davies, back after eight weeks out, score three of the 12 tries, all converted by Irish international Paul Burke. Lloyd Paget scored Seven's try. Swansea third choice scrum half Ed Lewsey crossed for a hat-trick of tries in a 48-0 victory at Crynant.

NO PRIMA DONNAS, WARNS COACH

Cardiff's new coach Lynn Howells says there is no room for prima donnas in the club. He states that international players will be treated exactly the same as their youth team members. No-one can expect an automatic place in the team. Selection has to be earned and everyone must play for the club and not themselves.

The big cooker
for big appetites

Cannon COOKERS

15.12

Cannon
Cambridge Double Oven

UNMISTAKABLE QUALITY

The Cambridge 600mmDouble Oven

This year,
Welsh Rugby
will be watched by
a wider audience...

(The new Sanyo wide-screen television range,
now available from quality retailers throughout Wales.)

For further details www.sanyo.co.uk

SWALEC CUP 1998-99

FOURTH ROUND

Aberavon 49, Carmarthen Q 22
Abercwmboi 5, Maesteg 29
Beddau 0, Whitland 35
Betws 3, Blackwood 15
Blaengarw 10, *Ynysybwl 10
Bonymaen 51, Newbridge 12
Bridgend 29, Treorchy 24
Builth Wells 5, Rumney 26
Cross Keys 25, Dunvant 14
Cwmavon 17, Bedwas 21
Cwmllynfell 13, Taffs Well 7
Dinas Powys 5, Pontypool Utd 16
Ebbw Vale 73, Treherbert 15
Glynneath 10, Trimsaran 25
Heol-y-Cyw 10, Tondu 27
Hirwaun 19, Kidwelly 9
(*Indicates through as away team)

Llandovery 22, Cardiff 40
Llanharan 19, Newport 25
Monmouth 11, Llanhilleth 20
Narberth 19, Caerphilly 29
Oakdale 7, UWIC 12
Pencoed 11, Abertillery 25
Penygraig 10, Rhymney 8
Pontyclun 0, Llanelli 80
Pontypool 64, Rhigos 6
Pontypridd 71, Aberavon Q 15
Risca 8, Swansea 57
Talywain 9, Nantymoel 14
Tredegar 20, Merthyr 16
Wrexham 15, Neath 46
Ystradgynlais 32, Vardre 20
Ystrad Rhondda 19, SW Police 13

FIFTH ROUND

Bonymaen 82, UWIC 19
Caerphilly 53, Bedwas 10
Cardiff 33, Abertillery 3
Cross Keys 38, Trimsaran 7
Cwmllynfell 0, Pontypridd 41
Hirwaun 13, Tondu 36
Llanelli 100, Ynysybwl 0
Llanhilleth 26, Ystradgynlais 19

Maesteg 8, Blackwood 31
Nantymoel 0, Bridgend 29
Penygraig 3, Neath 47
Pontypool Utd 3, Ebbw Vale 61
Swansea 60, Newport 38
Tredegar 35, Rumney 14
Whitland 13, Pontypool 15
Ystrad Rhondda 7, Aberavon 37

SIXTH ROUND

Aberavon 12, Cardiff 20
Blackwood 9, *Tredegar 12
Bridgend 16, Swansea 43
Caerphilly 15, Ebbw Vale 20
(*denotes extra time)

Cross Keys 39, Tondu 11
Llanelli 91, Llanhilleth 0
Pontypool 15, Neath 14
Pontypridd 47, Bonymaen 12

SEVENTH ROUND

Pontypool 26, Cardiff 52
Pontypridd 17, Llanelli 22

Swansea 42, Ebbw Vale 14
Tredegar 12, Cross Keys 17

SEMI-FINALS

Cross Keys 3, Swansea 60
(At Pontypridd)

Llanelli 39, Cardiff 10
(At Bridgend)

FINAL

Swansea 37, Llanelli 10
(At Ninian Park, Cardiff)

Hoisted high - to become Welsh rugby player of the year. Llanelli's all-action Chris Wyatt feeds back from grand elevation at Wembley on the day that England's Grand Slam ambitions crashed sensationally in injury time.

Huw Evans Picture Agency, Cardiff

Player of the Year

CHRIS WYATT

He roves the field and scatters the good seeds of success about him with care and deliberation. He is the one-arm bandit of the Wales team: Llanelli's lithe Chris Wyatt always caught the eye among the cognoscenti during the 1998-99 season for club and country; popping up one-handed passes for supporting attackers or diving and reaching out with a long, long arm to secure a stretch try. The reliable Chris snapped up 14 tries for the Scarlets during the season in 26 games and his mobility and shrewd reading of developing attacks made him a key figure in a re-emerging Wales pack alongside another exciting runner with the ball, crunching Craig Quinnell.

Chris cracked the mould with his selection as top player: for the previous six years the award had been monopolised by the backs. So a forward had broken into the glamour spot once more - and not a back-row bobby dazzler, at that. The last second rower to be chosen by the members of the Welsh Rugby Writers' Association was Phil Davies, another Llanelli player, in 1989. Wyatt was voted to this special hall of fame by a huge majority, reflecting the impressive impact he made among the professional critics.

Neath signed Shane Williams from Amman Utd and the flying wing was never out of the limelight with his thrilling tries and explosive running. He was a worthy choice for the Most Promising Player award in a close run thing with other popular candidates in Bath scrum half Gareth Cooper, Aberavon's Cerith Rees and Rhys Williams, a star of Wales's Junior World Cup Team.

The Most Overlooked Player award went to Caerphilly's Brett Davey by as clear a margin as Chris Wyatt registered his top spot. It was virtually a one-horse race for the full back, who has set National League records for most points in a season and most points in a match.

PREVIOUS PLAYERS OF THE YEAR

1969 G.O. EDWARDS	1979 T.D. HOLMES	1989 PHIL DAVIES
1970 RAY HOPKINS	1980 D.S. RICHARDS	1990 ARTHUR EMYR
1971 BARRY JOHN	1981 CLIVE BURGESS	1991 SCOTT GIBBS
1972 J.P.R. WILLIAMS	1982 GWYN EVANS	1992 EMYR LEWIS
1973 T.P. DAVID	1983 T.D. HOMES	1993 IEUAN EVANS
1974 T.J. COBNER	1984 M. TITLEY	1994 NEIL JENKINS
1975 T.M. DAVIES	1985 MARK RING	1995 NEIL JENKINS
1976 T.M. DAVIES	1986 J. DAVIES	1996 ROB HOWLEY
1977 P. BENNETT	1987 STUART EVANS	1997 ROB HOWLEY
1978 T.J. COBNER	1988 ROB NORSTER	1998 ALLAN BATEMAN

NZ TAKE GOLD FROM FIJI: WALES REACH LAST 8

New Zealand won the Commonwealth Games gold medal for seven-a-side rugby in September 1998 when the event was staged for the first time and proved a huge success. They defeated Fiji in the final 21-12 in Kuala Lumpur. Wales reached the quarter-final stage before going out 38-14 to the All Blacks. Jonah Lomu crossed for a second half hat-trick of tries and that was the end of Welsh hopes of keeping matters close. Ironically, Wales put together their best performance after being hammered and humiliated 45-7 by Canada. The 20,000 watchers at the Petaling Jaya Stadium saw Dafydd James and Scott Gibbs score against the All Blacks. Arwel Thomas and Craig Warlow each converted one try.

The Welsh squad were: Scott Gibbs, Arwel Thomas (Swansea), Gareth Wyatt, Dafydd James (Pontypridd), Craig Warlow, Chris Wyatt (Llanelli), Gareth Thomas, Jamie Ringer (Cardiff), Matthew Robinson (Newport), Gareth Cooper (Bath). Wales used Scott Gibbs and Gareth Thomas as forwards, and in the final New Zealand employed giant wing Jonah Lomu as a powerhouse prop.

Wales unsurprisingly went down 54-7 to Fiji in their opening pool contest, Craig Warlow converting Dafydd James's try, but there was 72-0 victory over Swaziland. Gareth Wyatt and Gareth Thomas went on as replacements and each contributed two of the 12 tries. It was noted that Fiji did not do so well as Wales against the Swazi's - it was only 71-0! The Welsh effort against Canada was dire indeed. Gareth Thomas's try was the only response in that 45-7 drubbing. However, the 62-0 win over Cayman Islands enabled Wales to scrape into the quarter-finals. Team manager John Ryan reflected, "If we can't send our best prepared side, perhaps we should not be competing in the top tournaments."

Quarter-finals: NZ defeated Wales 38-14, Western Samoa defeated South Africa 26-5, Fiji defeated Canada 26-19, Australia defeated England 49-14.

Semi-finals: NZ defeated Western Samoa 19-14, Fiji defeated Australia 28-14.

Final: NZ defeated Fiji 21-12.

Fiji retained the Hong Kong Sevens title in March 1999 21-12 against New Zealand in a fiercely contested final in front of some 30,000. Fiji put out Canada 14-7 in the quarter-final and then Australia 45-5 in the semi-final; NZ defeated Argentina and then Western Samoa to reach the final. It was Fiji's ninth victory at Hong Kong.

Caerphilly GSOB won the 50th Old Penarthians Sevens with a record score in the final 55-12 (nine tries) against Old Illtydians. Exotically named Samurai Seven won the Cwmtawe Sevens at their first attempt. They put out Llanelli 26-19 in the semi-final and then defeated holders Bonymaen 42-26 in the final. A sudden death try by Taniela Qauqau in the first few seconds of extra time gave Penguins, packed with Fijian players, 40-35 victory over Saracens in the Middlesex Sevens. Saracens led 14-0, 21-7 and 28-14. In the semi-final, San Isidro lost to Penguins 28-7 after Enrique Picot was sent off for felling Waisale Serevi in the first half.

Turns things round quicker than Graham Henry.

With one of the fastest spin speeds in the game, the Hotpoint Ultima Washer Dryer gives you an unbeatable wash every time. Not only that, it's as reliable as Neil Jenkins and as well-built as Scott Gibbs. Check out the rest of the team on the Hotpoint website or call us on **08701 50 60 70**.

www.hotpoint.co.uk

Tackle two jobs at once with a Creda Build-Under Double Oven

The perfect replacement for a single oven

You know the problem, half the team want Rack of Lamb and the other half want Kebabs and you've only got a single oven. Answer, substitute the single oven for a Creda Twin Cavity oven which offers a main oven and separate grill cavity - ideal for roasting and grilling at the same time.

Check out the wide choice of styles and colours on the Creda Website www.creda.co.uk or call us on 08701 54 64 74.

GARIN AND HIS PROPS DEFUSE ARGY SCRUM

Before the Welsh team left for Argentina, coach Graham Henry observed, "We had a good end to the Five Nations, but we are still an average side. Argentina is a very tough country to tour. They have not lost many series at home and even the best sides have found it hard going. It will be excellent preparation for the World Cup." By the end of the trip, he was a contented man with his team having become the first British outfit to whitewash the Pumas 2-0 on their home pampas.

Although Scott Gibbs had to withdraw with a broken bone in his hand (Matthew Watkins took his place), and Pontypridd full back Kevin Morgan also pulled out with injury (Byron Hayward was called up), it was a powerful team that confronted what was approved as the best scrummagers in world rugby. That reputation was wrecked by batting Garin Jenkins and his props. The front row held the key to victory while Chris Wyatt and Craig Quinnell were heroes in the second row with their all round skills. Brett Sinkinson proved a tireless and tenacious breakaway, invariably first to the scene of action, and the courage and determination of the whole side was praised by the critics as being quite exceptional.

But events opened unpromisingly with defeat. Buenos Aires Province, the Argentine champions and winners against England, France (twice) and South Africa during the last decade, triumphed 31-29 after the lead changed five times. Arwel Thomas kicked 19 points. "Hopefully, we can be competitive against Argentina next weekend," muttered a worried coach.

 Tour Party

Manager : David Pickering   *Coach :* Graham Henry   *Assistant Coach :* Lynn Howells

Backs : Rob Howley (capt), Gareth Thomas, Leigh Davies, Nick Walne (Cardiff), Neil Boobyer, Byron Hayward, Stephen Jones (Llanelli), Matthew Robinson, Mark Taylor, Arwel Thomas, Rhodri Jones (Swansea), Dafydd James, Neil Jenkins (Pontypridd), Shane Howarth (Sale), Allan Bateman (Northampton), Matthew Watkins (Newport), David Llewellyn (Ebbw Vale).

Forwards: Darren Morris, Ben Evans, Chris Anthony, Garin Jenkins, Andy Moore, Colin Charvis (Swansea), Andrew Lewis, David Young, Jonathan Humphreys, Craig Quinnell (Cardiff), Chris Wyatt, Mike Voyle, Scott Quinnell, Ian Boobyer (Llanelli), Geraint Lewis, Martyn Williams (Pontypridd), Peter Rogers (Newport), Brett Sinkinson (Neath), Richard Arnold (Newcastle), Gareth Llewellyn (Harlequins).

The second match produced a 69-44 success over Tucuman; but the Welsh management were dismayed by what they called "woeful defence." Matthew Robinson went in for four tries to secure his Test place in preference to Gareth Thomas, and Byron Hayward supplied 24 goal points. After surging into a 20-3 lead in just 11 minutes, Wales found themselves in arrears 25-20 as Tucuman snapped up 22 points in an explosive 10-minute spell.

"The Pumas will be favourites", warned skipper Rob Howley before the first Test: and with Wales trailing 23-0 after the opening 35 minutes, no-one was going to argue with his forecast. Neil Jenkins, who had not played for eight weeks following a shoulder operation, had his first clearance kick charged down and it almost cost a try. "They tore us apart", recalled Howley, but he was cheerful enough with a final score of 36-26 after an unforgettable recovery from the brink of defeat.

"When you are 23-0 up, you should never lose a Test", pointed out coach Henry, who could hardly believe his team had turned the game around so dramatically. Neil Jenkins, who admitted he was rusty, missed his first two penalty shots (hitting the post with the second); but just before the interval Wales clawed their way back with first a Jenks penalty goal and then a Dafydd James try following a Scott Quinnell charge. Jenkins converted with magnificent judgement.

HOWARTH'S INSPIRED DROP-GOAL

Another Jenkins penalty goal early in the second half and a superb conversion of Brett Sinkinson's try raised spirits enormously. A long Jenkins penalty shot made it 23-all. Again Wales had to level matters, this time with a memorable drop-goal from some 45 yards by Shane Howarth to make it 26-all. Next it was a try by Chris Wyatt, striding to the posts from Mark Taylor's battering-ram burst, and Wales were ahead for the first time some eight minutes from the end. Jenks swung over the extra points and added a fourth penalty goal to the joy of 300 Welsh supporters among the crowd of 16,500.

A second defeat came 47-34 to Argentina A and coach Henry summed up: "They played a more fluent and attractive game than we saw from the full Argentine side in the first Test. We came up against a very passionate and physical side who played a very direct style." Welsh ball retention was deplorable and it was meltdown in defence. Arwel Thomas provided 19 goal points.

The second Test promised a backlash from the Pumas. "They will throw the kitchen sink at us", warned coach Henry. Home hooker Frederico Mendez confirmed that view. "This time, no more Mr Nice Guy", he growled ominously. "It will be a very different story this time." But it wasn't. The magnificent front row of Garin Jenkins and props Ben Evans and Peter Rogers had the home scrum in disarray again.

Even after initiating a massed brawl and a heated slice of argy-bargy that spilled over into the home dug-out, the Pumas, then behind by 8-3, found themselves 23-9 down before they rallied with a late try to set up an exciting finish. Argentine captain Pedro Sporleder, who was yellow-carded together with Mauricio Reggiardo and Wales's Peter Rogers, blamed the punch-up on Dafydd James illegally killing the ball.

The Welsh try midway through the opening half appropriately was scored by the fearless and ferocious Garin Jenkins, dodging a couple of tackles when Allan Bateman put him away from close range after the centre charged down a clearance. All the other points came from the other Jenkins: Neil fired in a sweet dropped goal and planted over five penalty shots for 18 points and a 23-16 verdict.

MATCH DETAILS

May 29, 1999. Buenos Aires Province defeated Wales by 31 (2G, 4PG, 1T) to 29 (2G, 5PG) at BA Cricket and Rugby Club ground.

BUENOS AIRES PROVINCE: D. Albanese; O. Bartolucci, J. Orengo, J. Miranda, T. Solari; J. Cilley, N. Miranda (capt); F. Guateri, M. Ledesma, M. Scelzo, P. Sporleder, G. Ugartemendia, R. Martin, P. Camerlinckx, L. Ostiglia.

WALES: S. Howarth; G. Thomas, A. Bateman, L. Davies, D. James; A. Thomas, R. Howley (capt); P. Rogers, G. Jenkins, C. Anthony, M. Voyle, C. Wyatt, C. Charvis, G. Lewis, B. Sinkinson.

Referee: Chris White (England).

Scorers: For BAP, Rolando Martin, Octavio Bartolucci, Tomas Solari (tries), Jose Luis Cilley (4PG, 2con). For Wales, Allan Bateman, Geraint Lewis (tries), Arwel Thomas (5PG, 2con).

June 1, 1999. Wales defeated Tucuman Province by 69 (9G, 2PG) to 44 (4G, 2PG, 2T) at Tucuman Estadium Atletico.

TUCUMAN: L. Gravano; L. Rojas, P. Hamilton, J Rodriguez, M. Pfister; T. Molinuevo, L. Molinuevo; L de Chazal, M. Coll, O. Hasan, J. Macome, O. Portillo, J. Satamarina, H. Dande, E. Padua (capt). Reps: S. Retondo for Rodriguez, J. Martinez for Coll, J Belloto for Satamarina.

WALES: N. Boobyer; N. Walne, M. Taylor, S. Jones, M. Robinson; B. Hayward, D. Llewellyn; A. Lewis, J. Humphreys, D. Young, A. Moore, G. Llewellyn, R. Arnold, G. Lewis, M. Williams (capt). Reps: M. Watkins for Taylor, D. Morris for A. Lewis, C. Anthony for Young, I. Boobyer for G. Lewis.

Referee: Pablo Deluca (Argentina).

Full back Shane Howarth, another New Zealander with a Welsh grandfather, made an impact as a dashing attacker when new coach Graham Henry picked him out of the Sale team.

Huw Evans Picture Agency, Cardiff.

Scorers: For Tucuman, Pablo Garcia Hamilton (2), Tristan Molinuevo, Leandro Molinuevo, Leonardo Gravano, E. Padua (tries), Tristan Molinuevo (2PG, 4con). For Wales, Matthew Robinson (4), Mark Taylor (2), Neil Boobyer (2), Geraint Lewis (tries), Byron Hayward (2PG, 9con).

June 5, 1999. Wales defeated Argentina by 36 (3G, 1DG, 4PG) to 26 (2G, 4PG) at Stadio Ferro Carril Oeste, Buenos Aires.

ARGENTINA: D. Albanese; O. Bartolucci, E. Simone, L. Arbizu, E. Jurado; G. Quesada, A. Pichot; R. Grau, F. Mendez, M. Reggiardo, P. Sporleder (capt), A. Allub, I. Lobbe, P. Camerlinckx, R. Martin. Reps: O. Hasan for Grau, L. Ostiglia for Allub, G. Longo for Camerlinckx.

WALES: S. Howarth; M. Robinson, M. Taylor, A. Bateman, D. James; N. Jenkins, R. Howley (capt); P. Rogers, G. Jenkins, B. Evans, C. Quinnell, C. Wyatt, C. Charvis, S. Quinnell, B. Sinkinson. Reps: A. Lewis for Rogers, D. Young for Evans.

Referee: Brian Campsall (England).

Scorers: For Argentina, Gonzalo Quesada, Octavio Bartolucci (tries), Quesada (4PG, 2con). For Wales, Dafydd James, Brett Sinkinson, Chris Wyatt (tries), Neil Jenkins (4PG, 3con). Shane Howarth (1DG).

June 8, 1999. Argentina A defeated Wales by 47 (3G, 1DG, 6PG, 1T) to 34 (2G, 5PG, 1T) at Independence Park, Rosario.

ARGENTINA A: D. Giannantonio; P. Grande, J. Fernandez Miranda, G. Camardon, M. Pfister; F. Contepomi, N. Fernandez Miranda (Capt.); F. Alberdi, M. Ladesma, M. Scelzo, G. Llanes, R. Perez, S. Phelan, G. Longo, A. Petrilli. Reps: J. Nunez for Camardon, G. Astride for Alberdi, G. Gonzacez Bonorino for Scelzo, O. Portillo for Llanes.

WALES: N. Boobyer; N. Walne, L. Davies, S. Jones, G. Thomas; A. Thomas, R Jones; D. Morris, J. Humphreys, D. Young, M. Voyle, A. Moore, R. Arnold, G. Lewis, M. Williams (capt). Reps: M. Watkins for G. Thomas, B. Hayward for A. Thomas, D. Llewellyn for R. Jones, A. Lewis for Morris, C. Anthony for Young, G. Llewellyn for Moore, I. Boobyer for Lewis.

Referee: Wayne Erickson (Australia).

Scorers: For Argentina A, Juan Fernandez Miranda, Gonzalo Camardon, Nicolas Fernandez Miranda, Patrico Grande (tries), Felipe Contepomi (6PG, 3con), Camardon (1DG). For Wales, Rhodri Jones, Neil Boobyer, Nick Walne (tries), Arwel Thomas (5PG, 2 con).

June 12, 1999. Wales defeated Argentina by 23 (1DG, 5PG, 1T) to 16 (1G, 3PG) at Stadio Ferro Carril Oeste, Buenos Aires.

ARGENTINA: D. Albanese; O. Bartolucci, J. Orengo, L. Arbizu, G. Camardon; F. Contepomi, A. Pichot; R. Grau, F. Mendez, M. Reggiardo, P. Sporleder (capt), I. Lobbe, R. Martin, G. Longo, M.A. Ruiz. Reps: J.L. Cilley for Contemponi, M. Ledesma for Mendez, O. Hasan for Reggiardo, A. Allub for Lobbe, L. Ostiglia for Martin.

WALES: S. Howarth; G. Thomas, A. Bateman, M. Taylor, D. James; N. Jenkins, R. Howley (capt); P. Rogers, G. Jenkins, B. Evans, C. Quinnell, C. Wyatt, G. Lewis, S. Quinnell, B. Sinkinson. Reps: J. Humphreys for G. Jenkins, A. Lewis for Rogers, D. Young for B. Evans.

Referee: Chris White (England)

Scorers: For Argentina, Jose Orengo (1T), Jose Luis Cilley (1con), Felipe Contepomi (3PG). For Wales, Garin Jenkins (1T), Neil Jenkins (1DG, 5PG).

ENGLAND FOIL RECORD BID: GALLANT WALES JUST FAIL

The unbeaten Springboks confidently anticipated completing a record 18th consecutive Test victory (they shared the record of 17 with New Zealand) and in so doing collect a fifth grand slam of successes on a tour of the British Isles when they faced England at Twickenham in their final match. England had lost 18-0 to South Africa in Cape Town five months earlier on their disastrous tour in the southern hemisphere; but now they made the supreme effort and shocked the tourists 13-7 in a contest of spine-tingling tension from first to last.

This defeat confirmed the opinions of those who recognised after the Wales match that the Springboks were nowhere near so impressive as their teams of the past. Wales, with a tenacious performance, exposed weaknesses in a memorable encounter at Wembley and this time there was no disgrace for a gallant side that lost only 28-20. Indeed, Wales could have snatched what would have been their first victory over the Boks.

A male streaker from the 55,000 crowd caused a stoppage of some five minutes at a time when Wales were in front and it was considered that this broke Welsh concentration and took pressure off the visitors. It turned out to be a South African streaker!

GARETH'S SPARKLING TRY

Five months earlier, Wales had been pulverised 96-13 by SA in Pretoria and the world champions were obvious favourites again. There was speculation that Wales would be pleased with a job well done if they confined the Springboks' winning margin below the 30 points mark. In the event, fired by new coach Graham Henry, a New Zealander signed on a five-year contract at £250,000 per annum; Wales took the game to the tourists in amazing fashion. A sparkling try by Gareth Thomas and three penalty goals from Neil Jenkins (who passed 600 international points in the process) saw Wales surge ahead 14-0. Jenkins added two penalty shots and Wales led 20-17 with only three minutes remaining.

But the Springboks finished strongly, retaining vital possession as heroic defenders tired and Franco Smith equalised with a penalty kick when Scott Quinnell was yellow-carded for a stray elbow job. Then, cruelly, Joost van der Westhuizen darted through to make a try for Andre Venter in injury time and Smith added a penalty goal with the last kick of the match.

The tourists had been awarded a penalty try in controversial circumstances when hooker Jonathan Humphreys stood up as the tourists were driving a close-up scrum. Many thought a penalty kick would have been in order for the offence, but Australian referee Stuart Dickinson decided otherwise.

Wales, who had never previously fielded a heavier pack than the Springboks, included only four of the team that had been obliterated in Pretoria. They were Dafydd James, Mark Taylor, Colin Charvis and Chris Wyatt, one of the seven replacements used. SA coach Nick Mallett described Wales in Pretoria as one of the "worst sides I have ever seen." Now he commented, "We knew the side we saw in the summer was a pale shadow. It was really a club team. I am very relieved to have won again. The way Wales played made us make a lot of mistakes. We must look long and hard at our game."

In contrast, Wales were elated, and with every justification. "We are not going to be the whipping boys of international rugby any more," asserted skipper Rob Howley. Craig Quinnell (slimmed down from 21 stone to just over 19 stone) was a charging inspiration with Scott Quinnell also determined to dispel suspicions that the brothers lacked fitness and appetite for hard work. Charvis was another outstanding figure in a revitalised pack. There was a first cap for full back Shane Howarth (eligible through a Welsh grandfather), who had played four times for New Zealand. He began shakily, but emerged as a key figure.

WALES v SOUTH AFRICA

November 14, 1998. South Africa defeated Wales by 28 (2G, 3PG, 1T) to 20 (5PG, 1T) at Wembley Stadium.

WALES: S. P. Howarth (Sale); G. Thomas (Cardiff), M. Taylor (Swansea), I. S. Gibbs (Swansea), D. R. James (Pontypridd); N. R. Jenkins (Pontypridd), R. Howley (Cardiff, capt); A. L. P. Lewis (Cardiff), J. M. Humphreys (Cardiff), C. T. Anthony (Swansea), J. C. Quinnell (Richmond), C. Wyatt (Llanelli), C. L. Charvis (Swansea), L. S. Quinnell (Llanelli), M. E. Williams (Pontypridd). Reps: D. Morris (Swansea) for Lewis, B. Evans (Swansea) for Anthony.

SOUTH AFRICA: P. C. Montgomery; C. S. Terblanche, A. H. Snyman, F. Smith, P. W. G. Rossouw; H. W. Honiball, J. H. van der Westhuizen; R. B. Kempson, J. Dalton, A. C. Garvey, K. Otto, M. G. Andres, J. Erasmus, G. H. Teichmann (capt), A. G. Venter. Reps: O le Roux for Garvey, R. Skinstad for Andrews.

Referee: Stuart Dickinson (Australia).

Scorers: For Wales, Gareth Thomas (1T), Neil Jenkins (5PG). For SA, Joost van der Westhuizen, Andre Venter (tries), penalty try, Franco Smith (3PG, 2con).

Only 35,000 turned out at Murrayfield, which indicated the lack of faith by Scottish rugby fans. Accordingly, the Springboks were 35-10 winners. However, coach Jim Telfer ruminated, "We gave away two soft tries and if you take away those 14 points, it would be a better reflection on where we are compared to them. I don't think South Africa would say it was an easy victory, if they were honest."

Scotland undoubtedly raised spirits with the dashing manner of their aggressive first half rucking and concerted drive. They nosed in front 7-3 with a try at the posts by Duncan Hodge from a close-up lineout. He converted and added a penalty goal. Alas for their hopes: the tourists dominated the second half, though skipper Gary Teichmann admitted his team were a collection of talented individuals and not a finely tuned cohesive unit.

Gareth Thomas crashes over the Springboks' line to score as Andre Synman's tackle comes in too late at Wembley in 1998. It was Thomas's 14th try in 29 games, a strike rate that even Wales's record try-getter Ieuan Evans could not approach.

How Evans Picture Agency, Cardiff

SCOTLAND v SOUTH AFRICA

November 21, 1998. South Africa defeated Scotland by 35 (2G, 2PG, 3T) to 10 (1G, 1PG) at Murrayfield.

SCOTLAND: D. J. Lee (London Scottish); A. V. Tait (Newcastle), M. J. M. Mayer (Edinburgh Reivers), J. Leslie (Glasgow Caledonians), C. A. Murray (Edinburgh Reivers); D. W. Hodge (Edinburgh Reivers), B. W. Redpath (Edinburgh Reivers, capt); T. J. Smith (Glasgow Caledonians), G. C. Bulloch (Glasgow Caledonians), A. P. Burnell (London Scottish), S. Murray (Bedford), G. W. Weir (Newcastle), P. Walton (Newcastle), E. W. Peters (Bath), A. C. Pountney (Northampton). Reps: G. P. J. Townsend (Brive) for Lee, K. M. Logan (Wasps) for Tait, G. Armstrong (Newcastle) for Redpath, D. I. W. Hilton (Bath) for Burnell M. Leslie (Edinburgh Reivers) for Walton.

SOUTH AFRICA: P. C. Montgomery; C. S. Terblanche, A. H. Snyman, C. Stewart, P. W. G. Rossouw; H. W. Honiball, J. H. van der Westhuizen; R. B. Kempson, J. Dalton, A. C. Garvey, K. Otto, M. G. Andrews. J. Erasmus, G. H. Teichmann (capt), R. B. Skinstad. Reps: A. H. le Roux for Garvey, A. G. Venter for Otto.

Referee: Chris White (England)

Scorers: For Scotland, Duncan Hodge (1T, 1PG, 1con). For SA, Stefan Terblanche, Joost van der Westhuizen, Andre Snyman, Pieter Rossouw, Bobby Skinstad (tries), Percy Montgomery (2PG, 2con).

The tourists defeated Ireland 27-13 to equal the NZ record of 17 successive victories set between 1965-1970. In front of a capacity 48,000 crowd, the Irish pack gave an inspired performance. They were slightly heavier than the Springboks in the scrum and were soon troubling their opponents after teams and spectators stood in silent memory of the victims of the Omah terrorist bomb outrage. Ireland wore white jerseys to obviate a clash with Springbok green.

"We had the game for the taking," said skipper Paddy Johns. "But a lapse of concentration in just seven minutes cost us when we let South Africa in for 17 points." Springbok coach Mallett observed, "Ireland only moved the ball once. They do not have the athletes who can exploit broken play like South Africa. We have individuals who can do things. We have opportunities; we take them. The opposition have dominated us, but not taken their chances."

IRELAND v SOUTH AFRICA

November, 28, 1998. South Africa defeated Ireland by 27 (3G, 2PG) to 13 (1G, 2PG) at Lansdowne Road.

IRELAND: C. M. P. O'Shea (London Irish); J. P. Bishop (London Irish), J. C. Bell (Dungannon), K. M. Maggs (Bath), G. Dempsey (Terenure Coll); E. P. Elwood (Galwegians), C. D. McGuinness (St Mary's Coll); J. M. Fitzpatrick (Dungannon), K. G. M. Wood (Harlequins), P. M. Clohessy (Young Munster), P. S. Johns (Saracens, capt), M. E. O'Kelly (London Irish), D. O. Cuinneagain (Sale), V. C. P. Costello (St Mary's Coll), A. J. Ward (Ballynahinch). Reps: R. Corrigan (Lansdowne) for Fitzpatrick, R. P. Nesdale (Newcastle) for Wood, J. Davidson (Castres) for O'Kelly.

SOUTH AFRICA: P. C. Montgomery; C. S. Terblanche, A. H. Snyman, C. Stewart, P. W. G. Rossouw; H. W. Honiball, J. H. van der Westhuizen; R. B. Kempson, J. Dalton, A. C. Garvey, K. Otto, M. G. Andrews. J. Erasmus, G. H. Teichmann (capt), R. B. Skinstad. Reps: A. H. le Roux for Kempson, N. Drotske for Dalton, A. G. Venter for Andrews, R.B. Kempson for Garvey.

Referee: Clayton Thomas (Wales).

Scorers: For Ireland, Keith Wood (1T), Eric Elwood (2PG, 1con). For SA, Johan Erasmus, Bobby Skinstad, Joost van der Westhuizen (tries), Percy Montgomery (2PG, 3con).

England had not impressed in winning 23-15 against Italy in the World Cup qualifiers, and then lost 12-11 to Australia a week before facing the Springboks. A sell-out attendance of 75,000 expected a titanic tussle and were not disappointed. It was no classic, such as the unforgettable drawn match with the All Blacks a year earlier; but a raw, rugged battle saw England emerge triumphant 13-7 and dash South African hopes of ending their tour on a high with a grand slam of international match successes and, of course, that record 18th consecutive victory.

South Africa's forwards just could not exert dominance and England's pack, with impish delight at the way things were going, refused to accept any liberties by their opponents and tormented them at every turn. They were the dogged heroes of Twickenham on a day of great elation.

An early try by Pieter Rossouw on the overlap, as he evaded Nick Beale's tackle, was converted by Percy Montgomery. It served to stimulate England to more tenacious efforts and they swiftly equalised with an imaginative and well-rehearsed move.

It saw fly half Mike Catt kick wide and flat out to the left touch-line. There, wing Dan Luger jumped to meet the ball and knocked it down and away from marker Terblanche. In swooped Jeremy Guscott to snap up the ball in a flash and he was away before the startled, stretched defence could cut across to envelop him. A lovely try indeed, superbly crafted, and Matt Dawson, emergency kicker in the absence of Paul Grayson, converted.

So it was level pegging at half time and England came out fired up for the rousing climax. Two penalty goals by Dawson, in the 64th and 70th minutes, were the only further scores, though South Africa almost crossed at the end only for Luger to save matters when he got a desperate hand to Snyman's pass intended for the unmarked Terblanche.

England coach Clive Woodward commented, "This win is encouraging - no more than that. The gulf between us and the southern hemisphere is not so much in playing. It is in the structure of the game. Man for man, we are just as good as them. Administration is where the gulf is."

ENGLAND v SOUTH AFRICA

December 5, 1998. England defeated South Africa by 13 (1G, 2PG) to 7 (1G) at Twickenham.

ENGLAND: N. D. Beal (Northampton); T. Underwood (Newcastle), P. R. de Glanville (Bath), G. C. Guscott (Bath), D. D. Luger (Harlequins); M. J. Catt (Bath), M. J. S. Dawson (Northampton); J. Leonard (Harlequins), R. Cockerill (Leicester), D. J. Garforth (Leicester), M. O. Johnson (Leicester), T. A. K. Rodber (Northampton), L. B. N. Dallaglio (Wasps, capt), R. A. Hill (Saracens), N. A. Back (Leicester). Reps: D. L. Rees (Sale) for Underwood, A. S. Healey (Leicester) for Rees, A. D. King (Wasps) for de Glanville, M. E. Corry (Leicester) for Catt, D. J. Grewcock (Saracens) for Rodber.

SOUTH AFRICA: P. C. Montgomery; C. S. Terblanche, A. H. Snyman, C. Stewart, P. W. G. Rossouw; H. W. Honiball, J. H. van der Westhuizen; R. B. Kempson, J. Dalton, A. C. Garvey, K. Otto, M. G. Andrews, J. Erasmus, G. H. Teichmann (capt), R. B. Skinstad. Reps: W. Swanepoel for van der Westhuizen, A. H. le Roux for Kempson, le Roux for Garvey, A. G. Venter for Andrews.

Referee: Paddy O'Brien (New Zealand).

Scorers: For England, Jeremy Guscott (1T), Matt Dawson (2PG, 1con). For SA, Pieter Rossouw (1T), Percy Montgomery (1con).

Argy scrum power makes it
so torrid for battling Wales

WALES 43,   ARGENTINA 30

Wales were warned they would be up against the world's most ferocious scrummagers when they faced Argentina at Stradey Park on November 21, 1998. So it proved: the home scrum was subject to a merciless squeeze, battling on the retreat for much of the game and conceding a penalty try. Events began promisingly for Wales, who expected victory after their impressive display against South Africa a week earlier. Wales fielded the same team that started against the Springboks and roared into a 20-3 lead.

Two Neil Jenkins penalty goals were followed by a Mark Taylor try as the centre arrowed through with a hand-off. Jenkins converted. Combined passing put Colin Charvis across for Jenkins to add the points and provide a third penalty shot. The plan was unfolding to order and no-one was concerned when Felipe Contepomi popped over his second penalty goal. Two more Jenkins penalties winged between the posts and victory was being shaped with a 26-6 lead.

Then things went wrong. Scrum half Pichot pounced from a driving scrum; and another pressure scrum saw Scott Quinnell's pass go loose in in-goal for Felipe Contepomi's gift try. Next, a scrum collapsed and the penalty try was converted. Suddenly, it was 26-25 and half time.

The turning point came 17 minutes into the second half. Scott Gibbs tore through and Martyn Williams was the link to release Charvis for his second try. Jenkins converted and added the points to Dafydd James's try. Pedro Sporleder crossed for the Pumas; but Jenkins's fifth penalty shot sealed it and Wales had survived the terror of the monster scrum.

Welsh players confessed it was a more exacting match than that against the Springboks. "We showed we can play with real flair," said Howley. "We had to box clever, but I was delighted with our second half performance. Howley suffered a nasty gash on the forehead from a kick, but stayed on to direct events coolly. Attendance was reduced to 10,500 for safety reasons.

WALES: S. P. Howarth (Sale); G. Thomas (Cardiff), I. S. Gibbs (Swansea), M. Taylor (Swansea), D. R. James (Pontypridd); N. R. Jenkins (Pontypridd), R. Howley (Cardiff, capt), A .L .P. Lewis (Cardiff), J. M. Humphreys (Cardiff), C. T. Anthony (Swansea), J .C. Quinnell (Richmond), C. Wyatt (Llanelli), C. L. Charvis (Swansea), L. S. Quinnell (Llanelli), M. E. Williams (Pontypridd). Reps: M. J. Voyle (Llanelli) for L. S. Quinnell, B. H. Williams (Richmond) for M. E. Williams.

ARGENTINA: M. Contepomi; I. Corleto, J. Orengo, L. Arbizu, F. Soler; F. Contepomi, A. Pichot; M. Reggiardo, F. Mendez, O. Hasan, P. Sporleder (capt), A. Allub, M. Durand, P. Camerlinckx, M. Ruiz. Reps: E. Simone for Orengo, D. Albanese for Soler, M. Ledesema for Reggiardo, R. Martin for Durand.

Referee: Alan Lewis (Ireland)

Scorers: For Wales, Colin Charvis (2), Mark Taylor, Dafydd James (tries), Neil Jenkins (5PG, 4con). For Argentina, Agustin Pichot, Felipe Contepomi, Pedro Sporleder (tries), penalty try, Felipe Contepomi (2PG, 2con).

All-action Colin Charvis swoops to score against Argentina at Stradey in 1998. The bustling Swansea back rower scored two tries in this floodlight match.

Huw Evans Picture Agency, Cardiff

4-TRY GARETH SPURS BARBARIANS

Pontypridd wing Gareth Wyatt scored four tries for the Barbarians in a 51-20 win over Combined Services at United Services Ground, Portsmouth. Siua Taumalolo, the Ebbw Vale full back, playing at fly half, also crossed, as did Cardiff full back Justin Thomas. Paul Williams (Cardiff) figured in the back row. Former Pontypridd hooker Jonathen Evans and ex-Newport No 8 Jan Machacek scored tries when the Baa-Baas defeated Leicester 38-24. Cardiff's Greg Kacala, on debut for Baa-Baas, crossed for a try in 51-19 success over East Midlands at Northampton. Other Welsh players on duty were Sven Cronk (Newport) and flanker Paul Williams (Cardiff). Barbarians' World XV beat England champion club Leicester 55-33 at Twickenham to round off the season.

ITALY HAMMERED IN THE WAY
THAT HANNIBAL DID IT

ITALY 21,   WALES 60

A record 30 points by Neil Jenkins and four tries by wing Gareth Thomas to equal the Welsh record in a match were the highlights of this scintillating victory watched by 9,000 at the Stadio Comunale Di Monigo, Treviso on March 20, 1999. Wales led only 18-16 at the interval; but with the wind behind them in the second half they rippled into breathtaking all-out action.

Italy were stunned by the margin of defeat. It was a disaster almost as devastating as Hannibal's triumphs at the Trebia, Trasimene and Cannae all rolled into one! Italy had battled so resolutely at Stradey Park in 1998 before losing 23-20 that they never imagined this latest encounter would produce a rout.

Coach Graham Henry had measured his praise for the famous victory in Paris in the previous match: this time he was more lavish. "We are maturing," he said. "We played with discipline and focus. It is not just that we are winning, but we are playing such exciting rugby. Nobody would have expected this result, but it shows what confidence can do."

Wales ran with adventure and vision and it was an amazing image transformation from the performances that resulted in defeats by Scotland and Ireland. This biggest Welsh success against the Azzurri produced seven tries, including a third in successive games for Craig Quinnell. Neil Jenkins included a fine try in his tally and set up two others while giving another commanding display. By taking his total of points for Wales to 704 only Australia's Michael Lynagh is ahead of him with 911. Jenks passed his previous best in a match of 24 against Canada in 1993 and then against Italy in 1994.

Chris Wyatt was a dominating influence in the lineout as well as making a vital tackle to prevent Cristian Stoica scoring a try with Italy leading 10-8. Wyatt's ball-carrying also makes him a key figure in a fast-emerging pack. All seven replacements were sent on, including new cap Nick Walne.

ITALY: J. Pertile; F. Roselli, C. Stoica, L. Martin, D. Dallan; D. Dominguez, A. Troncon; M. Cuttitta, A. Moscardi, F. Properzi, M. Giacheri, W. Cristofoletto, M. Giovanelli (capt), D. Scaglia, A. Sgorlon. Reps: M. Baroni for Stoica, A. Castellani for Properzi, S. Stocco for Cristofoletto, S. Saviozzi for Sgorlon.

WALES: S. Howarth (Sale); G. Thomas (Cardiff), M. Taylor (Swansea), S. Gibbs (Swansea), D. James (Pontypridd); N. Jenkins (Pontypridd), R. Howley (Cardiff, capt), P. Rogers (London Irish), G. Jenkins (Swansea), B. Evans (Swansea), C. Quinnell (Richmond), C. Wyatt (Llanelli), C. Charvis (Swansea), S. Quinnell (Llanelli), B. Sinkinson (Neath). Reps: N. Boobyer (Llanelli) for Taylor, N. Walne (Richmond) for James, D. Llewellyn (Ebbw Vale) for Howley, D. Morris (Swansea) for Rogers, B. Williams (Richmond) for G. Jenkins, M. Voyle (Llanelli) for C. Quinnell, G. Lewis (Pontypridd) for Charvis.

Referee: Rob Dickson (Scotland).

Scorers: For Wales, Gareth Thomas (4), Craig Quinnell, Rob Howley, Neil Jenkins (tries), Neil Jenkins (5PG, 5con). For Italy, Luca Martin, Andrea Sgorlon (tries), Diego Dominguez (3PG, 1con).

A one-man stampede! Craig Quinnell emerged as a try-scoring second row during the 1998-99 season, displaying a serious turn of pace and a gritty determination that brought high praise from shocked opponents. Here he sends shock waves through Italy's defence.

Huw Evans Picture Agency, Cardiff

Jenkins kicks Wales to historic first victory

WALES 29, SOUTH AFRICA 19

"I think our chances are remote," considered Wales coach Graham Henry as his team prepared to take on the world champions in the first match at the new Arms Park (called by some Millennium Stadium) on June 26, 1999. "For us, this is a match too far," he mused. "We would rather not play it." All this was psychological warfare. "I told the media that," he confessed. "But I told our players we could win!" And they did. It was a day of glory: a day of history.

Wales had waited 93 years for this first victory over South Africa. Of the previous 12 games since the first in 1906, 11 had been lost and the 1970 match drawn 6-all. A year before this fateful day, Wales had been blasted off the Loftus Versfeld, losers by a record 96-13. SA coach Nick Mallett called them the worst team he had ever seen. Now the Boks would pay.

This Welsh pack were heroes to a man. They took on Gary Teichmann's forwards and quelled them. Though they lost combative Craig Quinnell three minutes after a hectic punch-up suffering from a broken thumb, they found a deputy in Mike Voyle who fitted in expertly alongside the soaring Chris Wyatt.

Scott Quinnell played his most commanding game for Wales with Brett Sinkinson and Colin Charvis defiant defenders at his elbow. It was unbending defence that won it. Three times South Africa swarmed on the goal-line and seemed impossible to stop. Grimly, they were held out. Springbok hearts don't break easily; but after that they must have known fate was against them. It was psychological off the field; but face-to-face physicality on it.

Neil Jenkins yet again proved the complete controller: he contributed 19 goal points and put Gareth Thomas across in the corner from short range. Neil's line-kicking was faultless; enormous fliers that screamed down and drove the Springboks back. Mark Taylor's hand-off as he rounded his marker was a deft and delightful moment for the first try at the new ground. Neil's conversion of Gareth Thomas's try from the more difficult touchline was another delicacy to savour. What a way to open the new ground, watched by 27,500, and raise hopes of a World Cup campaign that would signal Wales are back with a vengeance.

WALES: S.P. Howarth (Sale); G. Thomas (Cardiff), M. Taylor (Swansea), A.G. Bateman (Northampton), D.R. James (Pontypridd); N.R. Jenkins (Pontypridd), R. Howley (Cardiff, capt); P.J.D. Rogers (Newport), G.R. Jenkins (Swansea), D. Young (Cardiff), J.C. Quinnell (Cardiff), C.P. Wyatt (Llanelli), C.L. Charvis (Swansea), L.S. Quinnell (Llanelli), B.D. Sinkinson (Neath). Reps: M.J. Voyle (Llanelli) for J.C. Quinnell, A.L.P. Lewis (Cardiff) for Rogers, J.M. Humphreys (Cardiff) for G.R. Jenkins.

SOUTH AFRICA: P. Montgomery; S. Terblanche, P. Muller, J. Mulder, P. Rossouw; B. van Straaten, W. Swanepoel; R, Kempson, N. Drotske, C. Visagie, S. Boome, K. Otto, C. Krige, G. Teichmann (capt), J. Erasmus. Reps: G. du Toit for van Straaten, D. von Hoesslin for Swanepoel, O le Roux for Kempson, A. Venter for Boome.

Referee: Ed Morrison (England).

Scorers: For Wales, Mark Taylor, Gareth Thomas (tries), Neil Jenkins (5PG, 2con). For SA, Werner Swanepoel, Percy Montgomery (tries), Braam van Straaten (2PG), Gaffie du Toit (1PG).

HAYWARD SETS IT ALL UP FOR
SMART STEPHEN TO SHINE

A virtuoso performance by Stephen Jones, playing in the centre, steered Llanelli to 41-18 victory over Pontypridd in the Challenge Trophy final at Stradey Park on January 30, 1999. He swept over for two tries and kicked five penalty goals and three conversions for a tally of 31 points. Byron Hayward set up both Jones's tries: first with a ripping break in the opening half, and then with the last scoring move of the game, a kick-on that Jones chased.

Andrew Lamerton's try, converted by Gareth Wyatt, gave Ponty a quick lead; but their only other points came from an interception gift try for Rhys Shorney and two Gareth Wyatt penalty goals. Salesi Finau, the Tongan centre, was sin-binned in the second half for 10 minutes, but he and full back Darril Williams were the other Scarlets' try-getters.

Ponty had to defend their title without six leading players. Skipper Neil Jenkins, Dafydd James, Martyn Williams, Kevin Morgan, Geraint Lewis and Ian Gough were all in the Wales squad preparing for the match against Scotland the following week and their club made the sacrifice of not selecting them in the interests of their country. Llanelli similarly did not call on their squad men, Chris Wyatt, Mike Voyle and Scott Quinnell.

BEDEVILLED BY RAIN

Pontypridd borrowed flank forward Gavin Owen and full back Robert Morgan from Treorchy with two Romanian players on the bench. Former Wales and Neath prop John Davies, who had joined from Richmond earlier in the week, went on as replacement Llanelli prop for Martyn Madden in the second half.

Llanelli won all four pool games, including the clash with the Bulls of Northern Transvaal, who were rated tournament favourites when they arrived. Ponty qualified for the final despite playing only three pool games. Their fixture against Edinburgh Reivers was called off because of a frozen pitch and then through a waterlogged ground. The whole competition, in its second season, was bedevilled with inclement weather. Opinion was that a three-week tourney in January was the wrong time of the season because of weather risks. Still, the rain relented for the final and some 4,000 witnessed a rousing, physical contest under the Stradey floodlights.

LLANELLI: Darril Williams; Wayne Proctor (capt), Salesi Finau, Stephen Jones, Garan Evans; Byron Hayward, Rupert Moon; Phil Booth, Jason Hyatt, Martyn Madden, Vernon Cooper, Tony Copsey, David Hodges, Hywel Jenkins, Ian Boobyer. Reps: John Davies for Madden, Iwan Jones for Boobyer.

PONTYPRIDD: Robert Morgan; Rhys Shorney, Jason Lewis, Andre Barnard, Simon Enoch; Gareth Wyatt, Paul John; Aled Griffiths, Andrew Lamerton, Ngalu T'au, Greg Prosser, Aaron Freeman, Matthew Lloyd, Dale McIntosh (capt), Gavin Owen. Reps: Mihai Vioeanu for Morgan, Henry Whitfield for Prosser, Rob Appleyard for Owen, S. Mordan for Enoch.

Referee: Peter Marshall (Australia).

There were no semi-finals this time. Instead, Bridgend and Edinburgh Reivers met in a third place play-off. Bridgend, unbeaten in their pool, but without enough bonus points to qualify for the final, were 25-23 winners. Adrian Durston, Gareth Cull and Owain Thomas scored Bridgend tries and Cull converted two and added two penalty goals for 15 points.

Another change was that the guest teams this time could qualify for the final. In the event, none did. Edinburgh were always dangerous, but the cancellation of their pool match at Pontypridd denied them a chance to challenge. The Reivers' only defeat was in this play-off after defeating Aberavon, Neath and blasting Caerphilly 64-0 at Beddau when the match was switched because Virginia Park was under water.

TWO-TRY MADDEN SHAKES BULLS

The previous season, the inaugural event, only one match was lost by Welsh clubs against the overseas teams (Ebbw Vale 22-10 to Argentine's Tucuman); but this time, although the visitors sent a number of their development squads, they proved much more successful. Rugby Canada defeated Aberavon 10-0 and Neath 14-11; Natal Wildebeests accounted for Neath 36-18 and Caerphilly 37-32; and Northern Transvaal Bulls beat Newport 39-24. This time, no Welsh clubs opposed each other until the final, contested by the two pool winners.

Llanelli's pool successes saw them defeat Northern Bulls 23-10 with two tries by prop Madden, Gauteng Falcons 36-15, Glasgow Caledonians 21-19 (through a Stephen Jones penalty goal two minutes from time) and Romania 57-12.

Pontypridd produced one of their most convincing displays to defeat Natal Wildebeests 37-14 in icy rain and mud. "It was like running around in a refrigerator," commented Natal skipper Craig McIntosh. Ponty and Edinburgh each took one point from their cancelled fixture. Rugby Canada were overwhelmed 52-10 with 22 points from Neil Jenkins and then Ponty pounded Georgia 69-7 for a place in the final.

EARLY BATH FOR STEVE WAKE

Bridgend opened with a 44-10 verdict against Romania and then squeezed in 17-15 over Falcons. A notable triumph came 28-5 against Northern Bulls with Gareth Cull kicking three penalty goals and converting two of the tries by Owain Thomas, Steve Ford and Steve Winn. Then it was another tight tussle to shade Glasgow 10-8 despite having scrum half Steve Wake ordered off. Cull converted a penalty try and added a penalty goal.

Ebbw Vale battled back from 12-0 down to defeat Falcons 25-19 with two tries by David Llewellyn and two South African players were in the sin-bin together! Fly half Scott Mitchell scored 16 points as Newport beat Romania 46-20. Caerphilly registered an outstanding victory 11-7 over Canada; Aberavon slammed Georgia 42-0 and Neath's only win was 59-14 against Georgia.

Find out about New Astra's award winning standards of quality, comfort and safety
–
Lo-*call* 0345 400800 for a brochure.

ASTRA. *Quality is a right. Not a privilege.*

VAUXHALL

Raising the Standard

ARTFUL ARWEL HITS TARGET
WITH 95 POINTS IN 5 GAMES

It was celebrations for Wales A and Under-21 teams as they achieved notable success, each completing Grand Slams at their levels. Wales A coach Dennis John, whose son Paul captained the A side, praised his squad for their professionalism. "We always aimed to play exciting, controlled rugby and I think we provided the necessary entertainment," he said. Absolutely true. This A team had a dazzling catalyst in Swansea outside half Arwel Thomas. As a goal kicker he was not far behind Neil Jenkins's amazing strike rate and finished the season with 95 A team points in five games. A daring, deceptive runner with a devastating dummy, Arwel was capable of ripping defences apart.

The campaign opened with a defeat. Wales led 19-13 with 10 minutes remaining against Argentina A at Sardis Road in November, only for the visitors to unleash relentless scrum power and steamroller to 28-19 victory. However, the lessons were absorbed and put to effective use for the rest of the season.

Anthony Sullivan, in his first representative match after just four RU appearances for Cardiff, crossed against the Argentines, Byron Hayward converted and flighted over four penalty goals; but few Welsh players shone and coach John set to work to hone the edge, physically and mentally.

WELSH KIWIS LEND A HAND

The test came against Scotland at Myreside. The home team dominated early, but were worn down as Arwel found the target with five penalty shots. Nick Walne snapped up the try in 20-8 victory to avenge the previous season's defeat. Forwards Brett Sinkinson and Richard Arnold, New Zealanders with Welsh grand-parents, impressed on their first appearances.

There were 7,000 at Ebbw Vale to see Paul John's team topple Ireland 40-29 with a controlling performance from Arwel Thomas, who contributed 25 goal points. Wales rallied after falling 18-17 behind by the interval. Nick Walne (2) and Jason Lewis were the try-getters.

A second half fightback brought Wales a 20-17 verdict over France at Perigueux after the home side established a 14-6 lead. The only try of the game was obtained by No 8 Richard Arnold to make sure after Arwel had landed his customary five penalty goals.

The only hiccup in the march to the Grand Slam against rival home countries came at Rovigo when Giovanni Preo planted over a penalty goal four minutes from the end for Italy to edge it 24-23. Arwel scored six penalty goals and wing Gareth Wyatt crossed for the try. Wales lost lock Andy Moore with injury just before half time and it proved a crucial blow.

Finally, a superb display brought 32-25 victory over England to claim the Grand Slam at Wrexham in April. England also were in the hunt for the Slam and fought tenaciously in a see-saw tussle. It thrilled 9,000 watchers and such was the intensity that the referee was busy flashing yellow cards in all directions.

Matthew Robinson and Martyn Williams were home try-getters and Arwel fired in 22 points with six penalty goals and two conversions. England menaced in the third minute of stoppage time when Peter Mensah surged away. He had a couple of yards start on Kevin Morgan, but the fleet-footed full back overhauled him and dragged Mensah down with a try-saving tackle that will linger long in the memory.

WALES A 19, ARGENTINA A 28. Wales: K. Morgan (Pontypridd); A. Sullivan (Cardiff), J. Lewis (Pontypridd), S. Jones (Llanelli), W. Proctor (Llanelli); B. Hayward (Ebbw Vale), P. John (Pontypridd); A. Griffiths (Pontypridd), G. Jenkins (Swansea), L. Mustoe (Cardiff), C. Billen (Ebbw Vale), I. Gough (Pontypridd), G. P. Lewis (Pontypridd), N. Thomas (Bath), J. Forster (Pontypridd). Reps: C. Morgan (Cardiff), S. John (Llanelli), R. McBryde (Llanelli), C. Stephens (Bridgend), S. Eggar (Neath).

SCOTLAND A 8, WALES A 20. Wales: D. Weatherley (Swansea); A. Sullivan (St Helens RL), L. Davies (Cardiff), J. Lewis (Pontypridd), N. Walne (Richmond); A. Thomas (Swansea), P. John (Pontypridd, capt); P. Rogers (London Irish), G. Jenkins (Swansea), B. Evans (Swansea), S. Moore (Cardiff), A. Moore (Swansea), O. Williams (Cardiff), R. Arnold (Newcastle), B. Sinkinson (Neath). Reps: B. Hayward (Llanelli), A. Griffiths (Pontypridd), L. Jones (Swansea).

WALES A 40, IRELAND A 29. Wales: D. Weatherley (Swansea); N. Walne (Richmond), S. Winn (Bridgend), J. Lewis (Pontypridd), A. Sullivan (St Helens RL); A. Thomas (Swansea), P. John (Pontypridd, capt); P. Rogers (London Irish), A. Lamerton (Pontypridd), B. Evans (Swansea), S. Moore (Cardiff), A. Moore (Swansea), O. Williams (Cardiff), R. Arnold (Newcastle), B. Sinkinson (Neath). Reps: L. Jones (Swansea), L. Davies (Cardiff), R. McBryde (Llanelli), C. Billen (Ebbw Vale).

FRANCE A 17, WALES A 20. Wales: B. Hayward (Llanelli); N. Walne (Richmond), J. Lewis (Pontypridd), L. Davies (Cardiff), A. Sullivan (St Helens RL); A. Thomas (Swansea), P. Morris (Swansea), A. Lamerton (Pontypridd), A. Metcalfe (Ebbw Vale), S. Moore (Cardiff), A. Moore (Swansea), G. Lewis (Pontypridd), R. Arnold (Newcastle), M. Williams (Pontypridd). Reps: R. McBryde (Llanelli), I. Gough (Pontypridd).

ITALY A 24, WALES A 23. Wales: K. Morgan (Pontypridd); M. Robinson (Swansea), J. Lewis (Pontypridd), S. Winn (Bridgend), G. Wyatt (Pontypridd); A. Thomas (Swansea), P. John (Pontypridd, capt); A. Lewis (Cardiff), R. McBryde (Llanelli), D. Young (Cardiff), I. Gough (Pontypridd), A. Moore (Swansea), R. Arnold (Newcastle), L. Jones (Swansea), M. Williams (Pontypridd). Reps: C. Billen (Ebbw Vale), N. Budgett (Ebbw Vale), B. Hayward (Llanelli).

WALES A 32, ENGLAND A 25. Wales: K. Morgan (Pontypridd); M. Robinson (Swansea), J. Lewis (Pontypridd), L. Davies (Cardiff), R. Rees (Swansea); A. Thomas (Swansea), P. John (Pontypridd, capt); D. Morris (Swansea), R. McBryde (Llanelli), C. Anthony (Swansea), I. Gough (Pontypridd), A. Moore (Swansea), G. Lewis (Pontypridd), R. Arnold (Newcastle), M. Williams (Pontypridd). Reps: Rhodri Jones (Swansea), A. Griffiths (Pontypridd), C. Billen (Ebbw Vale).

Super Stephen's 70 points inspires sizzling season of success

This fine season of success for Stephen Jones's team opened with a tense 22-20 win against Scotland at Bridgehaugh. Skipper Jones kicked five penalty goals and converted a penalty try. Trailing 15-6, Wales hit back to defeat Ireland 24-18 at Virginia Park. Alix Popham, Martin Giraud and Craig Morgan crossed and captain Jones fired in three penalty goals. France were next victims 10-6 in Bordeaux. Gareth Cooper's try was goaled by Jones, who added a penalty shot.

Wales were handsome 78-19 winners over Italy at Udine. Craig Morgan, Gareth Cooper, Matthew Wakins, Giraud, Andy Newman, Nathan Bonner-Evans, Gavin Thomas, Craig Hawkins and Popham crossed to add to the three tries by Sam Greenaway. Jones converted nine. It was 36-21 over England at the Gnoll to complete the Grand Slam. Gareth Williams, Bonner-Evans, Cooper and skipper Jones scored tries and Jones supplied four penalty goals and two conversions to bring his tally in five games to 70 points.

SCOTLAND U-21 20, WALES U-21 22.

Wales: C. Morgan (Cardiff); D. Rogers (Llanelli), M. Watkins (Newport), S. Winn (Bridgend), M. Giraud (L Welsh); S. Jones (Llanelli, capt), G. Cooper (Bath); Duncan Jones (Neath), G. Williams (UWIC), D. Sweet (Ynysybwl), A. Newman (Northampton), Deiniol Jones (Bath), A. Popham (Newport), N. Bonner-Evans (Newport), G. Thomas (Bridgend). Rep: G. Mason (Ebbw Vale).

WALES U-21 24, IRELAND U-21 8.

Wales: C. Morgan (Cardiff); S. Greenaway (Bridgend), M. Watkins (Newport), D. Hawkins (Bonymaen), M. Giraud (L Welsh); S. Jones (Llanelli, capt), G. Cooper (Bath); Duncan Jones (Neath), G. Williams (UWIC), D. Sweet (Ynysybwl), A. Newman (Northampton), Deiniol Jones (Bath), A. Popham (Newport), N. Bonner-Evans (Newport), G. Thomas (Bridgend). Rep: R. Francis (Neath).

FRANCE U-21 6, WALES U-21 10.

Wales: C. Morgan (Cardiff); S. Greenaway (Bridgend), D. Hawkins (Bonymaen), S. Winn (Bridgend), M. Giraud (L Welsh); S. Jones (Llanelli, capt), G. Cooper (Bath); Duncan Jones (Neath), G. Williams (UWIC), D. Sweet (Ynysybwl), A. Newman (Northampton), Deiniol Jones (Bath), N. Bonner-Evans (Newport), A. Popham (Newport), G. Thomas (Bridgend).

ITALY U-21 19, WALES U-21 78

Wales: C. Morgan (Cardiff); S. Greenaway (Bridgend), M. Watkins (Newport), D. Hawkins (Bonymaen), M. Giraud (L Welsh); S. Jones (Llanelli, capt), G. Cooper (Bath); Duncan Jones (Neath), G. Williams (UWIC), D. Sweet (Ynysybwl), A. Newman (Northampton), Deiniol Jones (Bath), A. Popham (Newport), N. Bonner-Evans (Newport), G. Thomas (Bridgend). Reps: C. Hawkins, S. Daniels, M. Giffin, R. Francis, G. Mason, G. Evans, M. Taylor.

WALES U-21 36, England U-21 21.

Wales: C. Morgan (Cardiff); S. Greenaway (Bridgend), M. Watkins (Newport), D. Hawkins (Bonymaen), M. Giraud (L Welsh); S. Jones (Llanelli, capt), G. Cooper (Bath); Duncan Jones (Neath), G. Williams (UWIC), D. Sweet (Ynysybwl), A. Newman (Northampton), Deiniol Jones (Bath), A. Popham (Newport), N. Bonner-Evans (Newport), G. Thomas (Bridgend). Rep: G. Mason (Ebbw Vale).

Swansea keep cup as ace kicker
Cerith pops up with 20 points

Outside half Cerith Rees, star of the Aberavon back division, spearheaded Swansea University to 35-15 success to retain the British Universities Sports Association Rugby Cup, sponsored by Halifax BS, at Twickenham on March 24, 1999. They defeated St Mary's College (London) after the team from Strawberry Hill (less than a mile from Twickenham) had led 8-5 at half time. Then Cerith Rees fashioned a notable victory with 20 points. He collected a friendly bounce from his chip-on to cross and added three conversions and three penalty goals. Ed Lewsey, skipper Ben Martin and James Baker also scored tries and Swansea were the first Welsh team to retain the cup since the 1930s.

SWANSEA UNIVERSITY: David Kendrick; Ben Davies, James Baker, Owen Jones, Adrian Cox; Cerith Rees, Ed Lewsey; Neil Hennessy, Steve James, James Meredith, Paul Langley, Tom Radbourne, Ben Martin (capt), Rhodri Griffiths, Gareth Roberts.

Welsh Universities secured the coveted Triple Crown of success during 1999. There was an impressive opener in Edinburgh with the Scots overwhelmed 44-18. Next up were Ireland at Llanrumney, holders of the Triple Crown at this level for the previous two seasons. But Wales gave another dashing display to win 26-8 with three drop shots by outside half Craig Warlow. He also converted tries by Tristan Bowen and hooker Steve Jones and popped over a penalty goal for a tally of 16 points.

Though they lost in France 20-17, Welsh Universities clinched the crown against English Universities 19-17 at Cyncoed. Hooker Steve Jones snapped up two tries and wing Paul John also crossed. Ceri Sweeney converted two tries and Wales, led by Llanelli scrum half Aled Thomas, held out against England's fightback.

Wales Students lost 26-7 to England Students at the Brewery Field. Centre Owen Jones (Swansea) scored the home try and Warlow (Trinity Coll) converted. Swansea defeated Cardiff 17-13 at Cardiff RFC ground in their annual charity Welsh Varsity Match. Trinity College retained the BUSA Challenge Trophy 17-8 against Wolverhampton.

Varsity Match
FIVE WINS IN A ROW EQUALS RECORD

Cambridge University registered a record-equalling fifth consecutive Varsity Match victory with a 16-12 verdict in the rain at Twickenham in front of 60,000 onlookers on December 8, 1998. Mark Denney and hooker Stefan Rodgers scored Cambridge tries and Paul Moran kicked two penalty goals. Nick Booth and Nick Humphries crossed for the Dark Blues and Booth converted one try.

TRIPLE CROWN TRIUMPH FOR BATTLING WALES YOUTH

Wales Youth recorded a highly-pleasing triple success in the Four Home Nations tourney in 1998-99. It followed their notable achievement in reaching the final of the World Junior Cup and exemplified the wealth of talent that promises a bright future for the game in Wales.

The opening fixture brought Wales a 15-10 decision against Ireland, who twice stole the lead and made the Welsh team battle all the way. Dafydd Lewis (Millfield) fired over a penalty goal and converted one of the tries by skipper and scrum half Andrew Williams (Dunvant) and back row forward Andy Powell (Brecon).

Gala, in the Scottish borders, was the venue for the clash with England and this time Wales were 17-9 winners. Tries came from Duncan Murray (Christ College, Brecon) and Owain Ford (Bridgend). David Owen (Treorchy) and Dafydd Lewis each converted one and Owen added a penalty goal.

DAFYDD SHOWS THE WAY

Finally, with the Triple Crown a tempting prize, Murrayfield was the scene for a tense contest with Scotland putting up spirited resistance. Their senior team had put a spoke in Wales's wheel earlier in the year and now the Scot's youth side made a supreme effort. However, Wales could not be denied and triumphed 16-11 after Scotland led 8-6 at half time. Dafydd Lewis landed three penalty goals and his third kick nosed his team in front 9-8. Then Christ College wing Owen Williams went in for the Welsh try and Lewis supplied the goal points for the celebrations to begin.

Australia Schools came to avenge the 19-12 defeat they had suffered at Ballymore, Brisbane in August 1994 and accomplished their aim in most impressive fashion 56-10. Whereas on their tour Down Under, the Welsh boys had performed superbly (losing just one of seven games), with outside half Darren Morris (Neath TC) kicking 14 points, including a conversion of a try by Millfield prop Phil Booth (who was outstanding for Llanelli in their SWALEC Cup semi-final victory over Cardiff in April 1999), this time Wales were overawed by the power and pace of the young Aussies. Despite the mud at the Brewery Field on January 16, 1999, the tourists produced a dazzling display of varied tactics and secured tries by Talaia (3), Playford (2), Smith, Hardy and Schliebs. Five were converted by Warwick, who added two penalty goals. Wales replied with tries by scrum half Dwayne Peel and hooker Matthew Rees, but failed to retain possession when it mattered most.

WALES SCHOOLS (senior group) v Australia Schools: Rhodri Morris (Llanhari); Kevin James (Neath Coll), Nathan Hopkins (Cardinal Newman), Dylan Pugh (Colston's), Matthew Cunningham (Colston's); Matthew Davies (Strade), Dwayne Peel (Maes-y-Yrfa, capt); Andrew Cowen (Hartridge), Matthew Rees (Tonyrefail), Greg Woods (Cwmcarn), Carl Bowen (Neath Coll), Grant Wilson (Cross Keys Coll), Jason Simpson (Llanhari), Michael Owen (Bryn Celynnog), Rhys Williams (Cross Keys Coll). Reps: Paul Fisher (Strade), Gethin Worgan (Llanhari), Gethin Jenkins (Bryn Celynnog), Andrew Clatworthy (Gorseinon Coll).

Further disappointments were to follow. Although there was a significant improvement against France at Graulhet in February, Wales lost 30-20. Skipper Dwayne Peel crossed for two tries and Robin Sowden-Taylor also snapped up a try. Gethin Worgan converted one and added a penalty goal in a battling performance. But after the battle it was surrender as Ireland were 41-0 winners at Ebbw Vale, where David Cox's try was disallowed. No-one found excuses for an outplayed home side. Then England repeated their victory of the previous winter, this time by a more convincing margin at 18-9 at Church Bank, Llandovery in April. Gethin Worgan's three penalty goals comprised the Welsh points and although Dwayne Peel made a few sharp runs, the Welsh backline failed to function smoothly.

Just as Wales had snatched that unforgettable one-point victory over England at Wembley with Neil Jenkins's goal kick of Scott Gibbs's scorching try right at the end, so England's boys stole the game from the Welsh boys at Stradey Park in April. Wales Under-16 had levelled matters at 20-all through a try by Ashley Copic (Tonyrefail) only for England's Mark Scrivener to plunge the home side into 23-20 defeat with a last-minute penalty shot. It was a cruel fate after the Welsh team had played with plenty of determination. Wing Paul Mackey (Bishopston) scored two tries for Wales and Michael Hook (Glanafan) converted one and struck a penalty goal.

TRY HAT-TRICK FOR WING RHODRI

Wales A Under-16 also lost in their encounter with England A. It was 19-11. Skipper David Williams (Bishop Gore) obtained the Welsh try and Horner was on target with two penalty goals. Alas, England's forwards proved much too strong on this occasion.

Wing Rhodri Gomer Davies (Lampeter) swooped for a hat-trick of tries in a 38-5 success against Portugal Under-16 at Coimbra in February. Alyn Lake (Llanhari), James Malpas (Corpus Christi) and Gareth Knox (Ystalyfera) also crossed for Wales.

Then the Welsh youngsters opposed Italy Under-17 at the Gnoll in March and won 27-12. Full back Gareth Knox, Rhodri Gomer Davies, No 8 Gareth Delve (Cardiff) and replacement scrum half Rhodri Jones (Pontypool) were the try-getters. Hook converted two and hit over a penalty shot.

TWO-TRY LUKE IS A
FESTIVAL WINNER

Trelales School (Bridgend) were 21-5 winners against Parc-y-Twyn in the final of the Welsh National 10-a-side Festival, sponsored by *The Western Mail,* at the Brewery Field. Luke Hathaway scored two tries and converted all three. Adam Symons was the other Bridgend try scorer. Rhys Williams crossed for the Burry Port school.

BRILLIANT ALL BLACKS BLAST ADVENTUROUS WALES HOPES

Wales made a memorable contribution to the Junior World Cup, held in Wales for the first time, and reached the final only to fall 25-0 to a dazzling New Zealand team in front of some 12,000 at Stradey Park on April 3, 1999. It was the second time in the final for the Welsh side (they had lost to Argentina 34-7 in 1996 with Pontypridd's Kevin Morgan and Gareth Wyatt in the team). Adam Jones's side thoroughly deserved their latest march to the final after taking the most difficult route: they defeated England, Argentina and then went through on elimination test in a 10-all draw with South Africa.

New Zealand, competing for the first time, shattered Welsh hopes with tries by wings Gerrard Fasaualu (2) and Junior Muliaina and back row Richard McCaw. Riki Flutey converted one and kicked a penalty goal. Although they won plenty of possession, the home side just could not break an all-engulfing defence, which twice clawed down full back Rhys Williams when the exciting runner was almost across. The rain and mud were not the conditions Wales wanted, but coach John Bevan praised his players as a talented and dedicated squad who relished the wide, fast game, never afraid to attack from long range.

WALES (v New Zealand): R. Williams; K. James, M. Price, J. Robinson, R. Johnston; C. Sweeney, R. Powell; D. Pattison, C. Thomas, G. Woods, D. Adams, A. Jones (capt), J. Bater, M. Owen, T. Morris. Reps: D. Peel, R. Mills, R. Davies, C. Bowen, A. Chiffi, M. Griffiths

TECHNICAL KO FOR BOKS

Wales launched their title bid with a dazzling 39-9 victory over England at the Gnoll. Ceri Sweeney supplied 19 points with a try, four conversions and two penalty goals. Other tries came from Richard Johnston (2) and James Bater and there was also a penalty try. The quarter-final produced a 29-5 success against Argentina, who had swamped Poland in their opening game 55-11. Wales overawed the Argentines at the Brewery Field, maintaining discipline despite frequent provocation. Johnston scored two tries again and full back Rhys Williams also crossed. Sweeney converted one and kicked three penalty goals. G. Worgan also put over a penalty shot.

The semi-final produced an unusual result. A penalty goal by Pontypridd fly half Sweeney, a minute into stoppage time at the Brewery Field, saw Wales level against South Africa 10-all. But that penalty shot proved a 'technical knock-out' because it counted more than a South African dropped goal in the elimination test and Wales were through. It was the third successive year for the young Springboks to go out of the tourney in drawn matches. Although Wales did not perform with the dynamic impact that had won their first two matches, they attacked at every possible opportunity for Sweeney to cross and convert. He hit the post with a penalty attempt, but his next kick sailed over and that was enough!

The Sweeney is controller as Pontypridd topple Newport

Ceri Sweeney, always a cool controller at outside half, dropped a goal, added a penalty shot and converted three tries for Pontypridd to defeat Newport 32-15 in the Welsh Youth U19 Challenge Cup final at Abertillery Park. Tom Potts, Jason Hallett, Ashley Copic and Gareth Keech were Ponty try-getters, and skipper Michael Owen and No 8 Damien Adams key figures in the victory. Gareth Chapman and Neil McKim crossed for Newport. D Blanks converted one and Matthew Howells landed a penalty goal.

Cardiff were winners of the Welsh Youth U18 MK Electric Districts Cup. They defeated Ogwr 24-3 at Waterton Cross. Owain Ashman supplied 14 points with a try, penalty goal and three conversions; full back Chris Anderson and wing Neil Dallymore were the other try scorers. Rhys Edwards kicked an Ogwr penalty goal.

Llanelli edged Swansea 11-8 to win the Welsh Youth U17 Cup at the Gnoll. Swansea had both props, Lee May and Tim Evans, ordered off for use of the boot in the second half, but Llanelli were always in command with more efficient team work and decision-making. Daniel Jones kicked two Llanelli penalty goals and scrum half Rob Glenn obtained their try. James Horner fired over the Swansea penalty shot and Robert Lawson crossed for their try. Llanelli also won the DG Griffiths Trophy by an 18-5 margin against Rhondda and East Glamorgan at Maesteg.

Wales U19 were 19-8 winners against France U19 at Newport with tries by No 8 Alix Popham, the outstanding player on view, who crossed twice, full back Rhys Williams and wing Neil McKim. Luke Richards converted two. There was also victory over Italy U19 at Frascati, but Wales lost at this level 25-19 to Romania in Bucharest. Wing Kevin James (Neath Coll) scored two tries and Ceri Sweeney also crossed and converted two of the tries.

RECORD-MAKER IEUAN CALLS IT A DAY

Ieuan Evans, the Bath and former Llanelli wing, announced his retirement from rugby in March 1999. He had been dogged by injuries yet again and considered very wisely that it was time to give his body a break from rough useage at the age of 35. Iuean gained a record 72 caps for Wales, led his country a record 28 times and scored a record 33 tries. He toured with the British Lions in 1989, 1993 and 1997. We remember with pride his distinguished service to the game and his country.

Llanhari hot-shots are first
winners of the league title

Llanhari were first winners of the Lloyds/TSB Schools' League when it was launched in 1998-99. They defeated powerful Neath College 37-10 in the final at the Gnoll on March 13. Centre Christian Lambert and Jason Simpson scored first half tries for the winners and Gethin Worgan converted one and kicked a penalty goal for a 15-0 lead. Neath wing Kevin James hit back with a dazzling try and lock Rhys Jones crossed; but Llanhari surged away with further tries by lock Dean Fitzgerald, wing Darren Hallett and flanker Justin Jones. Worgan converted two and added a second penalty shot.

Llanhari, who also won the Welsh Schools Sevens title 31-10 againt hosts Llandovery College, put out Llandovery in the league semi-final 27-12 while Neath College won their semi-final 23-13 against Maes-yr-Yrfa.

Neath College, however, made no mistake to win the Welsh Schools U-18 Cup, fighting off a stirring challenge from Cross Keys College with a 30-24 verdict at Dunvant. It was the sixth time for Neath to collect the prize in its 10 seasons. Skipper Carl Bowen, hooker Rhodri Hughes, fly half Richard Davies and scrum half Grant Hall were Neath try-getters. Matthew Turner converted two and kicked two penalty goals. Cross Keys captain Russell Smith, wing Iestyn Smith and prop Grant Hughes crossed and Simon Barber converted all three tries and put over a penalty goal.

Rhondda, in the final of the Dewar Shield for the first time since 1965, were winners with a 40-37 aggregate over two legs. They lost to Bridgend 18-16 at the Brewery Field, but won the return at Sardis Road 24-19 and the three-point overall margin gave them the shield for the first time since 1928.

In the first leg, No 8 Craig Morris and centre Matthew Harrison scored for Rhondda and Geraint Shalton kicked two penalty goals. Outside half Matthew Jones and second row Chris Davies obtained Bridgend tries. Matt Jones converted one and kicked two penalty goals. The return leg saw full back Rhys Morris score a corner try in the ninth minute of injury time for Rhondda's 24-19 success. Jason Male and Matthew Rees had also crossed and Shalton converted one and a penalty try. Matt Jones converted his try and added four penalty goals for Bridgend.

IEUAN LEADS BRIDGEND TO 15th TRIUMPH

Bridgend triumphed in the D C Thomas (U-11) Cup, sponsored by *The Western Mail*. It was their 15th victory, appearing in their 21st final, as they defeated Pontypool 20-5 at Ninian Park. Skipper and prop Ieuan Watkins (2), Ian Hearne and Lee Sims scored tries. Pontypool scored the most spectacular try with a 60-yard run by No 8 Owain Fisher.

SMOOTH STUART GUIDES BONYMAEN
TO THEIR FIRST TOVALI CUP
By Roy Woodward

A new name appears on the Tovali West Wales Cup as the West's two strongest sides, Dunvant and Bonymaen, reached their first ever and keenly anticipated final. The battle for the Division 1 title between the two Swansea sides was temporarily forgotten as a physical and often uncompromising Strady Park final resulted in Bonymaen winning 18-8.

Both sides showed a willingness to spread the ball, but Bonymaen profited from some weak Dunvant defence to score early tries by speedy wing Paul John and strong running centre David Hawkins. A series of friendly warnings from referee David Davies cooled the occasional fiery personal duels, and to their credit Dunvant never gave up, limiting the winners to those two first half tires.

Skipper Mark Glover led a somewhat inexperienced pack, including several dual registration players, who worked hard throughout against a Bonymaen eight ably led by skipper Chris Gittins. The back row of Andy Macpherson, Gerald Williams and Martin Thomas posed a constant threat to Dunvant though a young Simon Delaney, son of former Lanelli prop Laurence, worked hard in the Dunvant front row to help Glover gain a late consolation try after Leigh Cobner had kicked a penalty.

Bonymaen fly half Stuart Davies's intelligent distribution and accurate goal kicking helped seal the result with two well struck penalties and a conversion. Despite Dunvant pressing hard in the final minutes, it was Bonymaen's proud captain Chris Gittins who claimed the cup for coach Malcolm Dacey's team; though Dunvant gained the "holy grail" of promotion to the Premier division just four days later after Bonymaen's league defeat at Pontypool.

Previous cup holders Llandovery, were knocked out by Bonymaen in round 2, but possibly the most remarkable result of the competition was Division 4 side Brynamman's 23-18 quarter-final victory over the then Division 3 leaders Carmarthen Athletic, flanker Sion Caddel getting the winning try for the Amman Valley side after scrum half Rhodri Morgan and player of the year and No.8 Clive Llewellyn had scored earlier Brynamman tries.

BONYMAEN : Chris Lewis; Paul John, David Hawkins, Dean Evans, Chris Batsford; Stuart Davies, Graham Alexander; Andy May, Darran Poland, Mike Rees, Leigh Robbins, Chris Gittins (capt), Andrew McPherson, Gerald Williams, Martin Thomas. Reps: Daniel Hawkins, Gareth Jones, Karl Emmanuel, Chris Powell, Leigh Carlsen, Nigel Evans, Mark John.

DUNVANT : Lee Cobner; Emyr Harris, Mike Smith, Deiniol Evans, Berian Davies; Andrew John, Andrew Williams; Ben Grace, Simon Delaney, Gareth Williams, Andrew Gore, Mark Glover (capt), Stuart Jenkins, Matthew Evans, Anthony Thomas. Reps: Euros Evans, Dean Hughes, Ricky Davies, Peter Lewis, James Reynolds, Tristram Arnold.

In the West Area National Leagues, Carmarthen Quins won the long running Division 3 title race ahead of neighbours Carmarthen Athletic. Wing Warren Leach and experienced centre Anthony Dragone formed a formidable attacking force during the season, but influential skipper Graham Evans proved an inspiring leader and appropriately scored the last try in the Quin's promotion-clinching victory over Pencoed.

Two former giants of the West Wales League, Kidwelly, who recorded just four league wins, and Tumble, who won just two games, suffered relegation to Division 4, to be replaced in the third division by Cwmllynfell, who pipped BSC Port Talbot to the title by a point. Cwmllynfell recorded their 19th consecutive win by beating Cowbridge in their final game 23 - 12. Veteran fly half Mike Lewis again steered Cwmllynfell to an impressive third successive promotion campaign, the Swansea Valley side scoring a total of 86 tries during the campaign.

Mumbles deservedly won the Division 5 West Shield ahead of Skewen, both clubs exchanging places with Penygroes and Cowbridge who are relegated to Division 6 while Penclawdd totalled a thousand points for the season and created a club record of 183 tries to win the Division 6 title to move up to Division 5 along with runners-up Bynea. Loughor and Betws also gained promotion after winning the Division 7 league, Lougher losing just a single game during the entire campaign, ironically away to fellow promotion winners Betws in their last game of the season when the championship had already been secured.

The Pembrokeshire Cup final played at the Haverfordwest ground saw Division 2 sides Whitland and Tenby contest the cup for the second successive year, with Whitland winning again by 24 points to 18. Played in a gale force wind, referee Clayton Thomas had the benefit of "talking flags" from his touch judges - the first time a Pembrokeshire match had witnessed this innovation. Whitland showed a refreshing willingness to spread the ball to battle against the elements and go 24-3 ahead at the interval thanks to two tries by elusive wing Eifion Lewis, with lock Tristan Bowen and flanker Mike Buckinham also getting tries.

In the second half, it was Tenby's turn to face the strong wind and they crossed for three tries with wing Steve Hartland, scrum half Grant Jones and the former Bonymaen lock Pat Nolan all touching down. In a tense and exciting final quarter, Whitland held on to claim the cup in one of the most exciting finals seen for many years, despite the disappointing crowd.

WHITLAND : Barry Thomas; Phil Bowen, Nolan Goodman, Andrew Davies, Eifion Lewis; Rob Phillips (capt), Barry Thomas; Colin Moreshead, Steve Gerrard, Andrew Webster, Steve Thomas, Tristan Bowen, Mike Buckinham, Simon Egger, Alan Reynolds. Reps: Carl Morgan, David Ebsworth, Jason Stiles, Justin Jones, Spencer Rourke.

TENBY : Gavin Scotcher (capt); Steve Hartland, Paul Luger, Neil Truman, John Dodd; Justine Price, Grant Jones; Dai Balkwell, Richard Rossiter, Carl Nottingham, Pat Nolan, Richard Crockford, Andrew Thomas, Nicky Allen, Chris Morgan. Reps: Neil Powling, Dean Bowen, Dean Hadley, Mike Penfold, Dominic Subbiani.

In the National League, Pembrokeshire clubs generally experienced a tough season, though the cup finalists, along with Narberth, ended in creditable mid-table positions in Division 2. Cardigan endured a mixed season in Division 3, finishing in 9th position, though Newcastle Emlyn enjoyed their season, ending in the highest position of the Pembrokeshire clubs, third position in Division 4, behind promoted Cwmllynfell and BSC Port Talbot.

Deputy Gareth kicks the Bwl to their first Silver success

Div 4 Ynysybwl won the Worthington Silver Ball for the first time when they defeated Div 7 Central Nantymoel at Sardis Road on April 22, 1999; but Nanty rocked the favourites with a resolute revival after trailing 19-0 at the interval. Key kicker Stuart Lloyd, who had put over the decisive points in the Bwl's 11-8 semi-final success against Cwmavon, including the winning penalty shot at the end of extra time, was off target in the final. So Gareth Davies took over the duties and converted two tries before he made victory secure with a late penalty shot.

Nanty, 17-6 winners against Blaengarw in the semi-final, rallied with a heartening display as scrum half Andrew Teale heralded the fightback with their first try. Speedy wing Mike Richards added another and Steve Hughes fired over a penalty goal. But Gareth Davies's penalty kick clinched it. Their first half command brought tries by wing Lyndon Lewis, Andrew David and scrum half Jeff Lloyd and Davies added the points to two of them.

YNYSYBWL: Paul Hatch; Marcus Lloyd, Stuart Lloyd (capt), Andrew David, Lyndon Lewis; Gareth Davies, Jeffrey Lloyd; Gregory Ward, Andrew Pickering, Jason Williams, Gavin Jones, Neil David, Carl Morgan, John Reed, Jerrard Arnold. Reps: Mark Welsh, Rhys Lloyd, Terry Rice.

NANTYMOEL: Jason Turner; Mike Richards, Mark Hopkins, Mark Jones, Anthony Smith; Steve Hughes (capt), Andrew Teale; Ian Gunner, Neil Hopkins, Craig Morgan, Ian Strang, Alex Peever, Justin Newman, Dai Stacey, Kevin James. Reps: Jeremy Williams, Carl Hinder, Steve Thomas.

Referee: Paul Adams (Ebbw Vale).

Nantymoel won the trophy as top try scorers with 53 in 10 games following a 79-5 victory in their final match at Pontardawe. They scored 12 tries, four of them by wing Mike Richards. Abercwmboi finished in second place with 51 tries.

SILVER BALL WINNERS	
1956-57	Taibach
1957-58	Welsh Acads.
1958-59	Maesteg Celtic
1959-60	Seven Sisters
1960-61	Glynneath
1961-62	Glynneath
1962-63	Glynneath
1963-64	Llantwit Major
1964-65	Llantwit Major
1965-66	Cwmgwrach
1966-67	Cardiff Athletic
1967-68	Cardiff Athletic
1968-69	Cardiff Coll. of Ed.
1969-70	Cardiff Coll. of Ed.
1970-71	Senghenydd
1971-72	Senghenydd
1972-73	Abercynon
1973-74	Kenfig Hill
1974-75	Taffs Well
1975-76	Pyle
1976-77	Abercynon
1977-78	Pyle
1978-79	Bridgend Sports
1979-80	Bridgend Sports
1980-81	Bridgend Sports
1981-82	Aberavon Quins
1982-83	Swansea Ath.
1983-84	Cilfynydd
1984-85	Cilfynydd
1985-86	St. Peter's
1986-87	Tondu
1987-88	Neath Ath.
1988-89	Llantrisant
1989-90	Beddau
1990-91	Tondu
1991-92	Tondu
1992-93	Tondu
1993-94	Llantrisant
1994-95	Tonyrefail
1995-96	Resolven
1996-97	Gilfach Goch
1997-98	Gilfach Goch
1998-99	Ynysybwl

Ystrad deputies to the rescue, but Merthyr keep the cup

MID-DISTRICT: Merthyr retained the Mid-District Cup with a 34-23 decision against Ystrad Rhondda at Sardis Road. Merthyr should have played Abercynon, but Abercynon, the Div 2 champions, pulled out just six hours before kick-off. They had clinched the Div 2 title the day before the Mid-District Cup final and said another big game on the following day was a match too far. So Ystrad, who had lost 21-17 to Merthyr in the semi-final, stepped into the breach - and lost again to the same opponents. J. Bryant (2), R. Sheppeard, J. Coccimiglio and J. Price scored Merthyr tries. J. Lloyd converted three and kicked a penalty goal. For Ystrad, D. Thomas and C. Brown crossed for tries; Brown converted both, kicked two penalty goals and dropped a goal.

GWENT: Brynmawr registered their first Ben Francis Cup victory since 1947 with a 22-20 success over Newbridge at Rodney Parade. John Davies's try, converted by Rob Jenkins in the closing minutes, proved decisive. O. Milligan and G. Hughes were the other Brynmawr try-scorers. Jenkins converted two and S. Jones dropped a goal. G. Bisp and R. Bowen were Newbridge scorers, both tries being converted by J. Williams, who added two penalty goals. Rhymney had lost to Cross Keys in the earlier round, but were reinstated because Keys fielded an ineligible player. Newport set a club record score 104-3 over Trinant in the first round (Shaun Connor 34 points), but later withdrew.

EAST DISTRICT: Rumney were 47-28 winners over Llanharan to collect the East District Cup with Simon Davies scoring 22 points. He led the way with two tries and converted six. Other try scorers were Jason Fofana (2), Mike Peard, Chris Wills and Stuart Coles. Llanharan's tries came from Mark Roper, Adrian Evans and Gregory Jones. Wayne Jervis converted two and landed three penalty goals.

NORTH WALES: Wrexham won the NW Cup 83-0 at Mold against Rhyl, who fielded a scratch team because the first XV were away on tour. Andrew Evans and Chris Monks each scored three tries.

Welsh Counties Cup

FIRST VICTORY FOR KEVIN'S CARDIGANSHIRE

Cardiganshire, led by former Wales hooker Kevin Phillips, now playing as a flanker, won the Welsh Counties Cup for the first time with a 23-8 verdict over Pembrokeshire, who made a determined challenge in the wet conditions at Cardigan (there was even a snow flurry), but their only points came from a try by wing Phil Bowen and a Huw Evans penalty goal. Cardiganshire collected tries by Owen Wilson, Kevin Phillips and Lee Evans. Ioan Bebb converted one and kicked two penalty goals.

No better line up.

You won't find a better team to help your business.

Barclays Bank PLC.,
Cymru/Wales H.Q.,
P.O. Box 793
Barclays House,
Ty Glas Avenue,
Cardiff CF4 5FE.
Tel:- 01222 426426

CYMRU/WALES

Kicker Carwyn Jones hits target
for Wales and Llanelli

Welsh Districts were 28-20 winners of a keenly contested match against Germany in Hanover with Llandovery's Carwyn Jones in tip-top kicking form. He planted over three penalty goals and converted two of the tries. Skipper Steve Jones, the Llanrumney wing, crossed for all three tries as Wales, ahead by just one point at the halfway mark, piled on intense pressure in the second half.

It required extra time to decide the last Howell's Cup final of the twentieth century - and Llanelli and District triumphed 23-13 against Gwynedd at Dunvant. Llanelli put out Cardiff and District in the semi-final stage 26-11 and had to battle all the way to edge out the North Wales side.

Stuart Dole (Llangadog), Andrew Burm (Llandovery) and Geraint Jones (Carmarthen Ath) were try-scorers for the winners with Carwyn Jones on target with a conversion and two penalty shots. For Gwynedd, Gwyn Jones (Nant Conwy) crossed and Ynyr Jones (Bala) converted and kicked two penalty goals.

Welsh Women

WALES CRASH 83-11 AGAINST ENGLAND

England, bigger and stronger, won the inaugural Women's Five Nations championship as they stormed to an 83-11 victory over Wales at St. Helen's, Swansea in April with 13 tries. Wasps wing Sue Day scored five of them. Wing Jo Brownley crossed for the home try and Claire Williams kicked two penalty goals. So Wales are still looking for a first success against England after 14 meetings.

Wales lost 23-0 away to Scotland, but were 26-0 winners over Ireland at Llanelli. Louise Rickard (2), Ellie Green and Non Evans scored tries and Claire Williams converted three. France defeated Wales 34-5 with Jo Brownley the Welsh try-getter. Skipper Liza Burgess completed her 50th international match.

Wales finished sixth in the European Women's championships. They defeated Italy 28-17, but lost to Spain 14-8 and Kazakhstan 22-11. France beat Spain in the final.

£2M FOR FIVE YEARS' BEER RIGHTS

Bass Brewers have agreed a package worth £2m to be the sole beer supplier to the Millennium Stadium and to become the official beer suppliers to the Welsh Rugby Union. The five-year deal gives Bass exclusive rights to supply ales and lagers to the 17 bars, 6 restaurants and 125 hospitality boxes within the Stadium.

Two-try Michael fires Fforest
to their first cup triumph

Cefn Fforest No 8 Michael Coles was the key man with two memorable tries that edged Caerleon out 21-20 in a dramatic final at Virginia Park, Caerphilly on April 17, 1999. Fforest had never progressed beyond the last 16 previously, but took control through their powerful pack. However, they had to hang on after Gareth Richards, who had converted a try and landed two penalty goals, was ordered off. Robbie James took over as kicker and fired in Fforest's winning penalty shot. Caerleon, cup winners in 1981, trailed 18-3 at the interval, but hit back with a try by Andy Rice and five Darren Gregg penalty goals. Fforest's Paul Bowen was voted man of the match.

CEFN FFOREST: Robbie James; Jeff Rogers, David Davies, Lee Shankland, Martin Pewtner; Gareth Richards, Mark Dimmick; Derwyn Brown, Glyndwr Cox, Shaun Lewis, Paul Bowden, Ronald Jones, Lee Morgan, Michael Coles (capt), Mike Morgan.

CAERLEON: Richard Bader; Darren Gregg (capt), Michael Sims, Andrew Rice, Ian Coles; Richard Parcell, Michael Gregg; Craig Fuller, Boyd Dwyer, Stuart Pankhurst, Graham Thomas, Stephen Hayes, Richard Jones, Tim Derrett, Ian Wilkinson. Reps: Julian Knight, Richard Edwards, Mark Rostron.

Referee: Robert Mota (Taffs Well).

WELSH BREWERS CUP

1974 Girling defeated Baglan 16-3	1989 St. Alban's defeated Hartridge HSOB 13-10
1975 Girling defeated St. Joseph's 6-3	1990 Hartridge HSOB defeated Newtown 24-18
1976 Cross Keys Utd. defeated Caldicot 9-6	1991 Fairwater defeated CIAC 13-3
1977 CIAC defeated Cross Keys Utd. 16-3	1992 St. Albans defeated Fairwater 21-20
1978 Rumney defeated Nantyglo 25-9	1993 Birchgrove defeated Wattstown 26-19
1979 Rumney defeated Nantyglo 18-10	*(after extra time)*
1980 Tondu defeated Rumney 15-10	**PRYSG/WHITBREAD CUP**
1981 Caerleon defeated Rhydyfelin 12-9	1994 Wattstown defeated Hartridge 15-6
1982 Llantrisant defeated Glyncorrwg 18-9	1995 Banwen defeated Fairwater 16-11
1983 Baglan defeated Heol-y-Cyw 13-6	**WD NATIONAL CUP**
1984 Baglan defeated Cimla 12-6	1996 St. Alban's defeated Wattstown 15-12
1985 Glyncorrwg defeated Llanishen 16-12	1997 Cambrian W. defeated Wattstown 18-11
1986 Tonmawr defeated CIAC 9-6	**WORTHINGTON CUP**
1987 CIAC defeated Hartridge 26-3	1998 Bedlinog defeated Brynithel 13-5
1988 Bedlinog defeated Forgeside 9-6	1999 Cefn Fforest defeated Caerleon 21-20

SEMI-FINALS: Caerleon ended Nant Conwy's ambition of a first appearance in the final by a North Wales club with an exciting 26-24 victory at Maesteg. Skipper Darren Gregg, a former Newport player, collected all the winners' points. The wing scored three tries, converted one and fired over three penalty goals. There were shades of the epic France-Wales match, when Thomas Castaignede missed the last-minute penalty shot that would have pipped Wales. This time it was Nant Conwy who failed with a last-minute conversion attempt that would have tied the scores - and put Nant through on elimination test because they scored more conversions than Caerleon. The other semi-final was a more relaxed affair with Cefn Fforest comfortable 23-8 winners at Ynysfach Estate, Merthyr. Cefn tries were obtained by Mike Morgan, Shaun Lewis and Martin Pewtner. Gareth Richards converted one and kicked two penalty goals. For Caerau (Ely), Craig Meredith crossed and Gareth Llewellyn landed a penalty goal.

FIFTH ROUND: Cefn Fforest benefited from another off-target goal kick. Nick Dufty missed the crucial second penalty shot, so Abertysswg went out 5-3 as Martin Pewtner crossed for the home try. Darren Gregg and wing Darren Bader were the try scorers for Caerleon to put out Llanrumney 10-8. Nant Conwy were 17-0 winners against Bettws. Outside half Peruder Ellis, full back Huw Clwyd Jones and hooker Ieuan Edwards snapped up tries and Ellis converted one. Caerau (Ely) took an 8-0 verdict over Llangadog through a Peter Brito try and Stuart Tobin's penalty goal.

FOURTH ROUND: Dean Lewis's penalty goal could not save Wattstown, who were hoping for a record fifth cup title. They went out 8-3 at Cefn Fforest. Huw Clywd Jones's two tries enabled Nant Conwy to continue to carry the flag for North Wales as they defeated Dowlais 22-0. Adrian Williams supplied 17 points for Llangadog to overcome Markham 42-0. Robert Evans scored three tries. It was close for Caerau (Ely) before they held off a keen challenge from Pontrhydyfen to go through 10-7. Caerleon also found it a struggle to win 15-10 against Hafodyrynys while Llanrumney edged Glyncoch 21-19. Glyncoch always provide spirited resistance and had reached the last eight during the previous season. Three points was enough for Abertysswg to win with the only score at Beaufort and Bettws advanced via a 15-10 decision against battling Trefil.

THREE CHAMPS GO OUT IN FIRST ROUND

THIRD ROUND: Glyncorrwg, the 1985 winners, went out 19-10 at Wattstown. Llanrumney cut loose with a dynamic all-round display of blistering attack to crush Aberbeeg 77-0 while Cefn Fforest also unleashed their full power as a dominating force to destroy Aberavon Naval Club 45-0. But it was a hard furrow for Beaufort to plough before they scraped an anxious 6-5 decision against visitors Ferndale. Caerau (Ely) progressed 29-10 with home advantage over Aberfan. Caerleon, showing their obvious signs of class, won 24-0 at Clwb Rygbi Caerdydd. Nant Conwy by no means had it all their own way before accounting for tenacious visitors Bala 8-3. Glyncoch squeezed a 24-22 verdict at Treharris while one try, the only score, was enough to put Dowlais into the next round.

SECOND ROUND: Nant Conwy blasted Flint 84-0, but Cefn Fforest walked a tightrope at Aberbargoed before scraping in 23-22. Former winners Cardiff International AC failed 53-3 against visitors Hafodyrynys. Caerleon accounted for Bryncethin 20-3.

FIRST ROUND: Three former cup winners went out. Girling, winners in 1974 and champs again in 1975, lost 15-10 at Pontyfelin. Fairwater, top team in 1991, and who had figured in the final three times during a five-year period, failed 24-15 at Blackwood Stars. Cambrian Welfare, winners in 1997, were eclipsed 45-0 at Dowlais. Llangefni, who carried NW hopes into the semi-final the previous season, hammered Holyhead 61-0. Another big score saw Nant Conwy overwhelm Abergele 62-3.

Cefn Fforest, Worthington Welsh Districts cup winners 1999. Back row (left to right): S. Lewis, G. Cox, D. Brown, Ron Jones, P. Bowen, Lee Morgan, J. Preece. Middle row: M. Murphy, P. Probert, B. Norton, S. Williams, M. Pewtner, Michael Morgan, Roland Davies, R. James, R. Giles, R. Munday, M. Morris. Front row: Brian Jones, G. Cook, M. Dimmick, David Davies, G. Richards, Michael Coles (capt), G. Rogers, L. Shankland, G. Woods.

Wales News and Pictures

WORTHINGTON DISTRICTS CUP 1998-99

FIRST ROUND

Group One

New Panteg w/o v Whitehead
Barry Plastics 10, Caerau (Ely) 22

Cwm 8, Bettws 82
Brackla 19, Newport CS 16

Group Two

Hollybush 21, Blaina Utd 20
Wick w/o v O Tyleryans

Six Bells S w/o v Tongwynlais
Pontyfelin 15, Girling 10

Group Three

Crickhowell 28, Magor 10
St Joseph's 3, Caerleon 16

Glyncorrwg 9, Deri 8
Blackwood Stars 24, Fairwater 15

Group Four

Whitchurch 5, Trefil 15
Abersychan Alex 0, Forgeside 24

Llanrumney w/o v Newbridge Utd

Group Five

Porthmadog 11, Rhos 46
Nant Conwy 62, Abergele 3
Flint 36, Benllech 7
Harlech 14, BSC Shotton 48

Llangefni 61, Holyhead 0
Bala w/o v Llangoed
Machynlleth 62, Menai Bridge 7
Deeside 19, Bro Ffestiniog 0

Group Six

Llandrindod Wells 14, Porth 25

Llangadog 18, Mynydd Garreg 8

Group Seven

Blaenau w/o v Tywyn

Penlan 0, Ferndale 9

Group Eight

Dowlais 45, Cambrian Welfare 0

SECOND ROUND

Group One

Bettws 18, New Panteg 0
Cardiff East w/o v Raglan

Brackla 0, Aberbeeg 3
Caerau (Ely) 41, St Julian's 12

Group Two

Wick w/o v Tongwynlais
Markham 10, Llanedeyrn 7

Pontyfelin 3, Abertysswg 8
Beaufort 20, Hollybush 17

Group Three

Blackwood Stars w/o v Ely
Caerleon 20, Bryncethin 3

Aberbargoed 22, Cefn Fforest 23
Glyncorrwg w/o v Crickhowell

Group Four

Llanwern 6, Trefil 7
CIAC 3, Hafodyrynys 53

Clwb Rygbi 32, Forgeside 0
Llanrumney 45, NASH 0

Group Five

BSC Shotton 12, Machynlleth 64
Rhos 15, Deeside 13

Nant Conwy 84, Flint 0
Llangefni 10, Bala 13

Group Six

Aberavon Naval 16, Tref-y-Clawdd 13
Troedyrhiw 8, Cimla 13

COBRA 3, Llangadog 50
Llanbradach 5, Porth Quins 13

Group Seven

Ferndale 72, Rhayader 14
Pontrhydyfen w/o v Ferryside

Blaenau 7, Glyncoch 32
Aberfan 25, Penybanc 0

Group Eight

Penallta 18, Wattstown 35
Llanwrtyd Wells w/o v S Gower

Dowlais 60, Bryn Wands 0
Tregaron 10, Treharris 16

THIRD ROUND

Beaufort 6, Ferndale 5
Caerau (Ely) 29, Aberfan 10
Cefn Fforest 45, Aberavon NC 0
Cimla 0, Bettws 17
Clwb Rygbi 0, Caerleon 24
Llangadog 15, Blackwood Stars 5
Llanrumney 77, Aberbeeg 0
Machynlleth 0, Dowlais 5

Markham 15, Cardiff East 8
Nant Conwy 8, Bala 3
Pontrhydyfen 42, Rhos 7
Porth Quins 6, Trefil 17
S. Gower 0, Hafodyrynys 13
Treharris 22, Glyncoch 24
Wattstown 19, Glyncorrwg 10
Wick 7, Abertysswg 47

FOURTH ROUND

Beaufort 0, Abertysswg 3
Bettws 16, Trefil 10
Caerau (Ely) 10, Pontrhydyfen 7
Caerleon 15, Hafodyrynys 10

Cefn Fforest 8, Wattstown 3
Llangadog 42, Markham 0
Llanrumney 21, Glyncoch 19
Nant Conwy 22, Dowlais 0

FIFTH ROUND

Caerau (Ely) 8, Llangadog 0
Caerleon 10, Llanrumney 8

Cefn Fforest 5, Abertysswg 3
Nant Conwy 17, Bettws 0

SEMI-FINALS

Cefn Fforest 23, Caerau (Ely) 8
(At Merthyr)

Caerleon 26, Nant Conwy 24
(At Maesteg)

FINAL

Cefn Fforest 21, Caerleon 20
(At Virginia Park, Caerphilly)

Captain Dallaglio stands down after drugs accusations

Lawrence Dallaglio stepped down as England captain on May 24, 1999 following allegations in a Sunday newspaper that the Wasps' forward had been involved in drugs. Dallaglio denied the stories, but withdrew from the trip to Australia and Martin Johnson took over the captaincy. The RFU stated they would not consider any possible disciplinary action until they had made a full investigation.

Dallaglio admitted he had experimented with drugs as a teenager, but now was very much anti-drugs. He said he had foolishly misinformed the two undercover newspaper reporters who led him on. "I lied to impress them," he explained. England coach Clive Woodward said Dallaglio had been "naïve and stupid."

England lost the Centenary Test against Australia 22-15 watched by 81,000 at the new Sydney Olympic Stadium on June 26, 1999. A year earlier, England had crashed to a record and humiliating defeat 76-0 to the Wallabies in Brisbane, but there was never any likelihood of a similar experience this time. England fielded a stronger side and dominated the opening half, but Australia struck suddenly and eventually tries by Ben Tune (2), Joe Roff and skippper David Wilson, one converted by Roff, brought victory. Matt Perry scored both England tries and Jonny Wilkinson converted one and kicked a penalty goal.

England's team: M. Perry; D. Rees, J. Guscott, M. Catt, D. Luger; J. Wilkinson, K. Bracken; J. Leonard, R. Cockerill, D. Garforth, M. Johnson (capt), T. Rodber, R. Hill, M. Corry, N. Back. Reps: N. Beal for Perry, P de Glanville for Catt, M. Dawson for Bracken, P. Greening for Cockerill, V. Ubogu for Garforth, D. Grewcock for Rodber, B. Clarke for Corry.

Ireland lost their two Tests in Australia during June 1999. The first brought 46-10 defeat in Brisbane with former South African captain Tiaan Strause scoring three tries on his debut, going on as a replacement. Ben Tune, David Wilson and Dan Herbert also crossed in a record tally by the Aussies against Ireland. Nathan Spooner converted five tries and added two penalty goals. Kevin Maggs obtained a late try for the Irish and David Humphreys converted and kicked a penalty goal.

Australia trailed 14-9 in the second Test in Perth before a late onslaught brought a 32-26 decision. It was three tries to two in Ireland's favour (Peter Clohessy, Justin Bishop, Kevin Maggs). Humphreys converted one and supplied three penalty goals. Tim Horan and Chris Latham were home try-getters. Roff converted two and added three penalty goals; Nathan Spooner also landed three penalty shots in the wet conditions.

Key : E – England, S – Scotland, SA – South Africa, A – Australia, M – Maoris (1888), I – Ireland, F – France, NZ – New Zealand, NSW – New South Wales, R – Romania, FJ – Fiji, T – Tonga, WS – Western Samoa, C – Canada, N – Namibia, B – Barbarians, AR – Argentina, Z – Zimbabwe, J – Japan, P – Portugal, Sp – Spain, It – Italy.
*Denotes Replacement player

Ackerman, R. (Newport and London Welsh) NZ. 1980; E.S.A. 1981; (I.F.E.S. 1982; S.I.F.R. 1983; S.I.F.E.A. 1984; S.I.F.E.FJ 1985.

Alexander, E.P. (Cambridge Univ. and Brecon) S.85; E.S. 86; E.I. 87.

Alexander, W.H. (Llwynypia) I.E. 98; E.S.I. 99; S.I. 1901.

Allen, A. (Newbridge) F.E.I. 1990.

Allen, C.P. (Oxford Univ. and Beaumaris) E.S.84.

Andrews, F. (Pontypool) SA. 1912; E.S.I.; 1913.

Andrews, F.G. (Swansea) E.S.84.

Andrews, G. (Newport) E.S. 1926; E.F.I. 1927.

Anthony, Chris (Swansea) USA (1* and 2*). C*. T* 1997; SA.AR. 1998; S.I.* 1999.

Anthony, L. ((Neath)) E.S.F. 1948.

Appleyard, Rob (Swansea) C. R.T.NZ. 1997; It. *E.S.I.F. 1998.

Arnold, P. (Swansea) N. 1, 2, B. 1990; E.S.I.F.A.AR.A. 1991; F.Z. (2nd) 1993; Sp. FJ. 1994; SA 1995; B* 1996.

Arnold, W. (Llanelli) S. 1903.

Arthur, C.S. ((cardiff)) I.M. 88; E.91.

Arthur, T. (Neath) S.F.I. 1927; E.S.F.I. 1929; E.S.I.F. 1930; E.S.F.I. 1931; SA. 1931; E.S. 1933.

Ashton, C. (Aberavon) E.S.I. 1959, 1960; I. 1962.

Attewell, L. (Newport) E.S.F. 1921.

Back, M. (Bridgend) F*. E*.S.I. 1995.

Badger, O. (Llanelli) E.S.I. 95; E.96.

Baker, A. (Neath) I. 1921; E.S.F.I. 1923.

Baker, A.M. (Newport) S.F. 1909; S. 1910.

Bancroft, J. (Swansea). E.S.F.I. 1909; F.E.S.I. 1910; E.F.I. 1911; E.S.I. 1912; I. 1913; E.S.F. 1914.

Bancroft W.J. (Swansea) S.E.I. 90; E.S.I. 91, 92, 93, 94, 95, 96; E. 97; I.E. 98; E.S.I. 99, 1900, 1901.

Barlow, T.M. (Cardiff) I.84.

Barrell, R. (Cardiff) E.S.I. 1929; I. 1933.

Bartlett, J.D. (Llanelli and London Welsh) S. 1927; E.S. 1928.

Bassett, A. (Aberavon and Cardiff) I. 1934; E.S.I. 1935; E.S. 1938.

Bassett, J. (Penarth) E.S.F.I. 1929; E.S.I. 1930; E.S.F.I.SA. 1931; E.S.I. 1932.

Bateman, A. (Neath, Richmond & Northampton) S.I.N. (1, 2) 1990; SA. 1996; USA.S.F.E. R.NZ. 1997; It. E.S.I. 1998; S.AR (1 & 2) SA. 1999.

Bayliss, G. (Pontypool) S. 1933.

Bebb, D. (Carmarthen T.C. and Swansea) E.S.I.F. 1959; E.S.I.T.SA. 1960; E.S.I.F. 1961; E.S.F.I. 1962; E.F.NZ. 1963; E.S.F.SA. 1964; E.I.S.F. 1965; F.A. 1966; S.I.F.E. 1967.

Beckingham, G. (Cardiff) E.S. 1953; F. 1958.

Bennett, Ivor (Aberavon) I. 1937.

Bennett, M. (Cardiff) NZ.SA.FJ. 1995.

Bennett, P. (Cardiff Harlequins) E.S.91; S.I. 92.

Bennett, P. (Llanelli) F* 1969; N.A.S.F. 1970; S* 1972; NZ. 1972; E.S.I.F.A. 1973; S.I.F.E. 1974; S. *I. 1975; E.S.I.F. 1976; I.F.E.S. 1977; E.S.I.F. 1978.

Bergiers, R.T.E. (Llanelli) E.S.F.NZ. 1972; E.S.I.F.A. 1973; E. 1974; I. 1975.

Bevan, Griff (Llanelli) E. 1947.

Bevan, J.A. (Cambridge Univ.) E. 81.

Bevan, J.C. (Cardiff) E.S.I.F. 1971; E.S.F. 1972; NZ. 1972; E.S. 1973.

Bevan, J.D. ((Aberavon)) F.E.S.A. 1975.

Bevan, Sid (Swansea) 1904.

Beynon, Ben (Swansea) E.S. 1920.

Beynon, E. (Swansea) F.I. 1925.

Bidgood, R.A. (Newport) S. 1992; Z. (1st and 2nd), N.J.* 1993.

Biggs, N. (Cardiff) M. 88; I. 89, 92; E.S.I. 93; E.I. 94.

Biggs, S. (Cardiff) E.S. 95; S. 96; E. 97; I.E. 98; S.I. 99; I. 1900.

Birch, J. (Neath) S.F. 1911.

Birt, F.W. (Newport) E.S. 1911; E.S.I.SA. 1912; E. 1913.

Bishop, D.J. (Pontypool) A. 1984.

Bishop, E.H. (Swansea) S. 89.

Blackmore, J. (Abertillery) E. 1909.

Blackmore, S. (Cardiff) I.T.*C.A. 1987.

Blake, J. (Cardiff) E.S.I. 99, 1900, 1901.

Blakemore, R.E. (Newport) E. 1947.

Bland, A.F. (Cardiff) E.S.I. 87; S.I.M. 88; S.E.I. 90.

Blyth, L. (Swansea) SA. 1951; E.S. 1952.

Blyth, W.R. (Swansea) E. 1974; S. *1975; F.E.S.I. 1980.

Boobyer, N. (Llanelli) Z. (1st* and 2nd), N. 1993; F.T. 1994; F. 1998; It.* 1999.

Boon, R. (Cardiff) S.F. 1930; E.S.I.F.SA. 1931; E.S.I. 1932; E.I. 1933.

Booth, J. (Pontymister) I. 98.

Boots, G. (Newport) I.E. 98; I. 99; E.S.I. 1900, 1901, 1902, 1903; E. 1904.

Boucher, A.W. (Newport) E.S.I. 92, 93; E. 94, E.S.I. 95; E.I. 96; E. 97.

Bowcott, H.M. (Cardiff and London Welsh) S.F.I. 1929; E. 1930; E.S. 1931; E.I. 1933.

Bowdler, F.A. (Cross Keys) NSW 1927; E.S.I.F. 1928; E.S.F.I. 1929; E. 1930; SA. 1931; E.S.I. 1932; I. 1933.

Bowen, B. (S. Wales Police and Swansea) R. 1983; S.I.F.E. 1984; FJ. 1985; E.S.I.F.FJ.T.WS. 1986; C.E.NZ.USA. 1987; E.S.I.F., 1988; S.I. 1989.

Bowen, C. (Llanelli) E.S.I. 96; E. 97.

Bowen, D.H. (Llanelli) E. 82; E.S. 86; E. 87.

Bowen, G.E. (Swansea) S.I. 87, 88.

Bowen, W. (Swansea) S.F. 1921; E.S.I.F. 1922.

Bowen, Wm (Swansea) E.S. 86; E.S.I. 87; M. 88; S.I. 89; S.E.I. 90; E.S. 91.

Brace, D.O. (Newport, Oxford Univ. and Llanelli) E.S.I.F. 1956; E.S.F. 1957; S.I. 1960; I. 1961.

Braddock, K.J. (Newbridge) A. 1966; S.I. 1967.

Bradshaw, K. (Bridgend) E.S.I.F.SA. 1964; E.S.I.F. 1966.

Brewer, T.J. (Newport, Oxford Univ. and London Welsh) E. 1950; E.S. 1955.

Brice, A. (Aberavon and Cardiff) E.S.I. 99, 1900, 1901, 1902, 1903, 1904.

Bridges, C. (Neath) N. 1, 2, B. 1990; E.* I.F.A. 1991.

Bridie, R. (Newport) I. 82.

Britton, G. (Newport) S. 1961.

Broughton, A. (Treorchy) NSW. 1927; S. 1929.

Brown, Archie (Newport) I. 1921.

Brown, J. (Cardiff) E.S.I. 1907; E.S.F. 1908; E. 1909.

Brown, J. (Cardiff) I. 1925.

Brown, M. (Pontypool) R.1983; E.S.FJ(R). T.WS. 1986.

Bryant, D. (Bridgend) NZ. (1 and 2), WS.R. 1988; S.I.F.E. 1989.

Buchanan, A. (Llanelli) T.E. *NZ.A. 1987; I. 1988.

Buckett, I. (Swansea) T. 1994; USA.C. 1997.

Burcher, D. (Newport) I.F.E.S. 1977.

Burgess, R.C. (Ebbw Vale) I.F.E.S. 1977; I.F. 1981; F.E.S. 1982.

Burnett, R. (Newport) E. 1953.

Burns, J. (Cardiff) F.I. 1927.

Bush, P. (Cardiff) NZ. 1905; E. 1906; SA. 1906; I. 1907; E.S. 1908; S.I. 1910.

Butler, E.T. (Pontypool) F.E.S.I.NZ* 1980; S. 1982; E.S.I.F.R. 1983; S.I.F.E.A. 1984.

Cale, W.R. (Newbridge and Pontypool) E.S.I. 1949; E.S.I.F. 1950.

Carter, A.J. (Newport) E.S. 1991.

Cattell, A. (Llanelli) E. 1882; S. 1883.

Challinor, C. (Neath) E. 1939.

Charvis, Colin (Swansea) A.* SA. 1996; USA.S.I.F. 1997; It*.E.S.I.F.Z*.SA.SA.AR. 1998; S.I.F.It.E.AR (2) SA. 1999.

Clapp, T. (Newport) I.E. 82; S. 83; E.S.I. 84; E.S. 85; S.86; E.S.I. 87; S.I. 88.

Clare, J. (Cardiff) E.82.

Clarke, S.S. (Neath) I. 82; I. 87.

Cleaver, W.B. (Cardiff) E.S.I.F.A. 1947; E.S.F.I. 1948; I. 1949; E.S.I.F. 1950.

Clegg, B. (Swansea) F. 1979.

Clement, A. (Swansea) USA. 1987; E.NZ (1), WS(R), R. 1988; NZ. 1989; S(R).I.N. (1, 2) 1990; S*.A*.F.WS.AR.A. 1991; I.F.E.S. 1992; I*.F.J.C. 1993; S.I.F.Sp.C*.T.WS.It.SA. 1994; F.E.J.NZ.I. 1995.

Clement, W.H. (Llanelli) E.S.I. 1937, 1938.

Cobner, T.J. (Pontypool) S.I.F.E. 1974; F.E.S.I. 1975; A. 1975; E.S. 1976; F.E.S. 1977; E.S.I.F.A(1) 1978.

Coldrick, A.P. (Newport) E.S.I. 1911; E.S.F. 1912.

Coleman, E. (Newport) E.S.I. 1949.

Coles, F.C. (Pontypool) S.I.F. 1960.

Collins, J. (Aberavon) A.E.S.F. 1958; E.S.I.F. 1959; E. 1960; F. 1961.

Collins, R.G. (S. Wales Police, Cardiff, Pontypridd) E*.I.I.E.NZ.USA 1987; E.S.I.F.R. 1988; E.S.I. 1990; A.F.WS. 1991; C.FJ.T.WS.R.It.SA. 1994; F.E.S.I. 1995.

Collins, T. (Mountain Ash) I. 1923.

Cook, T. (Cardiff) S.I. 1949.

Cope, W. (Cardiff and Blackheath) S.96.

Copsey, A.H. (Llanelli) I.F.E.S.A. 1992; E.S.I.J.C. 1993; E*.P.Sp*.FJ.T.WS*. 1994.

Cornish, F.H. (Cardiff) E. 97; I.E. 98; I. 99

Cornish, R.A. (Cardiff) E.S. 1923; E. 1924; E.S.F. 1925; E.S.I.F. 1926.

Coslett, K. (Aberavon) E.S.F. 1962.

Cowey, B.T.V. (Newport) E.S.I. 1934; E. 1935.

Cresswell, B. (Newport) E.S.I.F. 1960.

Cummins, W. (Treorchy) E.S.I.F. 1922.

Cunningham, L.J. (Aberavon) E.S.I.F. 1960; E.S.F. 1962; I. 1962; NZ. 1963; E.S.I.F.SA. 1964.

Dacey, M. (Swansea) E.S.I.F.R. 1983; S.I.F.E.A. 1984; FJ.T.WS. 1986; F*.T. 1987.

Daniel, D.J. (Llanelli) S. 91; E.S.I. 94; I.E. 98; E.I. 99.

Daniel, L.T.D. (Newport) S. 1970.

Daniels, P.C.T. (Cardiff) A. 1981; I. 1982.

Darbishire, G. (Bangor) E. 81.

Dauncey, F.H. (Newport) E.S.I. 96.

Davey, Claude (Swansea and London Welsh) F. 1930; E.S.I.F.SA. 1931; E.S.I. 1932; E.S. 1933; E.S.I. 1934, 1935; NZ. 1935; S. 1936; E.I. 1937, 1938.

David, R. (Cardiff) I. 1907.

David, T.P. (Pontypridd and Llanelli) F.A. 1973; I.F. 1976.

Davidge, G. (Newport) F. 1959; S.I.F. 1960; SA. 1960; E.S.I. 1961; F. 1962.

Davies, Adrian (Neath and Cardiff) B*. 1990; A. 1991; Z. (1st and 2nd) J.C. 1993; FJ. 1994; J.I. 1995.

Davies, A.C. (London Welsh) I. 89.

Davies, A.E. (Llanelli) A. 1984.

Davies, Rev. Alban (Swansea and Llanelli) S.F.I. 1913; E.S.F.I. 1914.

Davies, B. (Llanelli) E. 95, 96.

Davies, Bailey (Oxford and Llanelli) E. 1907.

Davies, Carwyn (Llanelli) WS. 1988; S.I.(R).F. 1989.

Davies, C.H.A. (Llanelli and Cardiff) I. 1957; A.E.S.I. 1958; SA. 1960; E. 1961.

Davies, C.L. (Cardiff) E.S.I. 1956.

Davies, C.R. (Bedford) E. 1934.

Davies, Cliff (Cardiff) S.F.I.A. 1947; E.S.F.I. 1948; F. 1949; E.S.I.F. 1950; E.S.I. 1951.

Davies, Daph. (Bridgend) I. 1921, 1925.

Davies, D. Brian (Llanelli) I. 1962; E.S. 1963.

Davies, D.G. (Cardiff) E.S. 1923.

Davies, D.H. (Neath) S. 1904.

Davies, D. Hunt (Aberavon) E. 1924.

Davies, D. Idwal (Swansea) E. 1939.

Davies, D.J. (Neath) I. 1962.

Davies, D.M. (Somerset Police) E.S.I.F. 1950, 1951; SA. 1951; E.S.I.F. 1952; I.F.N.Z. 1953; E. 1954.

Davies, E. (Aberavon) A. 1947; I. 1948.

Davies, Evan (Maesteg) NZ. 1919.

Davies Ewan (Cardiff) E.F. 1912.

Davies, Geo (Swansea) E.S.I. 1990, 1901, 1905.

Davies, Glyn (Pontypridd and Cambridge Univ) S.A. 1947; E.S.F.I. 1948; E.S.F. 1949; E.S. 1951.

Davies, Graham (Llanelli) F.I. 1921; F. 1925.

Davies, Gwyn (Cardiff) F. 1928; E. 1929; S. 1930.

Davies, H. (Bridgend) S.I.F.E. 1984.

Davies, H. (Swansea) I.E. 98; S.I. 1901.

Davies, H.J. (Aberavon) S.I.S. 1959.

Davies, Harold (Newport) S. 1924.

Davies, Howard (Swansea and Llanelli) S.I. 1939; E.S.F.I. 1947.

Davies, Howel (Neath) E.S. 1912.

Davies, J. (Neath, Llanelli and Cardiff) E.FJ. 1985; E.S.I.F.FJ.T.WS. 1986; F.E.S.I.I.T*.C.E.NZ.A. 1987; F.S.I.F.NZ. (1 and 2). W.S.R. 1988; A. 1996; USA*.S*.F*.E. 1997.

Davies, J.D. (Neath) I.F. 1991, F*.Z.(2nd), J.C. 1993; S.I.F.E.P.Sp.C.WS.R.It.SA. 1994; F.E.J.NZ.I.SA. 1995; It.E.S.I.F.A.B.F.It. 1996; Z.SA. 1998.

Davies, J.H. (Aberavon) I. 1923.

Davies, I.T. (Llanelli) S.F.I. 1914.

Davies, Leigh (Neath and Cardiff) It.E.S.I.F.A.B.F.It*. 1996; USA (1and 2). C.R.T.NZ*. 1997; E*.I.F. 1998.

Davies, Len (Llanelli) F.S. 1954; I. 1955.

Davies, Leslie (Swansea) S.I. 1939.

Davies, Lyn (Bridgend) E.S.I. 1966.

Davies, Mark (Swansea) A. 1981; I. 1982; FJ. 1985.

Davies, M.J. (Oxford) S.I. 1939.

Davies N. Glyn (London Welsh) e. 1955.

Davies, Nigel (Llanelli) NZ. (2nd). WS. 1988; S.I. 1989; F. 1993; S.I.E.P.Sp.C.FJ.T*.WS.R.It. 1994; E.S.I.FJ. 1995; E.S.I.F.A. (1 and 2).B.F. 1996; E. 1997.

Davies. P.T. (Llanelli) E.FJ. 1985; E.S.I.F.FJ.T.WS. 1986; F.E.It.T.C.NZ. 1987; WS.R. 1988; S.I.F.E.NZ. 1989; F.E.S. 1990; I.F.A.F.WS.AR.A. 1991; F.Z. (1st) N. 1993; S.I.F.E.C.FJ*.WS.R.It. 1994; F.I. 1995.

Davies, R.H. (Oxford Univ, and London Welsh) S.I.F. 1957; A. 1958; E.S. 1962.

Davies, Stan (Treherbert) I. 1923.

Davies, Stuart (Swansea) I.F.E.S.A. 1992; E.S.I.Z. (1st and 2nd) N.J. 1993; F.J.I. 1995; I*.F. 1998.

Davies, Terry (Swansea and Llanelli) E.S.I.F. 1953; E.S.I.F. 1957; A.E.S.F. 1958; E.S.I.F. 1959; E.S.A. 1960; E.S.F. 1961.

Davies, T.G.R. (Cardiff & London Welsh) A. 1966; S.I.F.E. 1967; E.S. 1968; S.I.FNZ.(1 & 2)A. 1969; E.S.I.F. 1971; E.S.F. 1972; NZ. 1972; E.S.I.F.A. 1973; S.F.E. 1974; F.E.S.I. 1975; E.S.I.F. 1976; I.F.E.S. 1977; E.I.S.A. (1 & 2) 1978.

Davies. T.M. (London Welsh and Swansea) S.I.F.E.NZ.(1 and 2)A. 1969; SA.S.E.I.F. 1970; E.S.I.F. 1971; E.S.F. 1972; NZ. 1972; E.S.I.F.A. 1973; S.I.F.E. 1974; F.E.S.I. 1975; A. 1975; E.S.I.F. 1976.

Davies, W. (Cardiff) S. 96.

Davies, W. (Swansea) SA. 1931; E.S.I. 1932.

Davies, W.G. (Cardiff and Oxford Univ) A.(1 and 2)NZ. 1978; S.I.F.E. 1979; F.E.S.NZ. 1980; E.S.A. 1981; I.F.E.S. 1982; S.I.F. 1985.

Davies, W.T.H. (Swansea) I. 1936; E.I. 1937; E.S.I. 1939.

Davies, Willie (Aberavon) S.I. 1912.

Davis, C. (Newbridge) A.(2) 1978; E.S. 1981.

Davis, Mark (Newport) A. 1991.

Davis, W.E.N. (Cardiff) E.S.I. 1939.

Dawes, S.J. (London Welsh) I.F.SA. 1964; E.S.I.F. 1965; A. 1966; I.F. 1968; E.NZ.(2)A. 1969; SA.S.E.I.F. 1970; E.S.I.F. 1971.

Day, H. (Newport) I. 92; E.S. 93; S.I. 94.

Day, H.C. (Newport) S.I.F. 1930; E.S. 1931.

Day, T. (Swansea) E.S.I.F.SA. 1931; E.S.I. 1932; SI. 1934; E.S.I. 1935.

Deacon, T. (Swansea) I. 91; E.S.I. 92.

Delahay, W. (Bridgend and Cardiff) E.S.I.F. 1922; E.S.I.F. 1923; NZ. 1924; E.S.F.I. 1926; E.S.I.F. 1926; S. 1927.

Delaney, L. (Llanelli) I.F.E. 1989; E. 1990; F.WS.AR.A. 1991; I.F.E. 1992.

Devereaux, D. (Neath) A.E.S. 1958.

Devereux, J. (S. Glam Inst. and Bridgend) E.S.I.F.FJ.T.WS. 1986; F.E.S.I.C*.E.NZ.A. 1987; NZ. (1 and 2)R. 1988; S.I. 1989.

Diplock, R. (Bridgend) R. 1988.

Dobson, G. (Cardiff) S. 1900.

Dobson, T. (Cardiff) I.E. 98; E.S. 99.

Donovan, A. (Swansea) A.(2) 1978; I*.A. 1981; E.S. 1982.

Donovan, R. (S. Wales Constab.) F*. 1983.

Douglas, M.H.J. (Llanelli) S.I.F. 1984.

Douglas, W.M. (Cardiff) E.S. 86, 87.

Dowell, W. (Newport) E.S.I. 1907; E.S.F.I. 1908.

Dyke, J.C.M. (Penarth) SA. 1906.

Dyke, L.M. (Cardiff) I. 1910; S.F.I. 1911.

Edmunds, A. (Neath) I.(R), B. 1990.

Edwards, A.B. (London Welsh and Army) E.S. 1955.

Edwards, B. (Newport) I. 1951.

Edwards, D. (Glynneath) E. 1921.

Edwards, G.O. (Cardiff and Cardiff Training College) F.E. 1967; NZ. 1967; E.S.I.F. 1968; S.I.F.E.NZ.(1 and 2)A. 1969; SA.S.E.I.F. 1970; E.S.I.F. 1971; E.S.F. 1972; NZ. 1972; E.S.I.F.A. 1973; S.I.F.E. 1974; F.E.S.I. 1975; A. 1975; E.S.I.F. 1976; I.F.E.S. 1977; E.S.I.F. 1978.

Eidman, I. (Cardiff) S.R. 1983; I.F.E.A. 1984; S.I.FJ. 1985; E.S.I.F. 1986.

Elliott, J.E. (Cardiff) I. 94; I.E. 98.

Elsey, W.J. (Cardiff) E. 95.

Emyr, A. (Swansea and Cardiff) E.NZ. 1989; F.E.S.I.N.(1,2) 1990; F.F.WS.AR.A. 1991.

Evans, A.C. (Pontypool) E.I.F. 1924.

Evans, Ben (Swansea) SA.* 1998; F.It.E.AR. (1 & 2) 1999.

Evans, Bryn (Llanelli) E.S. 1933; E.S.I. 1936; E. 1937.

Evans, Bryn (Swansea) S. 1933.

Evans, Bryn S. (Llanelli) E. 1920; E.S.I.F. 1922.

Evans, C. (Pontypool) E. 1960.

Evans, David W. (Cardiff and Treorchy) F.E.NZ. 1989; F.E.S.I.B. 1990; A.F*.A. 1991; J*. 1995.

Evans, D. (Penygraig) S.I. 96; E. 97; E. 98.

Evans, D.B. (Swansea) E. 1926.

Evans, D.D. (Cheshire and Cardiff Univ.) E. 1934.

Evans, D.P. (Llanelli and Oxford Univ.) SA. 1960.

Evans, D.W. (Cardiff and Oxford Univ.) S.I. 89; E.I. 90; E. 91.

Evans, Emrys (Llanelli) E. 1937; S.I. 1939.

Evans, Frank (Llanelli) S. 1921.

Evans, Garan (Llanelli) SA. 1998.

Evans, G. (Cardiff) E.S.F.I.A. 1947; E.S.F.I. 1948; E.S.I. 1949.

Evans, G. (Newport) F*. 1977; FA*.(2) 1978.

Evans, Gwyn (Maesteg) S*.I.F.A. 1981; I.F.E.S. 1982; F.R. 1983.

Evans, Ieuan (Llanelli, Bath) F.E.S.I.I.C.E.MZ.A. 1987; E.S.I.F.NZ.(1 and 2) 1988; I.F.E. 1989; E.S.I.F.A.F.WS.AR.A. 1991; I.F.E.S.A. 1992; E.S.I.FJ.C. 1993; S.I.E.P.Sp.C.FJ.T.WS.R. 1994; E.S.I.J.NZ.I.SA.FJ. 1995; It.E.S.I.F.A.(1 and 2).B.F.A.SA. 1996; USA.S.I.F. 1997; It. 1998.

Evans, Iowerth (London Welsh) S.I. 1934.
Evans, Islwyn (Swansea) E.S.I.F. 1922.
Evans, J. (Llanelli) S.I. 96; E. 97.
Evans, J. (Blaina) E. 1904.
Evans, J. (Pontypool) E.S.I. 1907.
Evans, J.D. (Cardiff) I.F. 1958.
Evans, J, Elwyn (Llanelli) S. 1924.
Evans, J.R. (Newport) E. 1934.
Evans, Luc (Llanelli) F*. 1991.
Evans, O.J. (Cardiff) E.S. 87; S.I. 88.
Evans, Peter (Llanelli) E.F. 1951.
Evans, R. (Bridgend) S.I.F. 1963.
Evans, R. (Cardiff). S. 89.
Evans, Ricky (Llanelli) E.S.I.F. 1993;
  S.I.F.E.P.Sp.C.FJ.WS.R.It.SA 1994; F.NZ.I*.
  1995.
Evans, R.T. (Newport) F.I. 1947; E.S.I.F. 1950,
  1951.
Evans, S. (Neath and Swansea) F.E. 1985;
  FJ.T.WS. 1986; F.E.I.T. 1987.
Evans, T.G. (London Welsh) SA.S.E.I. 1970;
  E.S.F. 1972.
Evans, T.P. (Swansea) F.E.S.I. 1975; A. 1975;
  E.S.I.F. 1976; I. 1977.
Evans, Tom (Llanelli) I. 1906; E.S.I. 1907; I.A.
  1908; E.S.F.I. 1909; F.E.S.I. 1910; E.S.F.I.
  1911.
Evans, Tom (Swansea) I. 1924.
Evans, V. (Neath) I.F.S. 1954.
Evans, W.F. (Rhymney) I. 82; S. 83.
Evans, W.G. (Brynmawr) I. 1911.
Evans, W.H. (Llwynpia) E.S.F.I. 1914.
Evans, W.J. (Pontypool) S. 1947.
Evans, W.R. (Cardiff, Bridgend) A.E.S.I.F. 1958;
  SA. 1960; E.S.I.F. 1961; E.S. 1962; I. 1962.
Evans, W. Rice (Swansea) S. 90; E.S. 91.
Evans, Wynne (Llanelli) A. 1958.
Everson, W. (Newport) S. 1926.
Faulkner, A.G. (Pontypool) F.E.S.I. 1975; A.
  1975; E.S.I.F. 1976; E.S.I.F.A.(1 and 2)NZ.
  1978; S.I.F. 1979.
Faull, J. (Swansea) I.F. 1957; A.E.S.I.F. 1958;
  E.S.I. 1959; E.F. 1960.
Fauvel, T. (Aberavon) *NZ.(1) 1988.
Fear, A. (Newport) S.I. 1934, 1935.
Fender, N. (Cardiff) I.F. 1930; E.S.F.I. 1931.
Fenwick, S.P. (Bridgend) F.E.S. 1975; A. 1975;
  E.S.I.F. 1976; I.F.S. 1977; E.S.I.F.A. (1 and
  2). NZ. 1978; S.I.F.E. 1979; E.S.I.NZ. 1980;
  E.S. 1981.
Finch, E. (Llanelli) F.NZ. 1924; F.I. 1925; F. 1926;
  NSW. 1927; I. 1928.
Finlayson, A.J. (Cardiff) I.F.E. 1974.
Fitzgerald, D. (Cardiff) S.I. 94.
Ford, F.J.V. (Welsh Regt. and Newport) E. 1939.
Ford, I. (Newport) E.S. 1959.
Ford, S. (Cardiff) I.N. (1,2), B. 1990; E.S.I.A.
  1991.
Forward, A. (Pontypool and Mon. Police) S.
  1951; SA. 1951; E.S.I.F. 1952.
Fowler, I. (Llanelli) NZ. 1919.
Francis, G. (Llanelli) NZ. 1919; S. 1924.
Francis, P.W. (Maesteg) S. 1987.
Funnell, John (Ebbw Vale) Z*.SA. 1998.
Gabe, R.T. (Llanelli and Cardiff) I. 1901; E.S.I.
  1902, 1903, 1904, 1905; NZ. 1905; E.I. 1906;
  SA. 1906; E.S.I. 1907; E.S.F.I. 1908.

Gale, N.R. (Swansea and Llanelli) I. 1960;
  E.S.I.NZ. 1963; E.S.I.F.SA. 1964; E.S.I.F. 1965;
  E.S.I.F.A. 1966; E. 1967; NZ. 1967; E. 1968;
  NZ.(1* and 2)A. 1969.
Gallacher, I.S. (Llanelli) F. 1970.
Garrett, R.M. (Penarth) M. 88; S. 89; E.S.I. 90;
  S.I. 91; E. 92.
Geen, W.P. (Newport) SA. 1912; E.I. 1913.
George, E. (Pontypridd & Cardiff) S.I. 95; E. 96.
George, G.M. (Newport) E.S. 1991.
Gethin, Glyn (Neath) F. 1913.
Gibbs, Andrew (Newbridge and Llanelli) I.SA.
  1995; A. 1996; USA (1 and 2)C. 1997.
Gibbs, I.S. (Neath and Swansea) E.S.I.F.A.F.WS.
  AR.A. 1991; I.F.E.SA. 1992; E.S.I.F.J.C. 1993;
  It.A.SA. 1996; USA.S.I.F.T.NZ. 1997; It.E.S.
  SA.AR.. 1998; S.I.F.It.E. 1999.
Gibbs, R.A. (Cardiff) S.I. 1906; E.S. 1907;
  E.S.F.I. 1908; F.E.S.I. 1910; E.S.F.I. 1911.
Giles, S.R. (Aberavon) R. 1983; FJ* 1985; C. 1987.
Girling, B.E. (Cardiff) E. 81.
Goldsworthy, S. (Swansea) I. 84; E.S. 85.
Gore, J. (Blaina) I.F.NZ. 1924; E. 1925.
Gore, W. (Newbridge) S.F.I. 1947.
Gough, Ian (Newport & Pontypridd) SA. 1998; S.
  1999.
Gould, A.J. (Newport) E.S. 85, 86; E.S.I. 87; S.
  88 I. 89; S.E.I. 90; E.S.I. 92, 93; E.S. 94; E.S.I.
  96, 96; E. 97.
Gould, B. (Newport) I. 92; S.I. 93.
Gould, R. (Newport) I.E. 82; S. 83; E.S.I. 84; E.S.
  85; E. 86; E.S. 87.
Graham, T.C. (Newport) I. 90; S.I. 91; E.S. 92;
  E.S.I. 93; E.S. 94, 95.
Gravell, R.W.R. (Llanelli) F.E.S.I.A. 1975; E.S.I.F.
  1976; E.S.I.F.A. (1 and 2)NZ. 1978; S.I. 1979;
  I.F. 1981; F.E.S. 1982.
Gray, A.J. (London Welsh) E.S. 1968.
Greenslade, D. (Newport) S. 1962,
Greville, H. (Llanelli) A. 1947.
Griffin, Dr A. (Edinburgh Univ.) S. 83.
Griffiths, C. (Llanelli) E*. 1979.
Griffiths, D. (Llanelli) M. 88; I. 89.
Griffiths, G. (Llanelli) I. 89.
Griffiths, Gareth (Cardiff) E.S.I.F. 1953; NZ.
  1953; I.F.S. 1954; I.F. 1955; E.S. 1957.
Griffiths, J. (Llanelli) NZ.(2nd) 1988; S. 1989.
Griffiths, M. (Bridgend, Cardiff & Pontypridd) WS.R.
  1988; S.I.F.E.NZ. 1989; F.E.N. (1,2)B. 1990;
  I.F.F.WS.AR.A. 1991; I.F.E.SA. 1992; Z.(1st and
  2nd)N.J.C. 1993; F*.E.S.I.J.I. 1995; SA. 1998.
Griffiths, V.M. (Newport) S.I.F. 1924.
Gronow, B. (Bridgend) F.E.S.I. 1910.
Gwilliam, J.A. (Edinburgh Wanderers &
  Gloucester) A. 1947; I. 1948; E.S.I.F. 1949,
  1950; E.S.I.SA. 1951; E.S.I.F. 1952; E.I.F.
  1953; NZ. 1953; E. 1954.
Gwynn, D. (Swansea) E. 82; S. 87; E.I. 90; E.S. 91.
Gwynn, W.H. (Swansea) E.S.I. 84; E.S. 85.
Hadley, A.M. (Cardiff) R. 1983; S.I.F.E. 1984;
  F.E.FJ. 1985; E.S.I.F.FJ.T. 1986;
  S.*I.I.T.C.E.NZ.A.USA. 1987; E.S.I.F. 1988.
Hall, I. (Aberavon) NZ. 1967; SA.S.E. 1970; S.
  1971; S.I.F. 1974.
Hall, M. (Bridgend & Cardiff) *NZ.(1) NZ.(2nd)WS.R.
  1988; S.I.F.E.NZ. 1989; F.E.S. 1990;
  A.F.WS.AR.A. 1991; I.F.E.SA. 1992; E.S.I. 1993;
  S.I.F.E.P.Sp.C.T.R.It.SA. 1994; F.S.I.J.NZ.I. 1995.

Hall, W. (Bridgend) WS. 1988.

Hancock, F.E. (Cardiff) I.84; E.S. 85; S. 86.

Hannan, J. (Newport) M. 88; S.I. 89; S.E.I. 90; E. 91; E.S. 92, 93, 94, 95.

Harding, A.F. (Cardiff and London Welsh) E.S.I. 1902, 1903, 1904, 1905; NZ. 1905; E.S.I. 1906; SA. 1906; I. 1907; E.S. 1908.

Harding, G.F. (Newport) E. 81; E. 82; S. 83.

Harding, Rowe (Swansea) E.S.F.I. 1923; I.F.NZ 1924; F.I. 1925; E.I.F. 1926; E.S.F.I. 1927; E. 1928.

Harding, Theo (Newport) M. 88; S.I. 89.

Harris, D.J.E. (Pontypridd and Cardiff) I.F. 1959; S.I.F. 1960; SA. 1960; E.S. 1961.

Harris, Tal. (Aberavon) NSW. 1927.

Hathaway, G. (Newport) I.F. 1924.

Havard, Rev. W.T. (Llanelli) NZ. 1919.

Hawkins, F. (Pontypridd) I.F. 1912.

Hayward, Byron (Ebbw Vale) Z*.SA. 1998.

Hayward, D. (Newbridge) E.F. 1949; E.S.I.F. 1950; E.S.I.F. 1951; SA. 1951; E.S.I.F. 1952.

Hayward, D.J. (Cardiff) E. 1963; NZ. 1963; S.I.F.SA. 1964.

Hayward, G. (Swansea) S.F.I.A. 1908; E. 1909.

Hellings, R. (Llwynypia) E. 97; I.E. 98; S.I. 99; E.I. 1900; E.S. 1901.

Herrera, R. (Cross Keys) S.F.I. 1925; E.S.I.F. 1926; E. 1927.

Hiams, H. (Swansea) I.F. 1912.

Hickman, Arthur (Neath) E. 1930; S. 1933.

Hiddlestone, D. (Neath) E.S.I.F. 1922; NZ. 1924.

Hill, A.F. (Cardiff) S. 85; E.S. 86; S.I.M. 88; S. 89; S.I. 90; E.S.I. 93, 94.

Hill, Simon (Cardiff) Z.(1st and 2nd)N. 1993; I.*F.SA. 1994; F.SA. 1995; A.F*.It. 1996; E. 1997.

Hinam, S. (Cardiff) I. 1925; E.S.I.F. 1926.

Hinton, J.T. (Cardiff) I. 84.

Hirst, G.L. (Newport) S. 1912, 1913; E.S.F.I. 1914.

Hodder, W. (Pontypool) E.S.F. 1921.

Hodges, J.J. (Newport) E.S.I. 99, 1900; E.S. 1901; E.S.I. 1902, 1903; E.S. 1904; E.S.I. 1905; NZ. 1905; E.S.I. 1906.

Hodgson, G.T.R. (Neath) I. 1962; E.S.I.F. 1963; NZ. 1963; E.S.I.F.SA. 1966; S.I.F. 1966; I. 1967.

Hollingdale, B. (Swansea) SA. 1912; E. 1913.

Hollingdale, T. (Neath) NSW. 1927; E.S.I.F. 1928; E. 1930.

Holmes, T.D. (Cardiff) A.(2)NZ. 1978; S.I.F.E. 1979; E.S.I.NZ. 1980; A. 1981; I.F.E. 1982; E.S.I.F. 1983; E. 1984; S.I.F.E.FJ. 1985.

Hopkin, W.H. (Newport) S. 1937.

Hopkins, K. (Cardiff and Swansea) E. 1985; F.E.S.T.C.*USA. 1987.

Hopkins, Phil (Swansea) A. 1908; E.I. 1909; E. 1910.

Hopkins, R. (Maesteg) E*. 1970.

Hopkins, T. (Swansea) E.S.I.F. 1926.

Hopkins, W.J. (Aberavon) E.S. 1925.

Howarth, S.P. (Sale) SA.AR 1998; S.I.F.It.E.AR (1 & 2) SA. 1999.

Howells, Bryn (Llanelli) E. 1934.

Howells, G. (Llanelli) E.S.I.F. 1957.

Howells, W.H. (Swansea) S.I. 88.

Howley, R. (Bridgend and Cardiff) E.S.I.F.A.(1 and 2).B.F.It.A.SA. 1996; USA.S.I.F.E.T.*NZ. 1997; It.E.S.I.F.Z.SA.AR. 1998; S.I.F.It.E.AR (1 & 2) SA. 1999.

Hughes, D. (Newbridge) NZ. 1967; NZ.(2) 1969; SA.S.E.I. 1970.

Hughes, Gomer (Penarth) E.S.I. 1934.

Hughes, H. (Cardiff) S. 87, 89.

Hughes, K. (Cambridge Univ. and London Welsh) I. 1970; A. 1973; S. 1974.

Hullin, W. (Cardiff) S. 1967,

Humphreys, J. (Cardiff) NZ.I.SA.FJ. 1995; It.E.S.I.F.A.(1and 2).B.It.A.SA. 1996; S.I.F.E. T*.NZ*. 1997; It*.E*.S*.I*.F*.SA.AR 1998; S.AR (2*) SA.* 1999.

Hurrell, J. (Newport) F. 1959.

Hutchinson, F. (Neath) I.94; S.I. 96.

Huxtable, R. (Swansea) F.I. 1920.

Huzzey, V. (Cardiff) E.I. 98; E.S.I. 99.

Hybart, A.J. (Cardiff) E. 87.

Ingledew, H.M. (Cardiff) I. 90, E.S. 91.

Isaacs, I. (Cardiff) E.S. 1933.

Jackson, T.H. (Swansea) E. 95.

James, B. (Bridgend) E. 1968.

James, C. (Llanelli) A.F. 1958.

James, Dafydd (Bridgend and Pontypridd) A*.It.A.SA. 1996; I.T*. 1997; F*.Z.SA.SA.AR 1998; S.I.F.It.E.AR (1 & 2) SA. 1999.

James, D.R. (Treorchy) F.I. 1931.

James, David (Swansea) I. 91; S.I. 92; E. 99.

James, Evan (Swansea) S. 90; I. 91; S.I. 92; E. 99.

James, Maldwyn (Cardiff) A. 1947; E.S.F.I. 1948.

James, T.O. (Aberavon) I. 1935; S. 1937.

James, W.J. (Aberavon) E.S.I.F.R. 1983; S. 1984; S.I.F.E.FJ. 1985; E.S.I.F.FJ.T.WS. 1986; E.S.I. 1987.

James, W.P. (Aberavon) E.S. 1925.

Jarman, H. (Newport) E.S.I. 1910; E. 1911.

Jarrett, K.S. (Newport) E. 1967; E.S. 1968; S.I.F.E.NZ(1 and 2)A. 1969.

Jarvis, Lee (Cardiff) R*. 1997.

Jeffery, J.J. (Newport) NZ. 1967.

Jenkins, Albert (Llanelli) E.S.F.I. 1920; S.F. 1921; F. 1922; E.S.F.I. 1923; NZ 1924; S.I. 1928.

Jenkins, A.M. (Swansea) I. 95; E. 96.

Jenkins, D. (Treorchy) E.S.I.F. 1926.

Jenkins, D.R. (Swansea) NSW. 1927; E. 1929.

Jenkins, E. (Newport) S.I. 1910.

Jenkins, E. M. (Aberavon) S.F.I. 1927; NSW. 1927; E.S.I.F. 1928; F. 1929; E.S.I.F. 1930; E.S.F.I. 1931; SA. 1931; E.S.I. 1932.

Jenkins, G.R. (Pontypool and Swansea) F.WS.*AR.A. 1991; I.F.E.S.A. 1992; C. 1993; S.I.F.E.P.Sp.C.T.WS.R.It.SA. 1994; F.E.S.I.J. *SA.*FJ. 1995; *E. 1996; USA.USA.C. 1997; S.I.F.Z.SA*. 1998; I.*F.It.E.AR (1 & 2) SA. 1999.

Jenkins, J.C. (London Welsh) SA. 1906.

Jenkins, L. (Aberavon) S.F. 1923.

Jenkins, Leighton (Newport) I. 1954; E.S.I.F. 1956.

Jenkins, N.R. (Pontypridd) E.S.I.F. 1991; I.F.E.S. 1992; E.S.I.F.Z.(1st and 2nd)N.J.C. 1993; S.I.F.E.P.Sp.C.T.WS.R.It.SA. 1994; F.E.S.I. J.NZ.I.SA.FJ. 1995; F.A.(1 and 2).B.F.It.A*.SA. 1996; S.I.F.E.T.NZ. 1997; It.E.S.I.F.SA.AR 1998; S.I.F.It.E.AR (1 & 2) SA. 1999.

Jenkins, T-Pryce (London Welsh) S.I. 88.

Jenkins, V.G. (Oxford Univ. London Welsh and Bridgend) E.I. 1933; S.I. 1934; E.S. 1935; NZ. 1935; E.S.I. 1936; E. 1937; E.S. 1938; E. 1939.

Jenkins, W. (Cardiff) I.F. 1912; S.I. 1913.

John, A. (Llanelli) I. 1925; E.S.I. 1928.

John, B. (Llanelli and Cardiff) A. 1966; S. 1967; NZ. 1967; E.S.I.F. 1968; S.I.F.E.NZ.(1 and 2)A. 1969; SA.S.E.I. 1970; E.S.I.F. 1971; E.S.F. 1972.

John, D.E. (Llanelli) F.I. 1923; E.S.I. 1928.

John, G. (St Luke's College, Exeter) E.F. 1954.

John, J.H. (Swansea) E.S.I.F. 1926; E.S.F.I. 1927.

John, Paul (Pontypridd) T. 1994; B*. 1996; USA*.USA(1 and 2).C.R.T. 1997; Z*.SA 1998.

John, R. (Neath) E.S.I.F. 1950, 1951; SA. 1951; E.S.I.F. 1952; E.S.I.F. 1953; NZ. 1953; E. 1954.

John, Spencer (Llanelli and Cardiff) S.I. 1995; E*.T.NZ*. 1997.

Johnson, T. (Cardiff) E.F.I. 1921; E.S.F. 1923; E.S.NZ. 1924; E.S.F. 1925.

Johnson, W.D. (Swansea) E. 1953.

Jones, A.H. (Cardiff) E.S. 1933.

Jones, B.J. (Newport) I.F. 1960.

Jones, J. Bedwellty (Abertillery) E.S.F.I. 1914.

Jones, Bert (Llanelli) S.I. 1934.

Jones, Bob (Llwynypia) I. 1901.

Jones, C.W. (Bridgend) E.S.F. 1920.

Jones, Cliff (Cardiff) E.S.I. 1934, 1935; NZ. 1935; E.S.I. 1936, 1938.

Jones, D. (Neath) NSW. 1927.

Jones, Dan (Aberavon) E. 97.

Jones, David (Newport) E.S.I.F. 1926; E. 1927.

Jones, David (Swansea) E.F.I. 1947; E.S.I.F. 1949.

Jones, David (Treherbert) E.S.I. 1902, 1903, 1905; NZ. 1905; E.S. 1906; SA. 1906.

Jones, Derwyn (Cardiff) SA. 1994; F.E.S.J.NZ.I. SA.FJ. 1995; It.E.S.I.F.A.(1 and 2).B.It.A. 1996.

Jones, Desmond (Llanelli) E. 1948.

Jones, D.K. (Llanelli, Cardiff) E.S.F.I. 1962; E.F.NZ. 1963; E.S.SA. 1964; E.S.I.F. 1966.

Jones, D.N. Rocyn (St Mary's Hospital, Cambridge Univ. and Newport) I. 1925.

Jones, D.P. (Pontypool) I. 1907.

Jones, Edgar (Llanelli) F. 1930; E.S.I. 1933; E. 1935.

Jones, Elvet (Llanelli) S. 1939.

Jones, Gareth (Bridgend) SA. 1995.

Jones, Gary (Llanelli) NZ.(2nd) 1988; F.E.NZ. 1989; F. 1990.

Jones, Graham (Cardiff) S. 1930; I. 1933.

Jones, Graham (Ebbw Vale) S.I.F. 1963.

Jones, G.R. Rees (Oxford and London Welsh) E.S. 1934; I. 1935; NZ. 1935; E. 1936.

Jones, Gwyn (Llanelli and Cardiff) It.E.S.I.F.A. 1996; USA*.S*.USA(1 and 2).R.T.NZ. 1997.

Jones, Harold (Neath) E.S. 1929.

Jones, Harry (Penygraig) S.I. 1902.

Jones, Howel (Neath) I. 1904.

Jones, Howie (Swansea) I.F. 1930.

Jones, I.C. (London Welsh) I. 1968.

Jones, Iowerth (Llanelli) NSW. 1927; E.S.I.F. 1928.

Jones, Ivor (Llanelli) E.S. 1924; S.F.I. 1927; NSW. 1927; E.S.I.F. 1928; E.S.F.I. 1929; E.S. 1930.

Jones, J. (Aberavon) E. 1901.

Jones, J.A. (Cardiff) S. 83.

Jones, J.P. 'Tuan' (Pontypool) S. 1913.

Jones, Jim (Aberavon) NZ. 1919; E.S. 1920; S.F.I. 1921.

Jones, Joe (Swansea) F. 1924.

Jones, J.P. (Newport and Pontypool) A. 1908; E.S.F.I. 1909; F.E. 1910; E.F. 1912; F.I. 1913, 1920; E. 1921.

Jones, J. Strand (Llanelli and Oxford Univ.) E.S.I. 1902; E.S. 1903.

Jones, K.D. (Cardiff) SA. 1960; E.S.I. 1961; E.F. 1962; E.S.I. 1963; NZ. 1963.

Jones, Ken (Monmouth and L. Welsh) E. 1934.

Jones, Ken (Newport) E.S.F.I.A. 1947; E.S.F.I. 1948; E.S.I.F. 1949, 1950, 1951; SA. 1951; E.S.I.F. 1952, 1953; NZ. 1953; E.I.F.S. 1954; E.S.I.F. 1955, 1956; S. 1957.

Jones, Kingsley (Ebbw Vale) B.F.It.A. 1996; I*.E. 1997; S.I.F*.SA. 1998.

Jones, Lewis (Devonport Services and Llanelli) E.S.I.F. 1950; E.S. 1951; SA. 1951; E.I.F. 1952.

Jones, Lyn (Llanelli) Z.(1st and 2nd)N.J.C. 1993.

Jones, Mark (Neath and Ebbw Vale) S. 1987; NZ.*(2nd) 1988; S.I.E.F.NZ. 1989; F.E.S.I.N.(1,2)B. 1990; Z. 1998.

Jones, Marsden (Cardiff and London Welsh) E. 1921; NZ. 1924.

Jones, P. Baker (Newport) S. 1921.

Jones, Percy (Newport and Pontypool) SA. 1912; E.S.F. 1913; E.S.F.I. 1914.

Jones, R. (London Welsh) E. 1929.

Jones, R. (Swansea) I. 1901; E. 1902; E.S.I. 1904; E. 1905; F.I.A. 1908; E.S.F.I. 1909; F.E. 1910.

Jones, R.B. (Cambridge) E.S. 1933.

Jones, R.E. (Coventry) F.E. 1967; S.I.F. 1968.

Jones, Robert (Northampton) S.I.F. 1926.

Jones, R.N. (Swansea) E.S.I.F.FJ.T.WS. 1986; F.E.S.I.I.T.E.NZ.A.USA. 1987; E.S.I.F. NZ(1).WS.R. 1988; I.F.E.NZ. 1989; F.E.S.I. 1990; E.S.F.WS.AR.A. 1991; I.F.E.S.A. 1992; E.S.I. 1993; I.*P. 1994; F.E.S.I.NZ.I. 1995.

Jones, Roy (Swansea) NSW. 1927; F. 1928.

Jones, Stephen (Llanelli) SA*. 1998.

Jones, S.T. (Pontypool) S.I.F.R. 1983; S. 1984; E.S.F.NZ.(1 and 2) 1988.

Jones, T.B. (Newport) I.E. 82; S. 83; S. 84; E.S. 85.

Jones, Tom (Newport) E.S.I.F. 1922; E.S. 1924.

Jones, W. (Newport) I.E. 98.

Jones, W.I. (Llanelli) E.S.F.I. 1925.

Jones, W.J. (Llanelli) I. 1924.

Jones, W.K. (Cardiff) NZ. 1967; E.S.I.F. 1968.

Jones, Wyndham (Mountain Ash) I. 1905.

Jones-Davies, T.E. (London Welsh) E.I. 1930; E.S. 1931.

Jordan, H.M. (Newport) E.S. 85; S. 89.

Joseph, W. (Swansea) E.S.I. 1902, 1903; E.S. 1904; E.S.I.NZ. 1905; E.S.I. 1906; SA. 1906.

Jowett, F. (Swansea) E. 1903.

Judd, S. (Cardiff) E.S.I.F. 1953; NZ. 1953; E.F.S. 1954; E.S. 1955.

Judson, J.H. (Llandovery Coll.) E. 82; S. 83.

Kedzlie, Q.D. (Cardiff) S.I. 88

Keen, L. (Aberavon) F.E.S.I. 1980.

Knight, P. (Pontypridd) N.(1,2)B.* 1990; E.S. 1991.

Knill, F.M.D. (Cardiff) F*. 1976.

Lamerton, A.E. (Llanelli) F.Z.(1st and 2nd)N.J. 1993.

Lane, S. (Cardiff) A.(1* and 2) 1978; I*. 1979; S.I. 1980.

112

Lang, J. (Llanelli and Swansea) F.I. 1931; S.I. 1934; E.S.I. 1935; NZ. 1935; E.S.I. 1936; E. 1937.

Law, V.J. (Newport) I. 1939.

Lawrence, S. (Bridgend) S.I. 1925; S.I.F. 1926; E. 1927.

Legge, W.G. (Newport) I. 1937, 1938.

Leleu, J. (London Welsh and Swansea) E.S. 1959; F. 1960; SA. 1960.

Lemon, A. (Neath) I. 1929; S.I.F. 1930; E.S.F.I.SA. 1931; E.S.I. 1932; I. 1933.

Lewis, A.J.L. (Ebbw Vale) F. 1970; E.I.F. 1971; E.S.F. 1972; E.S.I.F. 1973.

Lewis, Andrew (Cardiff) It.E.S.I.A*. 1996; It.E.S.I.F.SA.AR 1998; F.*E*AR (1* & 2*) SA* 1999.

Lewis, A.R. (Abertillery) E.S.I.F. 1966; A. 1966; I. 1967.

Lewis, Bryn (Swansea) I. 1912, 1913.

Lewis,Clem (Cardiff) E. 1912; S.F.I. 1913; E.S.F.I. 1914; I. 1921; E.S. 1923.

Lewis, C.P. (Llandovery) I.E. 82; S. 83; E.S. 84.

Lewis, D.H. (Cardiff) E.S. 86.

Lewis, Emyr (Llanelli and Cardiff) I.F.A.F.WS. AR.A. 1991; I.F.S.A. 1992; E.S.I.F.Z.(1st and 2nd)N.J.C. 1993; S.I.F.E.P.Sp.FJ.WS.R.It.SA. 1994; E.S.I.J.I. 1995; It.E.S.I.F. 1996.

Lewis, E.J. (Llandovery) E. 81.

Lewis, Geraint (Pontypridd) SA*. 1998; It.*AR (2) 1999.

Lewis, G. Windsor (Richmond) E.S. 1960.

Lewis, Howell (Swansea) S.F.I. 1913; E. 1914.

Lewis, J. (Llanelli) I. 87.

Lewis, J.R. (Cardiff) E.S.I.F. 1981; F.E.S. 1982.

Lewis, Mark (Treorchy) F. 1913.

Lewis, P.I. (Llanelli) A. 1984; S.I.F.E. 1985; E.S.I. 1986.

Lewis, Tom (Cardiff) E. 1926; E.S. 1927.

Lewis, W. (Llanelli) F. 1925.

Lewis, Windsor (London Welsh, Maesteg) I. 1926; E.F.I. 1927; NSW. 1927; F. 1928.

Llewellyn, David (Ebbw Vale) SA.* 1998; F.*It.* 1999.

Llewellyn, D.B. (Newport and Llanelli) SA.S.E.I.F. 1970; E.S.I.F. 1971; E.S.F. 1972; NZ. 1972.

Llewellyn, Gareth (Neath and Harlequins) NZ. 1989; E.S.I. 1990; E.S.A.* 1991; I.F.E.S.A. 1992; E.S.I.F.Z. (1st and 2nd) N.J.C. 1993; S.I.F.E.P.Sp.C.T. WS.R.It.SA. 1994; F.E.S.I.J. NZ.I. 1995; It.E.S.I.F.A. (1 and 2) B.F.It.A.SA. 1996; USA.S.I.F.E.USA (1 and 2).NZ. 1997; It.E. 1998.

Llewellyn, Glyn (Neath) N. (1, 2).B. 1990; E.S.I.F.A.F. 1991.

Llewellyn, P.D. (Swansea) I.F.A. 1973; S.E. 1974.

Llewellyn, W. (Llwynypia, London Welsh, Newport and Penygraig) E.S.I. 99, 1900, 1901, 1902; I. 1903; E.S.I. 1904, 1905; NZ. 1905.

Loader, Christian (Swansea) SA.FJ. 1995; F.A. (1 and 2).B.F.It.A.SA. 1996; USA. S.I.F.E.USA.R.T.NZ. 1997.

Lloyd, D.J. (Bridgend) E.S.I.F. 1996; A. 1966; S.I.F.E 1967; S.I.F. 1968; S.I.F.E.NZ(1)A. 1969; F. 1970; E.S.F. 1972; E.S. 1973j.

Lloyd, E. (Llanelli) S. 95.

Lloyd, G.L. (Newport) I. 96; S.I. 99; E.S. 1900; E.S. 1901; S.I. 1902; E.S.I. 1903.

Lloyd, P. (Llanelli) S.E. 90' E.I. 91.

Lloyd, R. ((Pontypool) S.F.I. 1913; E.S.F.I. 1914.

Lloyd, T. (Maesteg) I.F. 1953.

Lloyd, T.C. (Neath) F. 1909; F.I. 1913; E.S.F.I. 1914.

Lockwood, T.W. (Newport) E.S.I. 87.

Long, E. (Swansea) E.S.I. 1936; E.S. 1937; S.I. 1939.

Lyne, H.S. (Newport) S. 83; E.S.I. 84; E. 85.

Maddocks, H.T. (London Welsh) E.S.I. 1906; E.S. 1907; F. 1910.

Maddock, K. (Neath) E. 1957.

Main, D.R. (London Welsh) E.S.I.F. 1959.

Mainwaring, H.J. (Swansea) F. 1961.

Mainwaring, W.T. (Aberavon) S.I.F.E. 1967; NZ. 1967; E. 1968.

Major, W. (Maesteg) F. 1949; S. 1950.

Male, B.O. (Cross Keys, Pontypool and Cardiff) F. 1921; S. 1923; S.I. 1924; E.S.F.I. 1927; S.I.F. 1928.

Manfield, L. (Mountain Ash and Cardiff) S.I. 1939; A. 1947; E.S.F.I. 1948.

Mann, B.B. (Cardiff) E. 81.

Mantle, J. (Loughborough College and Newport) E.SA. 1964.

Margrave, F.L. (Llanelli) E.S. 84.

Martin, A.J. (Aberavon) A. 1973; S.I. 1974; F.E.S.I. 1975; A. 1975; E.S.I.F. 1976; I.F.E.S. 1977; E.S.I.F.A. (1 and 2).NZ. 1978; S.I.F.E. 1979; F.E.S.I.NZ. 1980; I.F. 1981.

Martin, W.J. (Newport) I.F. 1912; NZ. 1919.

Mason, J. (Pontypridd) NZ.* (2nd) 1988.

Mathias, R. (Llanelli) F. 1970.

Matthews, Rev. A.A. (Lampeter) S. 86.

Matthews, Chris (Bridgend) I. 1939.

Matthews, Jack (Cardiff) E.A. 1947; E.S.F. 1949; E.S.I.F. 1949, 1950, 1951.

May, P. (Llanelli) E.S.I.F.NZ.(1 and 2) 1988; WS. 1991.

McBryde, R. (Swansea and Llanelli) FJ. SA.* 1994; USA. 1997.

McCall, B.E.W. (Welch Regt. and Newport) E.S.I. 1936.

McCarley, A. (Neath) E.S.I. 1938.

McCutcheon, W. (Swansea) S. 91; E.S. 92; E.S.I. 93; E. 94.

McIntosh, Dale (Pontypridd) SA. 1996; E.* 1997.

Meek, N. (Pontypool) E.S.I. 1993.

Meredith, A. (Devonport Services) E.S.I. 1949.

Meredeith, B.V. (London Welsh and Newport) I.F.S. 1954; E.S.I.F. 1955, 1956, 1957; A.E.S.I. 1958; E.S.I.F. 1959; E.S.F. 1960; SA. 1960; E.S.I. 1961; E.S.F. 1962; I. 1962.

Meredith, C.C. (Neath) S. 1953; NZ. 1953; E.F.I.S. 1954; E.S.I.F. 1955; E.I. 1956; E.S. 1957.

Meredith, J. (Swansea) S.I. 88; E.S. 90.

Merry, G.E. (Pill Harriers) I.F. 1912.

Michael, G. (Swansea) E.S.F. 1923.

Michaelson, R.C.B. (Aberavon and Cambridge Univ.) E. 1963.

Miller, F. (Mountain Ash) I. 96; E.S.I. 1900, 1901.

Mills, F. (Swansea and Cardiff) E.S.I. 92, 93, 94, 95; E. 96.

Moon, Rupert (Llanelli) F.Z. (1st and 2nd) N.J.C. 1993; S.I.F.E.Sp.C.FJ.WS.R.It.SA 1994; E.* 1995.

Moore, Andrew (Swansea) *SA. FJ. 1995; S.I.F.A.SA. 1998.

Moore, Andy (Cardiff) J.SA.FJ. 1995; It. 1996.

Moore, Steve (Swansea and Moseley) C.* R.T. 1997.

Moore, W.J. (Bridgend) I. 1933.

Morgan, C.H. (Llanelli) I.F. 1957.

Morgan, C.I. (Cardiff and Bective Rangers) I.F. 1951; SA. 1951; E.S.I. 1952; S.I.F. 1953; NZ. 1953; E.I.S. 1954; E.S.I.F. 1955, 1956, 1957, 1958.

Morgan, D. (Llanelli) I. 95; E. 96.

Morgan, D. (Swansea) S. 85; E.S. 86; E.S.I. 87; I. 89.

Morgan, D.R. (Llanelli) E.S.F.I. 1962; E.S.I.F. 1963; NZ. 1963.

Morgan, E. (Llanelli) I. 1920; E.S.F. 1921.

Morgan, E. (London Welsh) E.S.I. 1902; I. 1903; E.S.I. 1904, 1905; NZ. 1905; E.S.I.SA. 1906; F. 1908.

Morgan, E. (Swansea) E.S.I. 1938; E. 1939.

Morgan, Edgar (Swansea) E.S.F.I. 1914.

Morgan, F.L. (Llanelli) E.S.I. 1938; E. 1939.

Morgan, H.J. (Abertillery) E.S.I.F. 1958; I.F. 1959; E. 1960; E.S.I.F. 1961; E.S.F.I. 1962; S.I.F. 1963; E.S.I.F. 1965; E.S.I.F. 1966; A. 1966.

Morgan, H.P. (Newport) E.S.I.F. 1956.

Morgan, Ivor (Swansea) A. 1908; E.S.F.I. 1909; F.E.S.I. 1910; E.F.I. 1911; S. 1912.

Morgan, J. (Llanelli) SA. 1912; E. 1913.

Morgan, Kevin (Pontypridd) USA (1 and 2).C.R.NZ. 1997; S.I.F. 1998.

Morgan, N. (Newport) S.I.F. 1960.

Morgan, P. (Aberavon) E.S.F. 1961.

Morgan, P. (Llanelli) S.*I.NZ.* 1980; I. 1981.

Morgan, R. (Newport) S. 1984.

Morgan, T. (Llanelli) I. 89.

Morgan, W. Guy (Swansea and Guy's Hospital) F.I. 1927; E.S.F.I. 1929; I.F. 1930.

Morgan, W.L. (Cardiff) S. 1910.

Moriarty, P. (Swansea) I.F.FJ.T.WS. 1986; F.E.S. I.I.T.C.E.NZ.A.USA. 1987; E.S.I.F.NZ(1) 1988.

Moriarty, R.D. (Swansea) A. 1981; I.F.E.S. 1982; E. 1983; S.I.F.E. 1984; S.I.F. 1985; FJ.T.WS. 1986; I.T.C.*E.NZ.A. 1987.

Morley, J.C. (Newport) E.S.F.I. 1929; E.I. 1930; E.S.F.I.SA. 1931; E.S.I. 1932.

Morris, Darren (Neath) A.SA*.SA.* 1998; S.I.It.* 1999.

Morris, G.L. (Swansea) I.E. 82; S. 83; E.S. 84.

Morris, H. (Cardiff) F. 1951; I.F. 1955.

Morris, Ivor (Swansea) E.S. 1924.

Morris, M. (South Wales Police and Neath) S.I.F. 1985; I.N.(1,2)B. 1990; I.F.W.S. 1991; E. 1992.

Morris, R.R. (Swansea and Bristol) S. 1933, 1937.

Morris, S. (Cross Keys) E.S.F.I. 1920; E.S.I.F. 1922; E.S.F.I. 1923; E.S.F.NZ. 1924; E.S.F. 1925.

Morris, W. (Abertillery) NZ. 1919; F. 1920; I. 1921.

Morris, W.D. (Neath) F.E. 1967; E.S.I.F. 1968; S.I.F.E.NZ(1 and 2)A. 1969; SA.S.E.I.F. 1970; E.S.I.F. 1971; E.S.F. 1972; NZ. 1972; E.S.I.A. 1973; S.I.F.E. 1974.

Morris, W.J. (Newport) S. 1965; F. 1966.

Morris, W.J. (Pontypool) S.I. 1963.

Morris, William (Llanelli) S.I. 96; E. 97.

Moseley, K. (Pontypool and Newport) NZ.(2nd).R. 1988; S.I. 1989; F. 1990; F.WS.AR.A. 1991.

Murphy, C. (Cross Keys) E.S.I. 1935.

Mustoe, L. (Cardiff) FJ. 1995; A. (1* and 2) 1996; USA (1 and 2).C.R.* 1997; E*.I*.F*. 1998.

Nash, D. (Ebbw Vale) SA. 1960; E.S.I.F. 1961; F. 1962.

Newman, C.H. (Newport) E. 81; I.E. 82; S. 83; E.S. 84, 85; E. 86, 87.

Nicholas, D. (Llanelli) E.S.I.F. 1981.

Nicholas, T.J. (Cardiff) NZ. 1919.

Nicholl, C.B. (Llanelli) I. 91; E.S.I. 92, 93; E.S. 94; E.S.I. 95, 96.

Nicholl, D.W. (Llanelli) I.94.

Nicholls, E.G. (Cardiff and Newport) S.I. 96; E. 97; E.I. 98; E.S.I. 99; S.I. 1900; E.S.I. 1901, 1902. I. 1903; E. 1904; I.NZ. 1905; E.S.I.SA. 1906.

Nicholls, F.E. (Cardiff Harlequins) I. 92.

Nicholls, H. (Cardiff) I. 1958.

Nicholls, S.H. (Cardiff) M. 88; S.I. 89; S. 91.

Norris, H. (Cardiff) F. 1963; F. 1966.

Norster, R.L. (Cardiff) S. 1982; E.S.I.F. 1983; S.I.F.E.A. 1984; S.I.F.E.FJ. 1985; FJ.T.WS. 1986; F.E.S.I.I.C.E.USA. 1987; E.S.I.F.NZ(1).WS 1988; F.E. 1989.

Norton, W.B. (Cardiff) I.F. 82; S. 83; E.S.I. 84.

O'Connor, A. (Aberavon and Oxford Univ) SA. 1960; E.S. 1961; F.I. 1962.

O'Connor, R. (Aberavon) E. 1957.

O'Neill, W. (Cardiff) S.I. 1904; E.S.I. 1905; E.I. 1907; E.S.F.I. 1908.

O'Shea, J.P. (Cardiff) S.I. 1967; S.I.F. 1968.

Oliver, G. (Pontypool) E.S.F.I. 1920.

Osborne, W.T. (Mountain Ash) E.S.I. 1902, 1903.

Ould, W.J. (Cardiff) E.S. 1924.

Owen, Albert (Swansea) E. 1924.

Owen, G. (Newport) I.F. 1955; E.S.I.F. 1956

Owen, R.M. (Swansea) I. 1901; E.S.I. 1902, 1903, 1904, 1905; NZ. 1905; E.S.I. 1906; SA. 1906; E.S. 1907; F.I.A. 1908; E.S.F.I. 1909; F.E. 1910; E.S.F.I. 1911; E.S. 1912.

Packer, H. (Newport) E. 91; S.I. 95; E.S.I. 96; E. 97.

Palmer, Frank (Swansea) E.S.I. 1922.

Parfitt, F.C. (Newport) E.S.I. 93, 94; S. 95; S.I. 96.

Parfitt, S. (Swansea) N.1*, B. 1990.

Parker, D. (Swansea) I.F.NZ. 1924; E.S.F.I. 1925; F.I. 1929; E. 1930.

Parker, T. (Swansea) NZ. 1919; E.S.I. 1920; E.S.F.I. 1921; E.S.I.F. 1922; E.S.F. 1923.

Parker, W. (Swansea) E.S. 99.

Parsons, G. (Newport) E. 1947.

Pascoe, D. (Bridgend) F.I. 1923.

Pask, A. (Abertillery) F. 1961; E.S.F.I. 1962; E.S.I.F. 1963; NZ. 1963; E.S.I.F.SA. 1964; E.S.I.F. 1965, 1966; A. 1966; S.I. 1967.

Payne, G.W. (Army and Pontypridd) E.S.I. 1960.

Payne, H. (Swansea) NZ 1935.

Peacock, H. (Newport) S.F.I. 1929; S.I.F. 1930.

Peake, E. (Chepstow) E. 81.

Pearce, G. (Bridgend) I.F. 1981; I*. 1982.

Pearson, T.W. (Cardiff and Newport) E.I. 91; E.S. 92; S.I. 94; E.S.I. 95; E. 97; I.E. 98; E. 1903.

Pegge, E.V. (Neath) E. 91.

Perego, M. (Llanelli) S. 1990; F.Z.(1st)N*. 1993; S.I.F.E.Sp. 1994.

114

Perkins, S.J. (Pontypool) S.I.F.R. 983; S.I.F.E.A. 1984; S.I.F.E.FJ. 1985; E.S.I.F. 1986.

Perrett, F. (Neath) SA. 1912; E.S.F.I. 1913.

Perrins, V.C. (Newport) SA.S. 1970.

Perry, W. (Neath) E. 1911.

Phillips, A. (Cardiff) E. 1979; F.E.S.I.NZ. 1980; E.S.I.F.A. 1981; I.F.E.S. 1982; C.E.A. 1987.

Phillips, B. (Aberavon) E.S.F.I. 1925; E. 1926.

Phillips, H. (Newport) E.S.F.I. 1927; NSW. 1927; E.S.I.F. 1928.

Phillips, H. (Swansea) F. 1952.

Phillips, K. (Neath) F.I.T.NZ.USA. 1987; E.NZ(1) 1988; NZ. 1989; F.E.S.I.N.(1,2)B. 1990; E.S.I.F.A. 1991.

Phillips, L.A. (Newport) E.S.I. 1900; S. 1901.

Phillips, Percy (Newport) E. 92; E.S.I. 93; E.S. 94.

Phillips, R. (Neath) USA. 1987; E.S.I.F.NZ.(1 and 2).WS. 1988; S.I. 1989.

Phillips, W.D. (Cardiff) E. 81; I. 82; E.S.I. 84.

Pickering, D.F. (Llanelli) E.S.I.F.R. 1983; S.I.F.E.A. 1984; S.I.F.E.FJ. 1985; E.S.I.F.FJ. 1986; F.E.S. 1987.

Plummer, R.C.S. (Newport) S.I.F. 1912; SA. 1912; E. 1913.

Pook, T. (Newport) S. 95.

Powell, G. (Ebbw Vale) I.F. 1957.

Powell, J. (Cardiff) I. 1906.

Powell, J. (Cardiff) I. 1923.

Powell, R.W. (Newport) S.I. 88.

Powell, W.C. (London Welsh) S.I.F. 1926; E.F.I. 1927; S.I.F. 1928; E.S.F.I. 1929; S.I.F. 1930; E.S.F.I.SA. 1931; E.S.I. 1932, 1935.

Powell, W.J. (Cardiff) E.S.F.I. 1920.

Price, B. (Newport) I.F. 1961; E.S. 1962; E.S.F. 1963; NZ. 1963; E.S.I.F.SA. 1964; E.S.I.F. 1965, 1966; A. 1966; S.I.F.E. 1967; S.I.F.NZ(1 and 2)A. 1969.

Price, G. (Pontypool) F.E.S.I.A. 1975; E.S.I.F. 1976; I.F.E.S. 1977; E.I.S.F.A.(1 and 2)NZ. 1978; S.I.F.E. 1979; F.E.S.I.NZ. 1980; E.S.I.F.A. 1981; I.F.E.S. 1982; E.I.F. 1983.

Price, M. (Pontypool and R.A.F.) E.S.I.F. 1959; E.S.I.F. 1960; E. 1962.

Price, R.E. (Weston) S.I. 1939.

Price, T.G. (Hendy, London Welsh and Llanelli) E.S.I.F. 1965; E.A. 1966; S.F. 1967.

Priday, A.J. (Gloucester) I. 958; I. 1961

Pritchard, Cecil (Pontypool) E.S.I.F. 1928; E.S.F.I. 1929.

Pritchard, Cliff (Newport and Pontypool) S.I. 1904; NZ. 1905; E.S. 1906.

Pritchard, C.M. (Newport) I. 1904; E.S.NZ. 1905; E.S.I.SA. 1906; E.S.I. 1907; E. 1908; F.E. 1910.

Proctor, W.T. (Llanelli) A. 1992; E.S.Z.(1st and 2nd).NC. 1993; I.C.FJ.WS.R.It.SA. 1994; S.I.NZ.FJ. 1995; It.E.S.I.A.(1 and 2).B.F.It.A. 1996; E*.USA (1 and 2).C.R. 1997; E*.S.I.F.Z. 1998.

Prosser, D.R. (Neath) S.I. 1935.

Prosser, Glyn (Neath) E.S.I. 1934; NZ. 1935.

Prosser, Greg (Pontypridd) NZ. 1995.

Prosser, J. (Cardiff) I. 1921.

Prosser, R. (Pontypool) S.F. 1956; E.S.I.F. 1957; A.E.S.I.F. 1958; E.S.I.F. 1959, 1960; SA. 1960; I.F. 1961.

Prothero, G.J. (Bridgend) S.I.F. 1964; E.S.I.F. 1965; E.S.I.F. 1966.

Pugh, C. (Maesteg) E.S.I.F.NZ. 1924; E.S. 1925.

Pugh, J. (Neath) USA. 1987; *S. 1988; S. 1990.

Pugh, Phil (Neath) NZ. 1989.

Pugsley, J. (Cardiff) E.S.I. 1910; E.S.I.F. 1911.

Pullman, J. (Neath) F. 1910.

Purdon, F. (Newport) E. 81; I.E. 82, S. 83.

Quinnell, Craig (Llanelli, Richmond & Cardiff) FJ. 1995; A*. 1996; USA*.S*.I*.E*. 1997; SA.AR. 1998; I.F.It.E.AR (1 & 2) SA. 1999.

Quinnell, D.L. (Llanelli) F.* 1972; NZ. 1972; E.S.A. 1973; S.F. 1974; E.* 1975; *I.F.E.S. 1977; E.S.I.F.A.(1)NZ. 1978; S.I.F.E. 1979; NZ. 1980.

Quinnell, Scott (Llanelli and Richmond) C. 1993; S.I.F.E.P.Sp.C.WS. 1994; USA.S.I.F.E. 1997; It.E.S*.Z.SA.AR. 1998; S.I.F.It.E.AR (1 & 2) SA. 1999.

Radford, W. (Newport) I. 1923.

Ralph, A.R. (Newport) F.I.S.A. 1931; E.S.I. 1932.

Ramsey, S.H. (Treorchy) E.96; E. 1904.

Randell, R. (Aberavon) I.F. 1924.

Raybould, W.H. (London Welsh and Newport) S.I.F.E. 1967; NZ. 1967; I.F. 1968; SA.E.I.F.* 1970.

Rayer, M.A. (Cardiff) WS.*AR.A.* 1991; E.*A. 1992; E.S.I.Z.(1st)N.J.* 1993; S.*I.*F.E.P.C.FJ.WS.R.It. 1994.

Rees, A. (Maesteg) E.S.F. 1962.

Rees, A.M. (London Welsh) E. 1934; E.S.I. 1935; NZ. 1935; E.S.I. 1936, 1937; E.S. 1938.

Rees, Aeron (Maesteg) NZ. 1919.

Rees, B.I. (London Welsh) S.I.F. 1967.

Rees, C.F.W. (London Welsh) I. 1974; A. 1975; NZ. 1978; F.A. 1981; I.F.E.S. 1982; E.S.I.F. 1983.

Rees, D. (Swansea) S.I.F. 1968.

Rees, Dan (Swansea) E. 1900; E.S. 1903, 1905.

Rees, E.B. (Swansea) NZ. 1919.

Rees, H. (Cardiff) S.I. 1937; E.S.I. 1938.

Rees, H.E. (Neath) S.I.F.E. 1979; F.E.S.I.NZ. 1980; E.S.I.F. 1983.

Rees, J. Conway- (Llanelli) S. 92; E. 93, 94.

Rees, J. Idwal (Swansea) E.S.I. 1934; S.NZ. 1935; E.S.I. 1936, 1937, 1938.

Rees, Joe (Swansea) E.S.F.I. 1920; E.S.I. 1921; E. 1922; E.F.I. 1923; E. 1924.

Rees, L. (Cardiff) I. 1933.

Rees, Peter (Llanelli) F.I. 1947.

Rees, P.M. (Newport) E.S.I. 1961; I. 1964.

Rees, Richard (Swansea) Z. 1998.

Rees, T. (Newport) S.I. 1935; NZ. 1935; E.S.I. 1936; E.S. 1937.

Rees, T.A. (Llandovery) E. 81.

Rees, T.E. (London Welsh) I.F. 1926; NSW. 1927; E. 1928.

Reeves, F. (Cross Keys) F.I. 1920; E. 1921.

Reynolds, A. (Swansea) N.(1,2*) 1990; A.* 1992.

Rhapps, J. (Penygraig) E. 97.

Richards, B. (Swansea) F. 1960.

Richards, Cliff (Pontypool) E.S.I.F. 1922; I. 1924.

Richards, D.S. (Swansea) F.E. 1979; F.E.S.I.NZ. 1980; E.S.I.F. 1981; I.F. 1982; E.S.I.F.* 1983.

Richards, E.S. (Swansea) E. 85; S.87.

Richards, Gwyn (Cardiff) S. 1927.

Richards, H. (Neath) T.* 1986; T.E.NZ. 1987.

Richards, Idris (Cardiff) E.S.F. 1925.

Richards, K. (Bridgend) SA. 1960; E.S.I.F. 1961.

Richards, M.C.R. (Cardiff) I.F. 1968; S.I.F.E.N.Z.(1 and 2)A. 1969.

Richards, Rees (Aberavon) S.F.I. 1913.

Richards, Rex (Cross Keys) F. 1956.

Richards, T.L. (Maesteg) I. 1923.

Richardson, S.J. (Aberavon) A.(2)* 1978; E. 1979.

Rickard, A. (Cardiff) F. 1924.

Ring, J. (Aberavon) E. 1921.

Ring, M.G. (Cardiff and Pontypool) E. 1983; A. 1984; S.I.F. 1985; I.I.T.A.USA. 1987; E.S.I.F.NZ(1 and 2) 1988; NZ. 1989; F.E.S.I.N. (1, 2)B. 1990; E.S.I.F.F.WS.AR.A. 1991.

Ringer, P. (Ebbw Vale and Llanelli) NZ. 1978; S.I.F.E. 1979; F.E.NZ. 1980.

Roberts, C. (Neath) I.F. 1958.

Roberts, D.E.A. (London Welsh) E. 1930.

Roberts, E. (Llanelli) E. 86; I.87.

Roberts, E.J. (Llanelli) S.I. 88, I. 89.

Roberts, G. (Cardiff) F.*E. 1985; I.T.C.E.A. 1987.

Roberts, H.M. (Cardiff) SA. 1960; E.S.I.F. 1961; S.F. 1962; I. 1963.

Roberts, J. (Cardiff and Cambridge Univ.) E.S.F.I. 1927; NSW. 1927; E.S.I.F. 1928; E.S.F.I. 1929.

Roberts, M.G. (London Welsh) E.S.I.F. 1971; I.F. 1973; S. 1975; E. 1979.

Roberts, T. (Risca and Newport) S.F.I. 1921; E.S.I.F. 1922; E.S. 1923.

Roberts, Willie (Cardiff) E. 1929.

Robins, J.D. (Birkenhead Park) E.S.I.F. 1950, 1951; E.I.F. 1953.

Robins, R. (Pontypridd) S. 1953; F.S. 1954; E.S.I.F. 1955; E.F. 1956; E.S.I.F. 1957.

Robinson, I.R. (Cardiff) F.E. 1974.

Robinson, M. (Swansea) S.I.F.AR (1) 1999.

Roderick, W.B. (Llanelli) I. 84.

Rogers, Peter (London Irish & Newport) F.It.E.AR (1 & 2) SA. 1999

Rosser, M. (Penarth) S.F. 1924.

Rowland, C.F. (Aberavon) I. 1926.

Rowlands, D.C.T. (Pontypool) E.S.I.F. 1963; NZ. 1963; E.S.I.F.SA. 1964; E.S.I.F. 1965.

Rowlands, G. (R.A.F. and Cardiff) NZ. 1953; E.F. 1954; F. 1956.

Rowlands, J. (Lampeter) E. 85.

Rowlands, K.A. (Cardiff) F.I. 1962; I. 1963; I.F. 1965.

Rowles, G.R. (Penarth) E. 92.

Rowley, Mark (Pontypridd) SA. 1996; USA.S.I.F.R. 1997.

Roy, Stuart (Cardiff) J.* 1995.

Russell, S. (London Welsh) USA. 1987.

Samuel, D. (Swansea) I. 91, 93.

Samuel, F. (Mountain Ash) S.I.F. 1922.

Samuel, J. (Swansea) I. 91.

Scourfield, T. (Torquay) F. 1930.

Scrines, F. (Swansea) E.S. 99; I. 1901.

Shanklin, J.L. (London Welsh) F. 1970; NZ.1972; I.F. 1973.

Shaw, G. (Neath) NZ. 1972; E.S.I.F.A. 1973; S.I.F.E. 1974; I.F. 1977.

Shaw, T. (Newbridge) R. 1983.

Shea, Jerry (Newport) NZ. 1919; E.S. 1920; E. 1921.

Shell, R.C. (Aberavon) A.* 1973.

Simpson, H.J. (Cardiff) E.S.I. 84.

Sinkinson, B. (Neath) F.It.E.AR (1 & 2) SA. 1999.

Skrimshire, R.T. (Newport) E.S.I. 99.

Skym, A. (Llanelli and Cardiff) E.S.I.F. 1928, 1930; E.S.F.I. 1931; SA. 1931; E.S.I. 1932, 1933; E. 1935.

Smith, J.S. (Cardiff) E.I. 84; E. 85.

Sparks, B. (Neath) I. 1954; E.F. 1955; E.S.I. 1956; S. 1957.

Spiller, W. (Cardiff) S.I. 1910; E.S.F.I. 1911; E.F. 1912; SA. 1912; E. 1913.

Squire, J. (Newport and Pontypool) I.F. 1977' E.S.I.F.A.(1)NZ. 1978; S.I.F.E. 1979; F.E.S.I.NZ. 1980; E.S.I.F.A. 1981; I.F.E. 1982; E.S.I.F. 1983.

Stadden, W.H. (Cardiff) I. 84; E.S. 86; I. 87; S.M. 88; S.E. 90.

Stephens, C.J. (Llanelli) I.F.E.A. 1992.

Stephens, Chris (Bridgend) E*. 1998.

Stephens, G. (Neath) E.S.I.F. 1912; SA. 1912; E.S.F.I. 1913; NZ. 1919.

Stephens, I. (Bridgend) E.S.I.F.A. 1981; I.F.E.S. 1982; I.F.E. 1984; A. 1984.

Stephens, Rev. J.G. (Llanelli) E.S.I.F. 1922.

Stephens, Rees (Neath) E.S.F.I. 1947; I. 1948; S.I.F. 1949; F. 1951; SA. 1951; E.S.I.F. 1952, 1953; NZ. 1953; E.I. 1954; E.S.I.F. 1955; S.I.F. 1956; E.S.I.F. 1957.

Stock, A. (Newport) F.NZ. 1924; E.S. 1926.

Stone, P. (Llanelli) F. 1949.

Summers, R.H.B. (Haverfordwest) E. 81.

Sutton, S. (Pontypool) F.E. 1982; F.E.S.I.C.NZ.*A. 1987.

Sweet-Escott, R.B. (Cardiff) S. 91; I. 94, 95.

Tamplin, W.E. (Cardiff) S.F.I.A. 1947; E.S.F. 1948.

Tanner, H. (Swansea and Cardiff) NZ. 1935; E.S.I. 1936, 1937, 1938, 1939; E.S.F.I. 1947, 1948; E.S.I.F. 1949.

Tarr, D.J. (Swansea) NZ. 1935.

Taylor, A.R. (Cross Keys) I. 1937, 1938; E. 1939.

Taylor, C.G. (Blackheath and Ruabon) E.S.I. 84; E.S. 85, 86; E.I. 87.

Taylor, Hemi (Cardiff) P.C.F.J.T.WS.*R.It.SA. 1994; E.S.J.NZ.I.SA.FJ. 1995; It.E.S.I.F.A.(1 and 2)It.A. 1996.

Taylor, J. (London Welsh) S.I.F.E. 1967; NZ. 1967; I.F. 1968; S.I.F.E.NZ(1)A. 1969; F. 1970; E.S.I.F. 1971; E.S.F. 1972; NZ. 1972; E.S.I.F. 1973.

Taylor, Mark (Pontypool and Swansea) SA. 1994; F.E.SA.* 1995; Z.SA.SA.AR. 1998; I.F.It.E.AR. (1 & 2) SA. 1999.

Thomas, A. (Newport) NZ. 1963; E. 1964.

Thomas, Alun (Cardiff and Llanelli) E.S.I.F. 1952; S.I.F. 1953; E.I.F. 1954; S.I.F. 1955.

Thomas, Arwel (Bristol and Swansea) It.E.S.I.F*.SA. 1996; USA.S.I.F.USA.(1 and 2).C.R.NZ*. 1997; It.E.S*.Z.SA. 1998.

Thomas, B. (Neath) E.S.I.F. 1963; NZ. 1963; E.S.I.F.SA. 1964; E. 1965; E.S.I. 1966; NZ. 1967; S.I.F.E.NZ.(1 and 2) 1969.

Thomas, Bob (Swansea) E.S.I. 1900; E.1901.

Thomas, C. (Bridgend) E.S. 1925.

Thomas, C.J. (Newport) I.M. 88; S.I. 89; S.E. 90; E.I. 91.

Thomas, D. (Aberavon) I.1961.

Thomas, D. (Swansea) S.I. 1930;T E.S.I. 1932; E.S. 1933; E. 1934; E.S.I. 1935.

Thomas, Denzil (Llanelli) I. 1954.

Thomas, **Dick** (Mountain Ash) SA. 1906; F.I. 1908; S. 1909.

Thomas, **D.J.** (Swansea) E. 1904; A. 1908; E.S.I. 1910; E.S.I.F. 1911; E. 1912.

Thomas, **D.L.** (Neath) E. 1937.

Thomas, **E.** (Newport) S.I. 1904; S.F.I. 1909; F. 1910.

Thomas, **G.** (Llanelli) E.S.F.I. 1923.

Thomas, **Gareth** (Bridgend and Cardiff) J.NZ.I.SA.FJ. 1995; F.A.(1 and 2).B.F.It.A. 1996; USA.S.I.F.E.USA.(1 and 2).C.R.T.NZ. 1997; It. E.S.I.F.SA.AR. 1988; F*.It.E.AR (2) SA. 1999.

Thomas, **Geo** (Newport) M. 88; I. 90; S. 91.

Thomas, **H.W.** (Swansea) SA. 1912; E. 1913.

Thomas, **Harold** (Llanelli) F. 1912.

Thomas, **Harold** (Neath) E.S.I. 1936, 1937.

Thomas, **Ifor** (Bryncethin) E. 1924.

Thomas, **Justin** (Llanelli and Cardiff) SA.FJ. 1995; It.E.S.I.F.B*. 1996; USA. 1997.

Thomas, **L.C.** (Cardiff) E.S. 85.

Thomas, **L.I.** (Newport) S. 94; E.I. 95.

Thomas, **M.C.** (Newport) F. 1949; E.S.I.F. 1950, 1951; SA. 1951; E.S.I.F. 1952; E. 1953; E.S.I.F. 1956; E.S. 1957; E.S.I.F. 1958; I.F. 1959.

Thomas, **Melbourne** (Bridgend and St. Bart's H.) NZ. 1919; S.F.I. 1921; F. 1923; E. 1924.

Thomas, **Nathan** (Bath) SA*. 1996; USA(1* and 2).C*.R.T.NZ. 1997; Z.SA. 1998.

Thomas, **R.C.C.** (Swansea and Cambridge Univ.) F. 1949; I.F. 1952; S.I.F. 1953; NZ. 1953; E.I.F.S. 1954; S.I. 1955; E.S.I. 1956; E. 1957; A.E.S.I.F. 1958; E.S.I.F. 1959.

Thomas, **Rees** (Pontypool) F.I. 1909; S.F. 1911; E.S. 1912; SA. 1912; E. 1913.

Thomas, **R.L.** (London Welsh and Llanelli) S.I. 89; I. 90; E.S.I. 91; E. 92.

Thomas, **S.** (Llanelli) A. 1966; S.I.F. 1968; E.NZ.(2)A. 1969; SA.S.E.I.F. 1970; E.S.I.F. 1971; E.S.F. 1972; NZ. 1972; E.S.I.F. 1973; E. 1974.

Thomas, **W.D.** (Llanelli) A. 1966; S.I.F. 1968; E.NZ. (2) A. 1969; SA.S.E.I.F. 1970; E.S.I.F. 1971; E.S.F.NZ. 1972; E.S.I.F. 1973; E. 1974

Thomas, **W.H.** (Llanelli and London Welsh) S. 85; E.S. 86, 87; S.I. 88; E.I. 90, S.I. 91.

Thomas, **W.J.** (Cardiff) F. 1961; F. 1963.

Thomas, **W.T.** (Abertillery) E. 1930.

Thomas, **Watcyn** (Llanelli and Swansea) E.S.F.I. 1927; E. 1929; E.S.SA. 1931; E.S.I. 1932, 1933.

Thompson, **J.** (Cross Keys) E. 1923.

Thorburn, **P.** (Neath) F.E.FJ. 1985; E.S.I.F. 1986; F.I.T.C.E.NZ.A.USA. 1987; S.I.F.WS.R(R). 1988; S.I.F.E.NZ. 1989; F.E.S.I.N.(1, 2) B. 1990; E.S.I.F.A. 1991.

Titley, **M.H.** (Bridgend) R. 1983; S.I.F.E.A. 1984; S.I.F.J. 1985; F.FJ.T.WS. 1986; F.E. 1990.

Towers, **W.H.** (Swansea) I. 87; M. 88.

Travers, **G.** (Pill Harriers and Newport) E.S.I. 1903, 1905; NZ. 1905; E.S.I.SA. 1906; E.S.I. 1907; E.S.I.F.A. 1908; E.S.I. 1909; S.I.F. 1911.

Travers, **W.H.** (Newport) S.I. 1937. E.S.I. 1938, 1939; E.S.I.F. 1949.

Treharne, **E.** (Pontypridd) E. 81; E. 82.

Trew, **W.** (Swansea) E.S.I. 1900; E.S. 1901; S. 1903, 1905, 1906; E.S. 1907; E.S.F.I.A. 1908; E.S.F.I. 1909; F.E.S. 1910; E.S.F.I. 1911; S. 1912; S.F. 1913.

Trott, **R.F.** (Cardiff) E.S.F.I. 1948; E.S.I.F. 1949.

Truman, **H.** (Llanelli) E. 1934, 1935.

Trump, **L.** (Newport) E.S.I.F. 1912.

Turnbull, **B.R.** (Cardiff and Cambridge Univ) I. 1925; E.S. 1927; E.F. 1928; S. 1930.

Turnbull, **M.J.** (Cardiff) E.I. 1933.

Turner, **P.** (Newbridge) I(R).F.E. 1989.

Uzzell, **H.** (Newport) E.S.I.F. 1912; S.F.I. 1913; E.S.F.I. 1914; E.S.F.I. 1920.

Uzell, **J.** (Newport) NZ. 1963; E.S.I.F. 1965.

Vickery, **W.** (Aberavon) E.S.I. 1938; E. 1939.

Vile, **T.H.** (Newport) E.S. 1908; I. 1910; I.F. 1912; SA. 1912; E. 1913; S. 1921.

Vincent, **H.C.** (Bangor) I. 82.

Voyle, **M.** (Newport and Llanelli) A*.B. 1996; E.USA.(1and 2)C.T.NZ. 1997; It.E.S.I.F.AR* 1998; S.*I.*It.*SA.* 1999.

Wakeford, **J.** (S.W. Police) WS.R. 1988.

Walker, **N.** (Cardiff) I.F.J. 1993; S.F.E.P.Sp. 1994; F.E. 1995; USA(1 and 2)C.R*.T.NZ. 1997; E. 1998.

Waldron, **R.** (Neath) E.S.I.F. 1965.

Waller, **P.D.** (Newport) A. 1908; E.S.F.I. 1909; F. 1910.

Walne, **Nick** (Richmond and Cardiff) It.*E. 1999.

Walters, **D.** (Llanelli) E. 1902.

Wanbon, **R.** (Aberavon) E. 1968.

Ward, **W.** (Cross Keys) S.I. 1934.

Warlow, **J.** (Llanelli) I. 1962.

Waters, **D.** (Newport) S.I.F. 1986.

Waters, **K.** (Newbridge) WS. 1991.

Watkins, **D.** (Newport) E.S.I.F. 1963; NZ. 1963; E.S.I.F.SA. 1964; E.S.I.F. 1965, 1966; I.F.E. 1967.

Watkins, **E.** (Blaina) S.I.F. 1926.

Watkins, **E.** (Cardiff) NZ. 1935; S.I. 1937; E.S.I. 1938; E.S. 1939.

Watkins, **E.** (Neath) E.S.I.F. 1924.

Watkins, **H.** (Llanelli) S.I. 1904; E.S.I. 1905; E. 1906.

Watkins, **I.** (Ebbw Vale) *E.S.I.F.NZ(2nd).R. 1988; S.I.F.E. 1989.

Watkins, **L.** (Llandaff) E. 81.

Watkins, **M.J.** (Newport) I.F.E. 1984; A. 1984.

Watkins, **S.J.** (Newport and Cardiff) S.I.F. 1964; E.S.I.F. 1965; E.S.I.F.A. 1966; S.I.F.E. 1967; NZ. 1967; E.S. 1968; S.I.F.E.NZ.(1) 1969; E. 1970.

Watkins, **W.** (Newport) F. 1959.

Watt, **W.** (Llanelli) E. 1914.

Watts, **D.** (Maesteg) E.S.F.I. 1914.

Watts, **J.** (Llanelli) E.S.I. 1907; E.S.F.I.A. 1908; S.F.I. 1909.

Watts, **Wallace** (Newport) E.S.I. 92, 93, 94; E.I. 95; E. 96.

Weatherley, **D.** (Swansea) Z. 1998.

Weaver, **D.** (Swansea) E. 1964.

Webb, **J.** (Abertillery) S. 1907; E.S.F.I.A. 1908; E.S.F.I. 1909; F.E.S.I. 1910; E.S.F.I. 1911; E.S. 1912.

Webb, **J.E.** (Newport) M. 88; S. 89.

Webbe, **G.** (Bridgend) T.*WS. 1986; F.E.S.T.USA. 1987; *F.NZ(1).R. 1988.

Webster, **R.** (Swansea) A. 1987; B. 1990; AR.A. 1991; I.F.E.S.A. 1992; E.S.I.F. 1993.

Wells, **G.** (Cardiff) E.S. 1955; I.F. 1957; A.E.S. 1958.

117

Westacott, D. (Cardiff) I. 1906.

Wetter, H. (Newport) SA. 1912; E. 1913.

Wetter, J. (Newport) S.F.I. 1914; E.S.Fl. 1920; E. 1921; I.NZ. 1924.

Wheel, G.A.D. (Swansea) I.E.* 1974; F.E.I. 1975; A. 1975; E.S.I.F. 1976; I.E.S. 1977; E.S.I.F.A.(1 and 2).NZ. 1978; S.I. 1979; F.E.S.I. 1980; E.S.I.F.A. 1981; I. 1982.

Wheeler, P.J. (Aberavon) NZ. 1967; E. 1968.

Whitefoot, J. (Cardiff) A. 1984; S.I.F.E.FJ. 1985; E.S.I.F.FJ.T.WS. 1986; F.E.S.I.I.C. 1987.

Whitfield, J. (Pill Harriers and Newport) NZ. 1919; E.S.F.I. 1920; E. 1921; E.S.I.F. 1922; S.I. 1924.

Whitson, G. (Newport) F. 1956; S.I. 1960.

Wilkins, G. (Bridgend) T. 1994.

Williams, Aled (Bridgend) N.2* 1990; FJ.* 1995.

Williams, Barry (Neath and Richmond) F. 1996; R.T.NZ. 1997; It.E.Z*.SA.AR.* 1998; S.*I.It.* 1999.

Williams, Bleddyn (Cardiff) E.S.F.I.A. 1947; E.S.F.I. 1948; E.S.I. 1949; I. 1951; SA. 1951; S. 1952; E.S.I.F. 1953; NZ. 1953; S. 1954; E. 1955.

Williams, Brian (Neath) S.I.B. 1990; E.S. 1991.

Williams, Bryn (Llanelli) S.F.I. 1920.

Williams, C. (Llanelli) NZ. 1924; E. 1925.

Williams, C. (Aberavon and Swansea) E.S. 1977; F.E.S.I.NZ. 1980; E. 1983.

Williams, C.D. (Cardiff, Neath) F.1955; F. 1956.

Williams, Darril (Llanelli) SA*. 1998.

Williams, D. (Ebbw Vale) E.S.I.F. 1963; E.S.I.F.SA. 1964; E.S.I.F. 1965; E.S.I. 1966; A. 1966; F.E. 1967; NZ. 1967; E. 1968; S.I.F.E.NZ(1 and 2)A. 1969; SA.S.E.I. 1970; E.S.I.F. 1971.

Williams, D.B. (Newport and Swansea) A.(1) 1978; E.S. 1981.

Williams, Eddie (Neath) NZ. 1924; F. 1925.

Williams, Evan (Aberavon) E.S. 1925.

Williams, Frank (Cardiff) S.F.I. 1929; E.S.I.F. 1930; F.I.SA. 1931; E.S.I. 1932; I. 1933.

Williams, G. (London Welsh and Llanelli) F. 1950; F.I.SA. 1931; E.S.I. 1932; I. 1933.

Williams, G.P. (Bridgend) NZ. 1980; E.S.A. 1981; I. 1982.

Williams, Gerald (Bridgend) I.F. 1981; E.*S. 1982.

Williams, Griff (Aberavon) E.S.I. 1936.

Williams, J. (Blaina) E.S.I.F. 1920; S.F.I. 1921.

Williams, J.F. (London Welsh) I.NZ. 1905; S. 1906; SA. 1906.

Williams, J.J. (Llanelli) F.*A. 1973; S.I.F.E. 1974; F.E.S.I. 1975; A. 1975; E.S.I.F. 1976; I.F.E.S. 1977; E.S.I.F.A.(1 and 2)NZ. 1978; S.I.F.E. 1979.

Williams, J.L. (Cardiff) SA. 1906; E.S.I.. 1907, 1908; A. 1908; E.S.F.I. 1909; I. 1910; E.S.F.I. 1911.

Williams, J.P.R. (London Welsh and Bridgend) S.I.F.E.NZ.(1 and 2)A. 1969; SA.S.E.I.F. 1970; E.S.I.F. 1971; E.S.F. 1972; NZ. 1972; E.S.I.F.A. 1973; S.I.F. 1974; F.E.SI. 1975; A. 1975; E.S.I.F. 1976; I.F.E.S. 1977; E.S.I.F.A.(1 and 2)NZ. 1978; S.I.F.E. 1979; NZ. 1980; E.S. 1981.

Williams, L. (Cardiff) S.I.F. 1957; E.S.I.F. 1958; E.S.I. 1959; F. 1961; E.S. 1962.

Williams, Les (Llanelli and Cardiff) E.S.F.I.A. 1947; I. 1948; E. 1949.

Williams, M. (Newport) F. 1923.

Williams, Martyn (Pontypridd) B.F.It.* 1996; It.E.Z. SA.AR. 1998; S.I. 1999.

Williams, Ossie (Llanelli) E.S.A. 1947; E.S.F.I. 1948.

Williams, Owain (Bridgend) N.2. 1990.

Williams, Ray (Llanelli) S. 1954; F. 1957; A. 1958.

Williams, R.D.G. (Abercamlais) E. 81.

Williams, R.F. (Cardiff) SA. 1912; E.S. 1913; I. 1914.

Williams, R.H. (Llanelli) I.F.S. 1954; S.I.F. 1955; E.S.I. 1956; E.S.I.F. 1957; A.E.S.I.F. 1958; E.S.I.F. 1959; E. 1960.

Williams, S. (Llanelli) E.S.F.I. 1947; S.F. 1948.

Williams, Sid (Aberavon) E.S.I.F. 1939.

Williams, Steve (Neath and Cardiff) T. 1994; E.A.(1 and 2).B.F.It.A.SA. 1996; USA.S.I.F.E. USA(1 and 2).C.R.T*.NZ*. 1997.

Williams, T. (Pontypridd) I.82.

Williams, T. (Swansea) S.I. 88.

Williams, Tom (Swansea) I. 1912; F. 1913; E.S.F.I. 1914.

Williams, Trevor (Cross Keys) S.I. 1935; NZ. 1935 E.S.I. 1936; S.I. 1937.

Williams, Tudor (Swansea) F. 1921.

Williams, W. (Crumlin) E.S.F.I. 1927.

Williams, W.A. (Newport) I.F. 1952; E. 1953.

Williams, W.E.O. (Cardiff) S.I. 87; S. 89; S.E. 90.

Williams, W.H. (Pontymister) E.S.I. 1900; E. 1901.

Williams, W.O. (Swansea) F. 1951; SA. 1951; E.S.I.F. 1952, 1953; NZ. 1953; E.I.F.S. 1954; E.S.I.F. 1955; E.S.I. 1956.

Williams, W.P.J. (Neath) I.F. 1974.

Williams-Jones, H. (S.W. Police and Llanelli) S(R). 1989; F(R).I. 1990; A. 1991; S.A. 1992; E.S.I.F.Z.(1st)N. 1993; FJ.T.WS.*It.* 1994; E*. 1995.

Willis, R. (Cardiff) E.S.I.F. 1950, 1951; SA. 1951; E.S. 1952; S. 1953; NZ. 1953; E.I.F.S. 1954; E.S.I.F. 1955.

Wiltshire, M.L. (Aberavon) NZ. 1967; E.S.F. 1968.

Windsor, R.W. (Pontypool) A. 1973; S.I.F.E. 1974; F.E.S.I.A. 1975; E.S.I.F. 1976; I.F.E.S. 1977;E.S.I.F.A.(1 and 2)NZ. 1978; S.I.F. 1979.

Winfield, H.B. (Cardiff) I. 1903; E.S.I. 1904; NZ. 1905; E.S.I. 1906; S.I. 1907; E.S.I.F.A. 1908.

Winmill, S. (Cross Keys) E.S.F.I. 1921.

Wintle, Matthew (Llanelli) It. 1996.

Wintle, R. (London Welsh) WS.(R). 1988.

Wooller, W. (Rydal School, Sale, Cambridge Univ. and Cardiff) E.S.I. 1933, 1935; NZ. 1935; E.S.I. 1936, 1937; S.I. 1938; E.S.I. 1939.

Wyatt, Chris (Llanelli) Z*.SA*.SA.AR. 1998; S.I.F.It.E.AR. (1 & 2) SA 1999.

Wyatt, Gareth (Pontypridd) T. 1997.

Wyatt, M. (Swansea) E.S.I.F. 1983; A. 1984; S.I. 1985; E.S.I. 1987.

Young, D. (Swansea and Cardiff) E.NZ.USA. 1987; E.S.I.F.NZ(1 and2)WS.R. 1988; S. 1989; A.SA. 1996; USA.S.I.F.E.R.NZ. 1997; It.E.S.I.F. 1998; I.E.*AR. (1* & 2*) SA. 1999.

Young, G.A. (Cardiff) E.S. 86.

Young, J. (Harrogate, Bridgend and London Welsh) S.I.F. 1968; S.I.F.E.NZ(1) 1969; E.I.F. 1970; E.S.I.F. 1971; E.S.F. 1972; NZ. 1972; E.S.I.F. 1973.

LEADING WELSH CAP-HOLDERS

	Matches		Matches		Matches
Ieuan Evans	72	N.R. Gale	25	Leigh Davies	18
Neil Jenkins	67	T.D. Holmes	25	W.J. Delahay	18
Gareth Llewellyn	62	B. John	25	Tom Evans	18
J.P.R. Williams	55	H. Tanner	25	Rupert Moon	18
Robert Jones	54	G. Travers	25	S.J. Perkins	18
G.O. Edwards	53	Delme Thomas	25	Alan Phillips	18
Phil Davies	46	Bleddyn Bowen	24	W. Wooller	18
T.G.R. Davies	46	R.T. Gabe	24	M. Voyle	18
Garin Jenkins	45	D.J. Lloyd	24	D.M. Davies	17
K.J. Jones	44	E. Gwyn Nicholls	24	Stuart Davies	17
Mike Hall	42	Hemi Taylor	24	Rowe Harding	17
Emyr Lewis	41	E.C. Davey	23	A.L.P. Lewis	17
G. Price	41	R.W. Gravell	23	J. Matthews	17
Scott Gibbs	39	J.A. Gwilliam	23	D.S. Richards	17
Mervyn Davies	38	J.J. Hodges	23	J.L. Williams	17
W. Proctor	38	D.F. Pickering	23	H. Williams-Jones	17
Anthony Clement	37	D.L. Quinnell	23	J.G. Boots	16
P. Thorburn	37	R.H. Williams	23	E.T. Butler	16
Denzil Williams	36	Jeff Young	23	A.H. Copsey	16
R.M. Owen	35	A. Ackerman	22	Cliff Davies	16
Gareth Thomas	35	Colin Charvis	22	R.A. Gibbs	16
D.I. Bebb	34	S.J. Dawes	22	W.W. Joseph	16
J.D. Davies	34	R.D. Moriarty	22	Ivor Jones	16
Rob Howley	34	R. Prosser	22	E. Morgan	16
A.J. Martin	34	B.L. Williams	22	Nigel Walker	16
B.V. Meredith	34	W.O. Williams	22	Mark Titley	15
W.D. Morris	34	T.J. Davies	21	J. Bassett	15
R.I. Norster	34	W. Gareth Davies	21	F.A. Bowdler	15
W.J. Bancroft	33	J. Devereux	21	M. Dacey	15
Mike Griffiths	33	W.J. James	21	Don Hayward	15
David Young	33	F.M. Jenkins	21	A.F. Hill	15
Jonathan Davies	32	Paul Moriarty	21	G.T.R. Hodgson	15
B.Price	32	Mike Rayer	21	R. Jones	15
Mark Ring	32	Brian Thomas	21	C.B. Nicholl	15
J.R.G. Stephens	32	D. Watkins	21	T. Parker	15
G. Wheel	32	W.R. Willis	21	Craig Quinnell	15
J.M. Humphreys	31	A.F. Harding	20	Mark Taylor	15
S.P. Fenwick	30	W. Llewllyn	20	H. Uzzell	15
J.J. Williams	30	S. Skym	20	H.B. Winfield	15
Phil Bennett	29	Arwel Thomas	20	Paul Arnold	15
Nigel Davies	29	J. Webb	20	Kevin Phillips	14
C.I. Morgan	29	Steve Williams	20	W.B. Cleaver	14
J. Squire	29	T.J. Cobner	19	L.J. Cunningham	14
W.J. Trew	29	Allan Bateman	19	J.P. Jones	14
Richie Collins	28	Ricky Evans	19	D.K. Jones	14
Scott Quinnell	28	A.G. Faulkner	19	Albert Jenkins	14
R.W. Windsor	28	J. Hannan	19	V.G.J. Jenkins	14
A.J. Gould	27	Dafydd James	19	C.C. Meredith	14
A.M. Hadley	27	E.R. John	19	J.C. Morley	14
H.J. Morgan	27	Derwyn Jones	19	C.M. Prtichard	14
W.C. Powell	27	Chris Loader	19	J. Idwal Rees	14
M.C. Thomas	27	S. Morris	19	D.C.T. Rowlands	14
A.E.I. Pask	26	J. Whitefoot	18	Wtcyn Thomas	14
J. Taylor	26	T. Arthur	18	F.L. Williams	14
R.C.C. Thomas	26	J. Bancroft	18		
S.J. Watkins	26	A.B. Price	18		

TRIPLE CROWN WINNERS

England 21 times - 1882-83, 1883-84, 1891-92, 1912-13, 1913-14, 1920-21, 1922-23, 1923-24, 1927-28, 1933-34, 1936-37, 1953-54, 1956-57, 1959-60, 1979-80, 1990-91, 1991-92, 1994-95, 1995-96, 1996-97, 1997-98.

Wales 17 times - 1892-93, 1899-1900, 1901-02, 1904-05, 1907-08, 1908-09, 1910-11, 1949-50, 1951-52, 1964-65, 1968-69, 1970-71, 1975-76, 1976-77, 1977-78, 1978-79, 1987-88.

Scotland 10 times - 1890-91, 1894-95, 1900-01, 1902-03, 1906-07, 1924-25, 1932-33, 1937-38, 1983-84, 1989-90.

Ireland 6 times - 1893-94, 1898-99, 1947-48, 1948-49, 1981-82, 1984-85.

GRAND SLAM WINNERS

England 11 times - 1912-13, 1913-14, 1920-21, 1922-23, 1923-24, 1927-28, 1956-57, 1979-80, 1990-91, 1991-92, 1994-95.

Wales 8 times - 1907-08, 1908-09, 1910-11, 1949-50, 1951-52, 1970-71, 1975-76, 1977-78.

France 6 times - 1967-68, 1976-77, 1980-81, 1986-87, 1996-97, 1997-98.

Scotland three times - 1924-25, 1983-84, 1989-90.

Ireland once - 1947-48.

INTERNATIONAL CHAMPIONSHIP WINNERS

Year	Winner	Year	Winner	Year	Winner
1883-84	ENGLAND	1924-25	SCOTLAND	1962-63	ENGLAND
1884-85	–	1925-26	IRELAND	1963-64	SCOTLAND
1885-86	ENGLAND		SCOTLAND		WALES
	SCOTLAND	1926-27	SCOTLAND	1964-65	WALES
1886-87	SCOTLAND		IRELAND	1965-66	WALES
1887-88	–	1927-28	ENGLAND	1966-67	FRANCE
1888-89	–	1928-29	SCOTLAND	1967-68	FRANCE
1889-90	ENGLAND	1929-30	ENGLAND	1968-69	WALES
	SCOTLAND	1930-31	WALES	1969-70	FRANCE
1890-91	SCOTLAND		ENGLAND		WALES
1891-92	ENGLAND	1931-32	WALES	1970-71	WALES
1892-93	WALES		IRELAND	1971-72	WALES
1893-94	IRELAND	1932-33	SCOTLAND	1972-73	FIVE WAY TIE
1894-95	SCOTLAND	1933-34	ENGLAND	1973-74	IRELAND
1895-96	IRELAND	1934-35	IRELAND	1974-75	WALES
1896-97	–	1935-36	WALES	1975-76	WALES
1897-98	SCOTLAND	1936-37	ENGLAND	1976-77	FRANCE
1998-99	IRELAND	1937-38	SCOTLAND	1977-78	WALES
1899-1900	WALES		ENGLAND	1978-79	WALES
1900-01	SCOTLAND	1938-39	WALES	1979-80	ENGLAND
1901-02	WALES		IRELAND	1980-81	FRANCE
1902-03	SCOTLAND	1946-47	WALES	1981-82	IRELAND
1903-04	SCOTLAND		ENGLAND	1982-83	FRANCE
1904-05	WALES	1947-48	IRELAND		IRELAND
1905-06	IRELAND	1948-49	IRELAND	1983-84	SCOTLAND
	WALES	1949-50	WALES	1984-85	IRELAND
1906-07	SCOTLAND	1950-51	IRELAND	1985-86	FRANCE
1907-08	WALES	1951-52	WALES		SCOTLAND
1908-0	WALES	1952-53	ENGLAND	1986-87	FRANCE
1909-10	ENGLAND	1953-54	ENGLAND	1987-88	WALES
1910-11	WALES		FRANCE		FRANCE
1911-12	ENGLAND		WALES	1988-89	FRANCE
	IRELAND	1954-55	WALES	1989-90	SCOTLAND
1912-13	ENGLAND		FRANCE	1990-91	ENGLAND
1913-14	ENGLAND	1955-56	WALES	1991-92	ENGLAND
1919-20	ENGLAND	1956-57	ENGLAND	1992-93	FRANCE
	SCOTLAND	1957-58	ENGLAND	1993-94	WALES
	WALES	1958-59	FRANCE	1994-95	ENGLAND
1920-21	ENGLAND	1959-60	FRANCE	1995-96	ENGLAND
1021-22	WALES		ENGLAND	1996-97	FRANCE
1922-23	ENGLAND	1960-61	FRANCE	1997-98	FRANCE
1923-24	ENGLAND	1961-62	FRANCE	1998-99	SCOTLAND

WELSH INTERNATIONAL RESULTS
AGAINST ENGLAND

Matches played 105   Wales 49 wins,   England 44,   12 drawn

1880-81 ENGLAND 7G, 1DG, 6T TO 0 (Blackheath)

1881-82 No Match

1882-83 ENGLAND 2G, 4T to 0 (Swansea)

1883-84 ENGLAND 1G, 2T to 1G (Leeds)

1884-85 ENGLAND 1G, 4T to 1G, 1T (Swansea)

1885-86 ENGLAND 1GM, 2T to 1G (Blackheath)

1886-87 DRAWN No Score (Llanelli)

1888-89 and 1888-89 No Matches

1889-90 WALES 1T(1) to 0 (Dewsbury)

1890-91 ENGLAND 2G, 1T (7) to 1G(3) (Newport)

1891-92 ENGLAND 3G, 1T (17) to 0 (Blackheath)

1892-93 WALES 1PG, 2T (12) to 1G 3T

1893-94 ENGLAND 4G, 1GM (24) to 1T (3) (Birkenhead)

1894-95 ENGLAND 1G, 3T (14) to 2T (6) (Swansea)

1895-96 ENGLAND 2G, 5T (25) to 0 (Blackheath)

1896-97 WALES 1G, 2T (11) to 0 (Newport)

1897-98 ENGLAND 1G, 3T (14) to 1DG, 1T (7) (Blackheath)

1898-99 WALES 4G, 2T (26) to 1T (3) (Swansea)

1899-1900 WALES 2G, 1PG (13) to 1T (3) (Gloucester)

1900-01 WALES 2G, 1T (13) to 0 (Cardiff)

1901-02 WALES 1PG, 2T (9) to 1G, 1T (8) (Blackheath)

1902-03 WALES 3G, 2T (21) to 1G (5) (Swansea)

1903-04 DRAWN ENGLAND 1G, 1PG, 2T (14) to WALES 2G, 1GM (14) (Leicester)

1904-05 WALES 2G, 5T (25) to 0 (Cardiff)

1905-06 WALES 2G, 2T (16) to 1T (3) (Richmond)

1906-07 WALES 2G, 4T (22) to 0 (Swansea)

1907-08 WALES 3G, 1DG, 1PG, 2T (28) to 3G, 1T (18) (Bristol)

1908-09 WALES 1G, 1T (8) to 0 (Cardiff)

1909-10 ENGLAND 1G, 1PG, 1T (11) to 2T (6) (Twickenham)

1910-11 WALES 1PG, 4T (15) to 1G, 2T (11) (Swansea)

1911-12 ENGLAND 1G, 1T (8) to 0 (Twickenham)

1912-13 ENGLAND 1G, 1DG, 1T (12) to 0 (Cardiff)

1913-14	**ENGLAND** 2g (10) to 1G, 1DG (9) (Twickenham)	1966-67	**WALES** 5G, 2PG, 1DG (34) to 4PG 3T (21) (Cardiff)
1919-20	**WALES** 1G, 2DG, 1T (19 to 1G (5) (Swansea)	1967-68	**DRAWN ENGLAND** 1G, 1PG, 1T (11) to 1G, 1DG, 1T (11) (Twickenham)
1920-21	**ENGLAND** 1G, 1DG, 3T (18) to 1T (3) (Twickenham)	1968-69	**WALES** 3G, 2PG, 1DG, 2T (30) to 3PG (9) (Cardiff)
1921-22	**WALES** 2G, 6T (28) to 2T (6) (Cardiff)	1969-70	**WALES** 1G, 1DG, 3T (17) to 2G, 1PG (13) (Cardiff)
1922-23	**ENGLAND** 1DG, 1T (7) to 1T (3) (Twickenham)	1970-71	**WALES** 2G, 2DG, 1PG, 1T (22) to 1PG, 1T (6) (Cardiff)
1923-24	**ENGLAND** 1G, 4T (17 to 3T (9) (Swansea)		**(Try upgraded to 4 pts)**
1924-25	**ENGLAND** 1PG, 3T (12) to 2T (6) (Twickenham)	1971-72	**WALES** 1G, 2PG (12) to 1PG (3) (Twickenham)
1925-26	**DRAWN** 1T (3) each (Cardiff)	1972-73	**WALES** 1G, 1PG, 4T (25) to 2PG, 1DG (9) (Cardiff)
1926-27	**ENGLAND** 1G, 1PG, 1GM (11) to 1PG, 2T (9) (Twickeham)	1973-74	**ENGLAND** 1G, 2PG, 1T (16) to 1G, 2PG (12) (Twickenham)
1927-28	**ENGLAND** 2G, (10) to 1G, 1T, (8) (Swansea)	1974-75	**WALES** 1G, 2PG, 2T (20) to 1T (4) (Cardiff)
1928-29	**ENGLAND** 1G, 1T (8) to 1T (3) (Twickenham)	1975-76	**WALES** 3G, 1PG (21) to 3PG (9) (Twickenham)
1929-30	**ENGLAND** 1G, 1PG, 1T (11) to 1T (3) (Cardiff)	1976-77	**WALES** 2PG, 2T (14) to 3PG (9) (Cardiff)
1930-31	**DRAWN ENGLAND** 1G, 2PG (11) to **WALES** 1G, 1GM, 1T (11) (Twickenham)	1977-78	**WALES** 3PG (9) to 2PG (9) (Twickenham)
1931-32	**WALES** 1G, 1DG, 1PG (12) to 1G (5) (Swansea)	1978-79	**WALES** 2G, 1DG, 3T (27) to 1PG (3) (Cardiff)
1932-33	**WALES** 1DG, 1T (7) to 1T (3) (Twickenham)	1979-80	**ENGLAND** 3PG (9) to 2T (8) (Twickenham)
1933-34	**ENGLAND** 3T (9) to 0 (Cardiff)	1980-81	**WALES** 1G, 1DG, 4PG (21) to 5PG, 1T (19) (Cardiff)
1934-35	**DRAWN ENGLAND** 1PG (3) to **WALES** 1T (3) (Twickenham)	1981-82	**ENGLAND** 3PG, 2T (17) to 1DG, 1T (7) (Twickenham)
1935-36	**DRAWN** No Score (Swansea)	1982-83	**DRAWN WALES** 2PG, 1DG, 1T (13) to **ENGLAND** 2PG, 1DG, 1T (13) (Cardiff)
1936-37	**ENGLAND** 1DG (4) to 1T (3) (Twickenham)	1983-84	**WALES** 1G, 2DG, 4PG (24) to 5PG (15) (Twickenham)
1937-38	**WALES** 1G, 2PG, 1T (14) to 1G, 1T (8) (Cardiff)	1984-85	**WALES** 2G, 1DG, 3PG (24) to 1G, 1DG, 2PG (15) (Cardiff)
1938-39	**ENGLAND** 1T (3) to 0 (Twickenham)	1985-86	**ENGLAND** 1DG, 6PG (21) to 1G, 1DG, 3PG (18) (Twickenham)
1946-47	**ENGLAND** 1G, 1DG (9) to 2T (6) (Cardiff)	1986-87	**WALES** 5PG, 1T (19) to 4PG 12 (Cardiff)
1947-48	**DRAWN ENGLAND** 1PG (3) to **WALES** 1T (3) (Twickenham)	1987	**WORLD CUP : WALES** 2G, 1T (16) to 1PG (3) (Brisbane)
	(Dropped goal revalued to 3 pts)	1987-88	**WALES** 1DG, 2T (11) to 1PG (3) (Twickenham)
1948-49	**WALES** 3T (9) to 1DG (3) (Cardiff)	1988-89	**WALES** 1G, 2PG (12) to 2PG, 1DG (9) (Cardiff)
1949-50	**WALES** 1G, 1PG, 1T (11) to 1G (5) (Twickenham)	1989-90	**ENGLAND** 3G, 4PG, 1T (34) to 1G (6) (Twickenham)
1950-51	**WALES** 4G, 1T (23) to 1G (5) (Swansea)	1990-91	**ENGLAND** 7PG, 1T (25) to 2PG (6) (Cardiff)
1951-52	**WALES** 1G, 1T (8) to 2T (6) (Twickenham)	1991-92	**ENGLAND** 3G, 2PG (24) to 0 (Twickenham)
1952-53	**ENGLAND** 1G, 1PG (8) to 1PG (3) (Cardiff)		**(Try upgraded to 5 pts.)**
1953-54	**ENGLAND** 3T (9) to 1PG, 1T (6) (Twickenham)	1992-93	**WALES** 1G, 1PG (10) to 2PG, 1DG (9) (Cardiff)
1954-55	**WALES** 1PG (3) to 0 (Cardiff)	1993-94	**ENGLAND** 1G, 1PG, 1T (15) to 1PG, 1T (8) (Twickenham)
1955-56	**WALES** 1G, 1T (8) to 1PG (3) (Twickenham)	1994-95	**ENGLAND** 1G, 2PG, 2T (23) to 3PG (9) (Cardiff)
1956-57	**ENGLAND** 1PG, (3) to 0 (Cardiff)	1995-96	**ENGLAND** 1G, 3PG, 1T (21) to 1G, 1PG, 1T (15) (Twickenham)
1957-58	**DRAWN ENGLAND** 1T (3) to **WALES** 1PG (3) (Twickenham)	1996-97	**ENGLAND** 4G, 2PG (34) to 1G, 2PG (13) (Cardiff)
1958-59	**WALES** 1G, (5) to 0 (Cardiff)	1997-98	**ENGLAND** 7G, 2PG, 1T (60) to 3G 1T (26) (Twickenham)
1959-60	**ENGLAND** 1G, 2PG, 1T (14) to 2PG (6) (Twickenahm)	1998-99	**WALES** 2G, 6PG (32) to 2G, 4PG, 1T (31) (Wembley)
1960-61	**WALES** 2T (6) to 1T (3) (Cardiff)		
1961-62	**DRAWN** No Score (Twickenham)		
1962-63	**ENGLAND** 2G, 1DG (13) to 1PG, 1T (6) (Cardiff)		
1963-64	**DRAWN** 2T Each (Twickenham)		
1964-65	**WALES** 1G, 1DG, 2T (14) to 1PG (3) (Cardiff)		
1965-66	**WALES** 1G, 2PG (11) to 1PG, 1T (6) (Twickenham)		

AGAINST SCOTLAND

Matches played 103   Wales 56 wins,   Scotland 45,   2 drawn

1882-83	**SCOTLAND** 3G to 1G (Edinburgh)	1884-85	**DRAWN** No Score (Glasgow)
1883-84	**SCOTLAND** 1DG, 1T to 0 (Newport)	1885-86	**SCOTLAND** 2G, 1T to 0 (Cardiff)

1886-87	**SCOTLAND** 4G, 8T to 0 (Edinburgh)
1887-88	**WALES** 1T to 0 (Newport)
1888-89	**SCOTLAND** 2T to 0 (Edinburgh)
1889-90	**SCOTLAND** 1G, 2T (5) to 1T (1) (Cardiff)
1890-91	**SCOTLAND** 1G, 2DG, 5T (15) to 0 (Edinburgh)
1891-92	**SCOTLAND** 1 G, 1t (7) to 1T (2) (Swansea)
1892-93	**WALES** 1PG, 3T (9) to 0 (Edinburgh)
1893-94	**WALES** 1DG, 1T (7) to 0 (Newport)
1894-95	**SCOTLAND** 1G (5) to 1GM (4) (Edinburgh)
1895-96	**WALES** 2T (6) to 0 (Cardiff)
1896-97 and 1897-98 No Matches	
1898-99	**SCOTLAND** 1GM, 2DG, 3T (21) to 2G (10 (Edinburgh)
1899-1900	**WALES** 4T (12) to 1T (3) (Swansea)
1900-01	**SCOTLAND** 3G, 1T (18) to 1G, 1T (8) (Inverleith)
1901-02	**WALES** 1G, 3T (14) to 1G (5) (Cardiff)
1902-03	**SCOTLAND** 1PG, 1T (6) to 0 (Inverleith)
1903-04	**WALES** 3G, 1PG, 1T (21) to 1T (3) (Swansea)
1904-05	**WALES** 2T (6) to 1T (3) (Inverleith)
1905-06	**WALES** 3T (9) to 1PG (3) (Cardiff)
1906-07	**SCOTLAND** 2T (6) to 1PG (3) (Inverleith)
1907-08	**WALES** 2T (6) to 1G (5) (Swansea)
1908-09	**WALES** 1G (5) to 1PG (3) (Inverleith)
1909-10	**WALES** 1G, 3T (14) to 0 (Cardiff)
1910-11	**WALES** 2G, 1DG, 6T (32) to 1DG, 2T (10) (Inverleith)
1911-12	**WALES** 2G, 2DG, 1T (21) to 2T (6) (Swansea)
1912-13	**WALES**, 1G, 1T (8) to 0 (Inverleith)
1913-14	**WALES** 2G, 2DG, 1PG, 1T (24) to 1G (5) (Cardiff)
1919-20	**SCOTLAND** 2PG, 1T (9) to 91G (5) (Inverleith)
1920-21	**SCOTLAND** 1G, 1PG, 2T (14) TO 2DG (8) (Swansea)
1921-22	**DRAWN SCOTLAND** 1PG, 2T (9) to **WALES** 1G, 1DG (9) (Inverleith)
1922-23	**SCOTLAND** 1G, 2T (11) to 1G, PG (8) (Cardiff)
1923-24	**SCOTLAND** 4G, 1PG, 4T (35) to 2G (10) (Inverleith)
1924-25	**SCOTLAND** 1G, 1DG, 5T (24) to 1G, 1PG, 2T (14) (Swansea)
1925-26	**SCOTLAND** 1G, 1PG, (8) to 1G (5) (Murrayfield)
1926-27	**SCOTLAND** 1G (5) to 0 (Cardiff)
1927-28	**WALES** 2G, 1T (13) to 0 (Murrayfield)
1928-29	**WALES** 1G, 3T (14) to 1DG, 1PG (7) (Swansea)
1929-30	**SCOTLAND** 1G, 1DG, 1T (12) to 1G, 2DG (9) (Murrayfield)
1930-31	**WALES** 2G, 1T (13) to 1G, 1T (8) (Cardiff)
1931-32	**WALES** 1PG, 1T (6) to 0 (Murrayfield)
1932-33	**SCOTLAND** 1G, 1PG, 1T (11) to 1T (3) (Swansea)
1933-34	**WALES** 2G, 1T (13) to 1PG, 1T (6) (Murrayfield)
1934-35	**WALES** 1DG, 2T (10) to 2T (6) (Cardiff)
1925-36	**WALES** 2G, 1T (13) to 1T (3) (Murrayfield)
1936-37	**SCOTLAND** 2G, 1T (13) to 2T (6) (Swansea)
1937-38	**SCOTLAND** 1G, 1PG (8) to 2T (6) (Murrayfield)

1938-39	**WALES** 1G, 1PG, 1T (11) to 1PG (3) (Cardiff)
1946-47	**WALES** 2G, 1PG, 3T (22) to 1G, 1PG (8) (Murrayfield)
1947-48	**WALES** 1G, 1PG, 2T (14) to 0 (Cardiff)
	(Droped goal revalued to 3 pts.)
1948-49	**SCOTLAND** 2T (6) to 1G (5) (Murrayfield)
1949-50	**WALES** 1DG, 1PG, 2T (12) to 0 (Swansea)
1950-51	**SCOTLAND** 2G, 1DG, 1PG 1T (19) to 0 (Murrayfield)
1951-52	**WALES** 1PG, 2PG (11) to 0 (Cardiff)
1952-53	**WALES** 1PG, 3T (12) to 0 (Murrayfield)
1953-54	**WALES** 1PG, 4T (15) to 1T (3) (Swansea)
1954-55	**SCOTLAND** 1G, 1DG, 1PG, 1T (14) to 1G, 1T (8) (Murrayfield)
1955-56	**WALES** 3T (9) to 1PG (3) (Cardiff)
1956-57	**SCOTLAND** 1DG, 1PG, 1T (9) to 1PG, 1T (6) (Murrayfield)
1957-58	**WALES** 1G, 1T (8) to 1PG (3) (Cardiff)
1958-59	**SCOTLAND** 1PG, 1T (6) to 1G (5) (Murrayfield)
1959-60	**WALES** 1G, 1PG (8) to 0 (Cardiff)
1960-61	**SCOTLAND** 1T (3) to 0 (Murrayfield)
1961-62	**SCOTLAND** 1G, 1T (8) to 1DG (3) (Cardiff)
1962-63	**WALES** 1DG, 1PG (6) to 0 (Murrayfield)
1963-64	**WALES** 1G, 1PG, 1T (11) to 1T (3) (Cardiff)
1964-65	**WALES** 1G, 2PG, 1T (14) to 2DG, 2PG (12) (Murrayfield)
1965-66	**WALES** 1G, 1T (8) to 1PG (3) (Cardiff)
1966-67	**SCOTLAND** 1G, 1DG, 1T (11) to 1G (5) (Murrayfield)
1967-68	**WALES** 1G (5) to 0 (Cardiff)
1968-69	**WALES** 1G, 2PG, 2T (17) to 1PG (3) (Murrayfield)
1969-70	**WALES** 2G, 1T (18) to 1DG, 1PG 1T (9) (Cardiff)
1970-71	**WALES** 2G, 1PG, 2TR (19) to 2PG, 2T (18) (Murrayfield)
	(Try upgraded to 4pts.)
1971-72	**WALES** 3G, 3PG, 2T (35) to 1G, 2PG (12) (Cardiff)
1972-73	**SCOTLAND** 1G, 1T (10) to 3PG (9) (Murrayfield)
1973-74	**WALES** 1G (6) to 0 (Cardiff)
1974-75	**SCOTLAND** 3PG, 1DG (12) to 2PG, IT (10) (Murrayfield)
1975-76	**WALES** 2G, 3PG, 1DG, 1T (28) to 1G (6) (Cardiff)
1976-77	**WALES** 2G, 2PG, (18) to 1G, 1DG (9) (Murrayfield)
1977-78	**WALES** 1DG, 1PG, 4T (22) to 2PG, 2T (14) (Cardiff)
1978-79	**WALES** 1G, 3PG, 1T (19) to 3PG, 1T (13) (Murrayfield)
1979-80	**WALES**, 1G, 1PG, 2T (17) to 1G (6) (Cardiff)
1980-81	**SCOTLAND** 2G, 1PG, (15) to 2PG (6) (Murrayfield)
1981-82	**SCOTLAND** 4G, 2DG, 1T (34) to 1G, 4PG (18) (Cardiff)
1982-83	**WALES** 1G, 3PG, 1T (19) to 1G 3PG (15) (Murrayfield)
1983-84	**SCOTLAND** 2G, 1PG (15) to 1G, 1PG (9) (Cardiff)
1984-85	**WALES** 1G, 1DG, 4PG, 1T (25) to 2G, 2DG, 1PG (21) (Murrayfield)
1985-86	**WALES** 5PG, 1DG, 1T (22) to 1PG, 3T (15) (Cardiff)

122

1986-87	**WALES** 2G, 2PG, 1DG (21) to 1G, 2PG, 1DG (15) (Murrayfield)
1987-88	**WALES** 2G, 2DG, 1PG, 1T (25) to 4PG, 2T (20) (Cardiff)
1988-89	**SCOTLAND** 1G, 2P, 1DG, 2T (23) to 1PG, 1T (7) (Murrayfield)
1989-90	**SCOTLAND** 3PG, 1T (13) to 1G, 1PG (9) (Cardiff)
1990-91	**SCOTLAND** 2G, 3PG, 1DG, 2T (32) to 1G, 2PG (12) (Murrayfield)
1991-92	**WALES** 1G, 3PG (15) to 1DG, 3PG (12) (Cardiff) **(Try upgraded to 5 pts.)**
1992-93	**SCOTLAND** 5PG, 1T (20) to 0 (Murrayfield)
1993-94	**WALES** 1G, 4PG, 2T (29) to 2PG (6) (Cardiff)
1994-95	**SCOTLAND** 2G, 4PG (26) to 1G, 2PG (13) (Murrayfield)
1995-96	**SCOTLAND** 1G, 3PG (16) to 3PG, 1T (14) (Cardiff)
1996-97	**WALES** 4G, 2PG (34) to 1G, 1DG, 3PG (19) (Murrayfield)
1997-98	**WALES** 1G, 4PG (19) to 1PG, 2T (13) (Wembley)
1998-99	**SCOTLAND** 2G, 3PG, 2T (33) to 2G, 2PG (20) (Murrayfield)

AGAINST IRELAND

Matches played 103   Wales 59 wins,   Ireland 38,   6 drawn

1881-82	**WALES** 2G, 2T to 0 (Dublin)
1882-83	No Match
1883-84	**WALES** 1DG, 2T to 0 (Cardiff)
1884-85 and 19885-86	No matches
1886-87	**WALES** 1DG, 1T to 3T (Birkenhead)
1887-88	**IRELAND** 1G, 1DG, 1T to 0 (Dublin)
1888-89	**IRELAND** 2T to 0 (Swansea)
1889-90	**DRAWN** 1G, (3) Each
1890-91	**WALES** 1G, 1DG (6) to 1DG, 1T (4) (Llanelli)
1891-92	**IRELAND** 1G, 2T (9) to 0 (Dublin)
1892-93	**WALES** 1T (2) to 0 (Llanelli)
1893-94	**IRELAND** 1PG (3) to 0 (Belfast)
1894-95	**WALES** 1G (5) to 1T (3) (Cardiff)
1895-96	**IRELAND** 1G, 1T (8) to 1DG (4) (Dublin)
1896-97	No match
1897-98	**WALES** 1G, 1PG, 1T (11) to 1PG (3) (Limerick)
1898-99	**IRELAND** 1T (3) to 0 (Cardiff)
1899-1900	**WALES** 1T (3) to 0 (Belfast)
1900-01	**WALES** 2G (10) to 3T (9) (Swansea)
1901-02	**WALES** 1G,1DG, 2T (15) to 0 (Dublin)
1902-03	**WALES** 6T (18) to 0 (Cardiff)
1903-04	**IRELAND** 1G, 3T (14) to 4T (12) (Belfast)
1904-05	**WALES** 2G (10) to 1T (3) (Swansea)
1905-06	**IRELAND** 1G, 2T (11) to 2T (6) (Belfast)
1906-07	**WALES** 2G, 1DG, 1PG, 4T (29) to 0 (Cardiff)
1907-08	**WALES** 1G, 2T (11) to 1G (5) (Belfast)
1908-09	**WALES** 3G, 1T (18) to 1G (5) (Swansea)
1909-10	**WALES** 1DG, 5T (19) to 1T (3) (Dublin)
1910-11	**WALES** 2G, 1PG, 1T (16) to 0 (Cardiff)
1911-12	**IRELAND** 1G, 1DG, 1T (12) to 1G (5) (Belfast)
1912-13	**WALES** 2G, 1PG, 1T (16) to 2G, 1PG (13) (Swansea)
1913-14	**WALES** 1G, 2T (11) to 1T (3) (Belfast)
1919-20	**WALES** 3G, 1DG, 3T (28) to 1DG (4) (Cardiff)
1920-21	**WALES** 1PG, 1T (6) to 0 (Belfast)
1921-22	**WALES** 1G, 2T (11) to 1G (5) (Swansea)
1922-23	**IRELAND** 1G (5) to 1DG (4) (Dublin)
1923-24	**IRELAND** 2G, 1T (13) to 1DG, 2T (10) (Cardiff)
1924-25	**IRELAND** 2G, 1PG, 2T (19) to 1T (3) (Belfast)
1925-26	**WALES** 1G, 2T (11) to 1G, 1PG (8) (Swansea)
1926-27	**IRELAND** 2G, 1PG, 2T (19) to 1G, 1DG (9) (Dublin)
1927-28	**IRELAND** 2G, 1T (13) to 2G (10) (Cardiff)
1928-29	**DRAWN** 1G (5) Each (Belfast)
1929-30	**WALES** 1PG, 3T (12) to 1DG, 1PG (7) (Swansea)
1930-31	**WALES** 1G, 1DG, 2T (15) to 1T (3) (Belfast)
1931-32	**IRELAND** 4T (12) to 1DG, 2T (10) (Cardiff)
1932-33	**IRELAND** 1DG, 1PG, 1T (10 to 1G (5) (Belfast)
1933-34	**WALES** 2G, 1T (13) to 0 (Swansea)
1934-35	**IRELAND** 2PG, 1T (9) to 1PG (3) (Belfast)
1935-36	**WALES** 1PG (3) to 0 (Cardiff)
1936-37	**IRELAND** 1G (5) to 1PG (3) (Belfast)
1937-38	**WALES** 1G, 1PG, 1T (11) to 1G (5) (Swansea)
1938-39	**WALES** 1DG, 1T (7) to 0 (Belfast)
1946-47	**WALES** 1PG, 1T (6) to 0 (Swansea)
1947-48	**IRELAND** 2T (6) to 1T (3) (Belfast) **(Drop goal revalued to 3pts.)**
1948-49	**IRELAND** 1G (5) to 0 (Swansea)
1949-50	**IRELAND** 2T (6) to 1PG (3) (Belfast)
1950-51	**DRAWN WALES** 1PG (3) to Ireland 1T (3) (Cardiff)
1951-52	**WALES** 1G, 1PG, 2T (14) to 1PG (3) (Dublin)
1952-53	**WALES** 1G (5) to 1T (3) (Swansea)
1953-54	**WALES** 1DG, 3PG (12) to 2PG, 1T (9) (Dublin)
1954-55	**WALES** 3G, 1PG, 1T (21) to 1PG (3) (Cardiff)
1955-56	**IRELAND** 1G, 1DG, 1PG (11) to 1PG (3) (Dublin)
1956-57	**WALES** 2PG (6) to 1G (5) (Cardiff)
1957-58	**WALES** 3T (9) to 1PG, 1T (6) (Dublin)
1958-59	**WALES** 1G, 1T (8) to 1PG, 1T (6) (Cardiff)
1959-60	**WALES** 2G (10 to 2PG, 1T (9) (Dublin)
1960-61	**WALES** 2PG, 1T (9) to 0 (Cardiff)
1961-62	**DRAWN IRELAND** 1DG (3) to **WALES** 1PG (3) (Dublin)
1962-63	**IRELAND** 1G, 1DG, 2PG (14) to 1DG, 1T (6) (Cardiff)
1963-64	**WALES** 3G (15) to 2PG (6) (Dublin)
1964-65	**WALES** 1G, 1DG, 1PG, 1T (14) to 1G, 1T (6) (Cardiff)
1965-66	**IRELAND** 1DG, 1PG, 1T (9) to 1PG, 1T (6) (Dublin)
1966-67	**IRELAND** 1T (3) to 0 (Cardiff)

1967-68	**IRELAND** 1PG, 1DG, 1T (9) to 1PG, 1DG (6) (Dublin)
1968-69	**WALES** 3G, 1PG, 1DG, 1T (24) to 1G, 2PG (12) (Cardiff)
1969-70	**IRELAND** 1G, 1DG, 1PG, 1T (14) to 0 (Dublin)
1970-71	**WALES** 1G, 1DG, 2PG, 3T (23) to 3PG (9) (Cardiff)
1971-72	No match
1972-73	**WALES** 1G, 2PG, 1T (16) to 1G, 2PG (12) (Cardiff)
1973-74	**DRAWN IRELAND** 3PG (9) to **WALES** 1G, 1PG (9) (Dublin)
1974-75	**WALES** 3G, 2PG, 2T (32) to 1T (4) (Cardiff)
1975-76	**WALES** 3G, 4PG, 1T (34) to 3PG (9) (Dublin)
1976-77	**WALES** 2G, 3PG, 1DG 1T (25) to 3PG (9) (Cardiff)
1977-78	**WALES** 4PG, 2T (20) to 3PG, 1DG, 1T, (16) (Dublin)
1978-79	**WALES** 2G, 4PG (24) to 2G, 3PG (21) (Cardiff)
1979-80	**IRELAND** 3G, 1PG (21) to 1PG, 1T (7) (Dublin)
1980-81	**WALES** 2PG, 1DG (9) to 2T (8) (Cardiff)
1981-82	**IRELAND** 1G, 2PG, 2T (20) to 1G, 1DG, 12PG (12) (Dublin)
1982-83	**WALES** 1G, 3PG, 2T (23) to 3PG (9) (Cardiff)
1983-84	**WALES** 1G, 4PG (18) to 3PG (9) (Dublin)
1984-85	**IRELAND** 2G, 3PG (21) to 1G, 1DG (9) (Cardiff)
1985-86	**WALES** 1G, 3PG, 1T (19) to 1G, 2PG (12) (Dublin)
1986-87	**IRELAND** 2G, 1PG (15) to 1PG, 2T (11) (Cardiff)
1987	**WORLD CUP : WALES** 2DG, 1PG, 1T (13) to 2PG (6) (Wellington)
1987-88	**WALES** 1G, 1DG, 1PG (12) to 1G, 1PG (9) (Dublin)
1988-89	**IRELAND** 1G, 3PG, 1T (19) to 3PG, 1T (13) (Cardiff)
1989-90	**IRELAND** 1G, 2T (14) to 2T (8) (Dublin)
1990-91	**DRAWN WALES** 2G, 2PG, 1DG (21) **IRELAND** 1G, 1DG, 3T (21) (Cardiff)
1991-92	**WALES** 3PG, 1DG, 1T (16) to 1G, 3PG (15) (Dublin) **(Try upgraded to 5 pts.)**
1992-93	**IRELAND** 1G, 3PG, 1DG (19) to 3PG, 1T (14) (Cardiff)
1993-94	**WALES** 4PG, 1T (17) to 5PG (15) (Dublin)
1994-95	**IRELAND** 1G, 1DG, 2PG (16) to 4PG (12) (Cardiff)
1995	**WORLD CUP : IRELAND** 3G, 1PG (24) to 2G, 1DG, 2PG (23) (Johannesburg)
1995-96	**IRELAND** 2G, 2PG, 2T (30) to 2G, 1PG (17) (Dublin)
1996-97	**IRELAND** 1G, 3PG, 2T (26) to 2G, 2PG, 1T (25) (Cardiff)
1997-98	**WALES** 3G, 3PG (30) to 1G, 3PG (16) (Dublin)
1998-99	**IRELAND** 2G, 2DG, 3PG (29) to 2G, 3PG (23) (Wembley)

* Includes 2 friendly matches

AGAINST FRANCE

Matches played 74*   Wales 39 wins,   France 32,   3 drawn

1907-08	**WALES** 1PG, 6T (36) to 1DG (4) (Cardiff)
1908-09	**WALES** 7G, 4T (47) to (1G (5) (Paris)
1909-10	**WALES** 8G, 1PG, 2T (49) to 1G, 2PG, 1T (14) (Swansea)
1910-11	**WALES** 3G (15) to 0 (Paris)
9911-12	**WALES** 1G, 3T (14) to 1G, 1T (8) (Newport)
1912-13	**WALES** 1G, 2T (11) to 1G, 1T (8) (Paris)
1913-14	**WALES** 5G, 2T (31) to 0 (Swansea)
1919-20	**WALES** 2T (6) to 1G (5) (Paris)
1920-21	**WALES** 2PG, 2T (12) to 1DG (4) (Cardiff)
1921-22	**WALES** 1G, 2T (11) to 1T (3) (Paris)
1922-23	**WALES** 2G, 1PG, 1T (16) to 1G, 1T (8) (Swansea)
1923-24	**WALES** 1DG, 2T (10) to 2T (6) (Paris)
1924-25	**WALES** 1G, 2T (11) to 1G (5) (Cardiff)
1925-26	**WALES** 1DG, 1T (7) to 1G (5) (Paris)
1926-27	**WALES** 2G, 5T (25) to 1DG, 1T (7) (Swansea)
1927-28	**FRANCE** 1G, 1T (8) to 1T (3) (Paris)
1928-29	**WALES** 1G, 1T (8) to 1T (3) (Cardiff)
1929-30	**WALES** 2DG, 1T (11) to 0 (Paris)
1930-31	**WALES** 5G, 1DG, 2T (35) to 1T (3) (Swansea)
1946-47	**WALES** 1PG (3) to 0 (Paris)
1947-48	**FRANCE** 1G, 2T (11) to 1PG (3) (Swansea) **(Dropped goal revalued to 3 pts.)**
1948-49	**FRANCE** 1G (5) to 1T (3) (Paris)
1949-50	**WALES** 3G, 1PG, 1T (21) to 0 (Cardiff)
1950-51	**FRANCE** 1G, 1PG (8) to 1T (3) (Paris)
1951-52	**WALES** 1DG, 2PG (9) to 1G (5) (Swansea)
1952-53	**WALES** 2T 96) to 1PG (3) (Paris)
1953-54	**WALES** 2G, 3PG (19) to 2G, 1PG (13) (Cardiff)
1954-55	**WALES** 2G, 2PG (16) to 1G, 1DG, 1PG (11) (Paris)
1955-56	**WALES** 1G (5) to 1T (3) (Cardiff)
1956-57	**WALES** 2G, 1PG, 2T (19) to 2G, 1T (13) (Paris)
1957-58	**FRANCE** 2G, 2DG (16) to 1PG, 1T (6) (Cardiff)
1958-59	**FRANCE** 1G, 1PG, 1T (11) to 1PG (3) (Paris)
1959-60	**FRANCE** 2G, 2T (16) to 1PG (8) (Cardiff)
1960-61	**FRANCE** 1G, 1T (8) to 2T (6) (Paris)
1961-62	**WALES** 1PG (3) to 0 (Cardiff)
1962-63	**FRANCE** 1G (5) to 1PG (3) (Paris)
1963-64	**DRAWN** 2G, 2PG (11) Each (Cardiff)
1964-65	**FRANCE** 2G, 1PG, 1DG, 2T (22) to 2G, 1T (13) (Paris)
1965-66	**WALES** 2PG, 1T (9) to 1G, 1T (8) (Cardiff)
1966-67	**FRANCE** 1G, 2DG, 1PG, 2T (20) to 1G, 2PG, 1DG (14) (Paris)
1967-68	**FRANCE** 1G, 1PG, 1DG, 1T (14) to 2PG, 1T (9) (Cardiff)
1968-69	**DRAWN FRANCE** 1G, 1PG (8) to **WALES** 1G, 1T (8) (Paris)
1969-70	**WALES** 1G, 2PG (11) to 2T (6) (Cardiff)
1970-71	**WALES** 1PG, 2T (9) to 1G (5) (Paris) **(Try upgraded to 4pts.)**
1971-72	**WALES** 4PG, 2T (20) to 2PG (6) (Cardiff)
1972-73	**FRANCE** 3PG, 1DG (12) to 1DG (3) (Paris)
1973-74	**DRAWN WALES** 3PG, 1DG, 1T (16) to **FRANCE** EPG, 1DG, 1T 16) (Cardiff)
1974-75	**WALES** 1G, 1PG, 4T (25) to 2PG, 1T (10) (Paris)
1975-76	**WALES** 5PG, 1T (19) to1G, 1PG, 1T (13) (Cardiff)

1976-77	**FRANCE** 1G, 2PG, 1T (16) to 3PG (9) (Paris)	1989-90	**FRANCE** 3G, 1PG, 2T (29) to 4PG, 1DG, 1T (19) (Cardiff)
1977-78	**WALES** 1G, 2DG, 1T (16) to 1DG, 1T (7) (Cardiff)	1990-91	**FRANCE** 3G, 2PG, 3T (36) to 1PG (3) (Paris)
1978-79	**FRANCE** 2PG, 2T (14) to 3PG, 1T (13) (Paris)	1991	(Friendly) **FRANCE** 2G, 2PG, 1T (22) to 1G, 1PG (9) (Cardiff)
1979-80	**WALES** 1G, 3T (18) to 1G, 1DG (9) (Cardiff)	1991-92	**FRANCE** 1G, 1DG, 1PG (12) to 3PG (9) (Cardiff)
1980-81	**FRANCE** 5PG, 1T (19) to 1G, 3PG (15) (Paris)		**(Try upgraded to 5pts.)**
1981-82	**WALES** 6PG, 1T (22) to 1G, 2PG (12) (Cardiff)	1992-93	**FRANCE** 1G, 3PG, 2T (26) to 1G, 1PG (10) (Paris)
1982-83	**FRANCE** 3PG, 1DG, 1T (16) to 1G, 1PG (9) (Paris)	1993-94	**WALES** 1G, 4PG, 1T (24) to 1G, 1PG, 1T (15) (Cardiff)
1983-84	**FRANCE** 1G, 4PG, 1DG (21) to 1G, 1T 2PG (16) (Cardiff)	1994-95	**FRANCE** 1G, 3PG, 1T (21) to 3PG (9) (Paris)
1984-85	**FRANCE** 2PG, 2T (14) to 1PG (3) (Paris)	1995-96	**WALES** 1G, 3PG (16) to 1G, 1PG, 1T (15) (Cardiff)
1985-86	**FRANCE** 2G, 1DG, 2T (23) to 5PG (15) (Cardiff)	1996	(Friendly) **FRANCE** 4G, 4PG (40) to 3G, 4PG (33) (Cardiff)
1986-87	**FRANCE** 1G, 2PG, 1T (16) to 3P (9) (Paris)	1996-97	**FRANCE** 2G, 1PG, 2T (27) to 2G, 1PG, 1T (22) (Paris)
1987-88	**FRANCE** 2PG, 1T (10) to 1G, 1PG (9) (Cardiff)	1997-98	**FRANCE** 5G, 2PG, 2T (51) to 0 (Wembley)
1988-89	**FRANCE** 3G, 2PG, 1DG, 1T (31) to 4PG (12) (Paris)	1998-99	**WALES** 2G, 5PG, 1T (34) to 2G, 3PG, 2T (33) (Paris)

AGAINST NEW ZEALAND

Matches played 17   Wales 3 wins,   New Zealand 14

1905-06	**WALES** 1T (3) TO 0 (Cardiff)	1978	**N.Z.** 3PG, 1T (13) to 4PG (12) (Cardiff)
1924-25	**N.Z.** 2G, 1PG, 2T (19) to 0 (Swansea)	1980	**N.Z.** 2G, 1PG, 2T (23) to 1PG (3) (Cardiff)
1935-36	**WALES** 2G, 1T (13) to 1G, 1DG, 1T (12) (Cardiff)	1987	World Cup : **N.Z.** 7G, 1PG, 1T, (4) to 1G (6) (Brisbane)
1953-54	**WALES** 2G, 1PG (13) to 1G, 1PG (8) (Cardiff)	1988	**N.Z.** 6G, 4T (52) to 1PG (3) (Christchurch)
1963-64	**N.Z.** 1PG, 1DG (6) to 0 (Cardiff)	1988	**N.Z.** 8G, 2PG (54) to 1G, 1PG (9) (Auckland)
1967	**N.Z.** 2G, 1PG (13) to 1PG, 1DG (6) (Cardiff)	1989	**N.Z.** 3G, 4PG, 1T (34) to 3PG (9) (Cardiff)
1969	**N.Z.** 2G, 1PG, 2T (19) to 0 (Christchurch)	1995	WORLD CUP : **N.Z.** 2G, 1DG, 4PG, 1T (34) to 1DG, 2PG (9) (Johannesburg)
1969	**N.Z.** 3G, 5PG, 1DG (33) to 2PG, 2T (12) (Auckland)	1996	**N.Z.** 4G, 2PG, 1DG, 1T (42) to 1G (7) (Wembley)
1972-73	**N.Z.** 5PG, 1T (19) to 4PG, 1T (16) (Cardiff)		
1974	**N.Z.* 1G, 2PG, (12) to 1PG (3) (Cardiff)		

AGAINST SOUTH AFRICA

Matches played 13   Wales 1 win,   South Africa 11,   1 drawn

1906	**S.A.** 1G, 2T (11) to 0 (Swansea)	1995	**S.A.** 3G, 3PG, 2T (40) to 2PG, 1T (11) (Johannesburg)
1912-13	**S.A.** 1PG (3) to 0 (Cardiff)	1996	**S.A.** 3G, 2PG, 2T (37) to 5PG, 1T (20) (Cardiff)
1931-32	**S.A.** 1G, 1T (8) to 1T (3) (Swansea)	1998	**S.A.** 9G, 1PG, 6T (96) to 1G, 2PG, (13) (Pretoria)
1951-52	**S.A.** 1DG, 1T (6) to 1T (3) (Cardiff)		
1960-61	**S.A.** 1PG (3) to 0 (Cardiff)	1998	**S.A.** 2G, 3PG, 1T (28) to 5PG, 1T (20) (Wembley)
1964	**S.A.** 3G, 2PG, 1DG (24) to 1PG (3) (Durban)	1999	**WALES** 2G, 5PG (29) to 3PG, 2T (19) (Cardiff)
1970	DRAWN 1PG, 1T (6) Each (Cardiff)		
1994	**S.A.** 1G, 1PG, 2T (20) to 4PG (12) (Cardiff)		

AGAINST AUSTRALIA

Matches played 19   Wales 8 wins,   Australia 11

1908-08	**WALES** 1PG, 2T (9) to 2T (6) (Cardiff)	1973-74	**WALES** 2G, 2PG, 3T (24) to 0 (Cardiff)
1927-28	**AUSTRALIA (NSW)** 3G, 1T (18) to 1G, 1T (8) (Cardiff)	1975-76	**WALES** 3G, 1PG, 1DG, 1T (28) to 1PG (3) (Cardiff)
1947-48	**WALES** 2PG (6) to 0 (Cardiff)	1978	**AUSTRALIA** 1G, 4PG (18) to 2T (8) (Brisbane)
1957-58	**WALES** 1PG, 1DG, 1T (9) to 1T (3) (Cardiff)	1978	**AUSTRALIA** 3PG, 2DG, 1T (19) to 2PG, 1DG, 2T (17) (Sydney)
1966-67	**AUSTRALIA** 1G, 1PG, 1DG, 1T (14) to 1G, 1PG, 1T (11) (Cardiff)	1981	**WALES** 1G, 1DG, 3PG (18) to 1G, 1PG, 1T (13) (Cardiff)
1969	**WALES** 2G, 2PG, 1T (19) to 2G, 2PG (16) (Sydney)		

1984	**AUSTRALIA** 3G, 2PG, 1T (28) to 1G, 1PG (9) (Cardiff)	1992	**AUSTRALIA** 1G, 2PG, 2T (23) to 2PG (6) (Cardiff)
1987	**WORLD CUP : WALES** 2G, 2PG, 1T (22) to 2G, 2PG, 1DG (21) (Rotorua)	1996	**AUSTRALIA** 6G, 3PG, 1T (56 to 2G, 2PG, 1T (25) (Brisbane)
1991	**AUSTRALIA** 6G, 1PG, 6T (63) to 1DG, 1PG (6) (Brisbane)	1996	**AUSTRALIA** 3G, 2PG 3T (42) to 1PG (3) (Sydney)
1991	**WORLD CUP : AUSTRALIA** 4G, 2PG, 2T (38) to 1PG (3) (Cardiff)	1996	**AUSTRALIA** 2G, 3PG, 1T (28) to 1G, 4PG (19) (Cardiff)

AGAINST MAORIS

Matches played 2   Wales 2 wins,   Maoris 0

| 1888-89 | **WALES** 1G, 2T (5) to 0 (Swansea) | 1982 | **WALES** 1G, 1DG, 4PG, 1T (25) to 1G, 3PG, 1T (19) (Cardiff) |
| Note : | A goal countd 3 pts., a try 1 pt. | | |

AGAINST N.Z. ARMY TEAMS

| 1919 | **N.Z. ARMY** 2PG (6) to 1PG (3) (Swansea) | 1946 | ***KIWIS** 1G, 2PG (11) to 1PG (6) (Cardiff) *No caps awarded |

AGAINST NAMIBIA

Matches played 3   Wales 3 wins

| 1990 | **WALES** 2G, 2PG (18) to 1G, 1PG (9) (Windhoek) | 1992 | **WALES** 2G, 3PG, 3T (38) to 2G, 3PG, (23) (Windhoek) |
| 1990 | **WALES** 3G, 3PG, 1DG, 1T (34) to 3G, 3PG, 1DG (30) (Windhoek) | | |

AGAINST TONGA

Matches played 5   Wales 5 wins

1974	**WALES** 2PG, 5T (26) to 1PG, 1T (7) (Cardiff)	1994	**WALES** 6PG (18) to 3PG (9) (Nuku'Alofa)
1986	**WALES** 1G, 3PG, (15) to 1PG, 1T (7) (Nuku'Alofa)	1997	**WALES** 2G, 4PG, 4T (46) to 1G, 1T (12) (Swansea)
1987	**WORLD CUP : WALES** 2G, 2PG, 1DG, 2T (29) to 1G, 2PG, 1T (Palmerston North)		

AGAINST CANADA

Matches played 9   Wales 8 wins,   Canada 1

1962	**WALES** U-23 1G, 1T (8) to 0 (Cardiff)	1989	**WALES** 4G, 1PG, 1T (31) to 3G, 1DG, 2T (29) (Edmonton)
1971	**WALES** 5G, 1DG, 1PG, 5T (56) to 1G, 1T (10) (Cardiff)	1993	**CANADA** 2G, 4PG (26) to 8PG (24) (Cardiff)
1973	**WALES** 8G, 2PG, 1T (58) to 1G, 2PG, 2T (20) (Toronto)	1994	**WALES** 3G, 4PG (33) to 5PG (15) (Toronto)
1980	**WALES** 1G, 1DG, 5PG (24) to 1PG, 1T (7) (Vancouver)	1997	**WALES** 2G, 3PG, 1T (28) to 2G, 1PG, 1DG, 1T (25) (Toronto)
1987	**WORLD CUP : WALES** 4G, 4T (40) to (3PG (9) (Invercargill)		

AGAINST USA

Matches played 4   Wales 4 wins

| 1987 | **WALES** 4G, 2PG, 4T (46) to 0 (Cardiff) | 1997 | **WALES** 2G, 2PG, 2T (30) to 2G, 2PG (20) (Wilmington) |
| 1997 | **WALES** 4G, 2PG (34) to 3PG, 1T (14) (Cardiff) | 1997 | **WALES** 1G, 2PG, 3T (28) to 2G, 3PG (23) (San Francisco) |

AGAINST WESTERN SAMOA

Matches played 4   Wales 2 wins,   Western Samoa 2

| 1986 | **WALES** 2G, 3PG, 1DG, 2T (32) to 2PG, 2T (14) (Apia) | 1991 | **WORLD CUP : W SAMOA** 1G, 2PG, 1T (16) to 1G, 1PG, 1T (13) (Cardiff) |
| 1988 | **WALES** 4G, 1T (28) to 1G (6) (Cardiff) | 1994 | **W. SAMOA** 2G, 5PG, 1T (34) to 3PG (9) (Apia) |

AGAINST ZIMBABWE

Matches played 3   Wales 3 wins

| 1993 | **WALES** 3G, 2PG, 1DG, 1T (35) to 3PG, 1T (14) (Bulawayo) | 1998 | **WALES** 3G, 1PG, 5T (49) to 2PG, 1T (11) (Harare) |
| 1993 | **WALES** 3G, 2PG, 3T (42) to 1G, 2PG (13) (Harare) | | |

AGAINST PORTUGAL

Matches   played   1   Wales   1   win

1994	**WALES** 11G, 5T (102) to 2PG, 1T (11) (Lisbon)

AGAINST BARBARIANS

Matches   played   3   Wales   1   win,   Barbarians   2

1915	**BARBARIANS** 4G, 2T (26) to 1DG, 2T (10) (Cardiff)	1996	**WALES** 3G, 2T (31) to 2T (10) (Cardiff)
1990	**BARBARIANS** 3G, 3PG, 1T (31) to 1G, 5PG, 1DG (24) (Cardiff)		

AGAINST ITALY

Matches   played   6   Wales   6   wins

1992	**WALES** 4g, 3T (43) to 1G, 1T (12) (Cardiff)	1996	**WALES** 2G, 4PG, 1T (31) to 1G, 5PG (22) (Rome)
1994	**WALES** 1G, 7PG, 1T (29) to 1G, 4PG (19) (Cardiff)	1998	**WALES** 2G, 3PG (23) to 2G, 2PG (20) (Llanelli)
1996	**WALES** 2G, 4PG, 1T (31) to 2G, 4PG (26) (Cardiff)	1999	**WALES** 5G, 5PG, 2T (60) to 1G, 3PG, 1T (21) (Treviso)

AGAINST ROMANIA

Matches   played   5   Wales   3   wins,   Romania   2

1979	**WALES** 2DG, 1PG, 1T (13) to 1G, 2PG (12) (Cardiff)	1994	**WALES** 1G, 3PG (16) to 3PG (9) (Bucharest)
1983	**ROMANIA** 1G, 2PG, 3T (24) to 2PG (6) (Bucharest)	1997	**WALES** 6G, 1PG, 5T (7) to 1G, 3PG (21) (Wrexham)
1988	**ROMANIA** 1G, 3PG (15) to 1G, 1PG (9) (Cardiff)		

AGAINST ARGENTINA

Matches played 7   Wales 5 wins,   Argentina 1,   1 drawn

1968	**ARGENTINA** 2PG, 1T (9) to 1G (5) (Buenos Aires)	1998	**WALES** 4G, 5PG (43) to 2G, 2PG, 2T (30) (Llanelli)
1968	**DRAWN : ARGENTINA** 2PG, 1T (9) **WALES** 2PG, 1T (9) (Buenos Aires)	1999	**WALES** 3G, 1DG, 4PG, (36) to 2G, 4PG (26) (Buenos Aires)
1976	**WALES** 4PG, 2T (20) to 1G, 3PG, 1T (19) (Cardiff)	1999	**WALES** 1DG, 5PG, IT (23) to 1G, 3PG (16) (Buenos Aires)
1991	**WORLD CUP : WALES** 4PG, 1T (16) to 1PG, 1T (7) (Cardiff)		

AGAINST FIJI

Matches   played   7   Wales   7   wins

1964	Wales 2G, 1PG, 5T (28) to 2G, 4T, (22) (Cardiff)	1985	Wales 3G, 2PG, 4T (40 to 1PG (3) (Cardiff)
1969	Wales 5G, 1DG, 1T (31) to 1G, 1PG, 1T (11) (Suva)	1986	Wales 1G, 1DG, 3PG, 1T (22) to 2G, 1PG (15) (Suva)
1970	Wales U-25 1G, 1T (8) to 1PG, 1T (6) (Cardiff)	1994	Wales 2G, 3PG (23) to 1PG, 1T (8) (Suva)
		1995	Wales 3PG, 2T (19) to 1G, 1PG, 1T (15) (Cardiff)

AGAINST JAPAN

Matches   played   6   Wales   6   wins

1973	**WALES** 9G, 2T (62) to 2PG, 2T (14) (Cardiff)	1983	**WALES** 3G, 1PG, 2T (29) to 1G, 2PG, 3T (24) (Cardiff)
1975	**WALES** 5G, 2PG, 5T (56) to 4PG (12) (Osaka)	1993	**WALES** 5G, 4T (55) to 1T (5) (Cardiff)
1975	**WALES** 10G, 2PG, 4T (82) to 2PG (6) (Tokyo)	1995	**WORLD CUP : WALES** 5G, 4PG, 2T (5) to 2T (10) (Bloemfontein)

AGAINST SPAIN

Matches   played   2   Wales   2   win

1983	**WALES** 7G, 1PG, 5T (65) to 2G, 1T (16) (Madrid)	1994	**WALES** 5G, 3PG, 2T (54) to 0 (Madrid)

Major Fixtures 1999-2000

(Some dates may be subject to change)

1999

AUGUST
18   Wales A v Canada A..Pontypridd
21   WALES v CANADA..Millennium Stadium
28   WALES v FRANCE..Millennium Stadium

SEPTEMBER
25   SWALEC Cup Round 1

OCTOBER
23   SWALEC Cup Round 2

NOVEMBER
6   Rugby World Cup Final (See page 14)..Millennium Stadium
20   SWALEC Cup Round 3

DECEMBER
7   Varsity Match..Twickenham
18   SWALEC Cup Round 4

2000

JANUARY
22   SWALEC Cup Round 5

FEBRUARY
4   Wales A v France A..Wrexham RFC
4   Wales U21 v France U21..Builth Wells
4   Wales Students v France Students..Stradey Park
5   WALES v FRANCE..Millennium Stadium
5   Italy v Scotland..tba
5   England v Ireland..Twickenham
18   Wales A v Italy A..Ebbw Vale*
18   Wales U21 v Italy U21..Rodney Parade
19   WALES v ITALY..Millennium Stadium
19   France v England..Paris
19   Ireland v Scotland..Dublin
26   SWALEC Cup Round 6

MARCH
3   England A v Wales A..tba
3   England U21 v Wales U21..tba
3   England Students v Wales Students..tba
4   ENGLAND v WALES..Twickenham
4   Scotland v France..Murrayfield
4   Ireland v Italy..Dublin
17   Wales A v Scotland A..Bridgend
17   Wales U21 v Scotland U21..Caerphilly
18   WALES v SCOTLAND..Millennium Stadium
18   Italy v England..Rome
19   France v Ireland..Paris
25   SWALEC Cup Quarter-finals
30   Ireland A v Wales A..tba
30   Ireland U21 v Wales U21..tba

APRIL
1   IRELAND v WALES..Dublin
1   France v Italy..Paris
2   Scotland v England..Murrayfield
15   European Cup Quarter-finals
22   SWALEC Cup Semi-finals

MAY
6   European Cup Semi-finals
20   SWALEC Cup Final..Millennium Stadium
27   European Cup Final..tba

Published by Buy As You View, Dinas Isaf, Williamstown, Rhondda, CF40 1NQ.
Printed by Hackman Printers Ltd., Cambrian Industrial Park, Clydach Vale, Rhondda, CF40 2XX.